INCLUSIONARY HOUSING PROGRAMS

INCLUSIONARY HOUSING PROGRAMS

POLICIES AND PRACTICES

Alan Mallach

Published in the United States of America
by the Center for Urban Policy Research
Building 4051 — Kilmer Campus
New Brunswick, New Jersey 08903

Library of Congress Cataloging in Publication Data

Mallach, Alan.
  Inclusionary housing programs.

  Bibliography: p. 278
  Includes index.
  1. Housing policy—United States. I. Title.
HD7293.M26   1984   363.5'8'0973   84-7055
ISBN 0-88285-100-4

CONTENTS

PREFACE

The effort of writing this book has been prompted by the conviction that the place of inclusionary housing programs in American housing and land use policy has become such that a serious and comprehensive treatment of the subject is not only timely, but overdue. This book seeks to provide that treatment. It is not a cookbook, with specific and detailed instructions on the design and conduct of inclusionary zoning ordinances and housing programs. It is, rather, an effort to discuss with reasonable objectivity the policy, programmatic, and technical issues associated with those programs, and to assess the national experience with inclusionary housing programs through 1983. A state or local official seeking to design an inclusionary program will find much that is useful in these pages, but will not find a model or a blueprint through which he or she will be explicitly guided.

Although the author has sought to be objective, the book is not without a point of view. Everything written on this subject, or on any comparably controversial topic, is animated by a point of view, even if efforts are made to disguise it. This book is no exception. It is grounded in a commitment to housing opportunity for all and to racial and economic integration as a central element in the provision of housing opportunity. These are practical, although highly ambitious, goals. For that reason, the book is written from a practical perspective; it seeks to evaluate the policies and programs under consideration as much from the standpoint of how they further those goals, as from abstract or idealized perspectives.

It would be impossible for me to acknowledge all of those who have contributed to making this book possible. In particular, I would like to express my appreciation to the many individuals with whom it has been an honor and a pleasure to work in this field for the past decade, and who have constantly given me ideas and readily served as sounding boards for my own ideas as they emerged. Among the many people in this group, I would like to mention in alphabetical order, rather than in any order of importance, Peter Abeles, of Abeles Schwartz & Associates, New York; Richard Bellman, Esq., of Steel & Bellman, New York; Carl Bisgaier, Esq., of Bisgaier & Pancotto, Cherry Hill, N.J.; Mary Brooks, San Pedro, California; Peter Buchsbaum, Esq., and Frank Petrino, Esq., of Sterns, Herbert & Weinroth, Trenton, N.J.; Philip Caton, of Clarke & Caton, Trenton; Steven Eisdorfer, Esq., and Kenneth Meiser, Esq., of the New Jersey Department of the Public Advocate, Trenton; Philip Elberg, Esq., of Medvin & Elberg, Newark, N.J.; Bruce Gelber, Esq., and Janet LaBella, Esq., of the National Committee Against Discrimination in Housing, Washington, D.C.; Thomas Hall, Esq., Henry Hill, Esq., and Michael Masanoff, Esq., of Brener, Wallack & Hill, Princeton, N.J.; Jonathan Lehrer-Graiwer, Esq., of the Western Center on Law & Poverty, Los Angeles, Calif.; John Nolon, of the Center for Community Development and Preservation, Tarrytown, N.Y.; Peter O'Connor, Esq., of Cherry Hill, N.J.; Crystal Sims, Esq., of the Orange County Legal Aid Society, Santa Ana, Calif.; and, above all, Paul Davidoff, of the Center for Metropolitan Action at Queens College, New York. To all of us who have worked for housing opportunity and integration since the beginning of the decade of the 1970s, Paul has been a constant source of ideas and insights, and above all, a conscience.

During the course of writing this book, innumerable people provided me information, over the telephone, in response to written requests, or in personal interviews. While I can only thank a few of them, I would like to note, among those who gave me much of their time and consideration, Valerie Glassford and Marilyn Zatz, of the Palo Alto Housing Corporation; John Gibson, of the Orange County Administrative Office; Frederic Kahane, of the Southern California Association of Governments; Lila Lieberthal, of the Carma-Sandling Group, Irvine, Calif.; Steven Mabs and Ruth Schwartz, of the California Department of Housing & Community Development; Peggy Schneble, of the City of Irvine, Calif.; Judith Swayne, Executive Assistant to Supervisor Riley, Orange County; and William Witte, of the Mayor's Office of Community Development, San Francisco. To these individuals, and to the very many others that I have not mentioned by name, my deepest thanks.

Finally, my special appreciation to Robin, whose companionship and moral support were always there, and who made the writing of this book far easier than it otherwise would have been.

Roosevelt, New Jersey
January 1984

1

Defining and Describing the Inclusionary Housing Program

The subject of this book is the provision of low- and moderate-income housing opportunities. It is grounded in two propositions: first, that the provision of decent housing for all Americans, whatever their income, is an important goal of American society; and second, that it is as important that those housing opportunities be provided in a manner that will foster both racial and economic integration, in the interest of a fairer and saner society.

The particular subject of the book is the provision of low- and moderate-income housing opportunities through the approach which has come to be known as the inclusionary housing program. This approach, still largely new and untested, represents a dramatic departure from past practice in housing and land use regulation. Perhaps for that reason it holds great promise of becoming the most significant means by which housing opportunities for lower-income households, in a racially and economically integrated environment, can and will be provided in the United States during the coming years. It has already been adopted, accompanied by considerable controversy, as a major element in land use and housing policy in California and in New Jersey — two states widely considered bellwether states, or guides to the future, in this field. At the same time, both the underlying proposition on which inclusionary housing programs depend and many of the specific features of such programs raise questions of law, public policy, and economic soundness that are yet unanswered. Unless these questions are resolved, this approach could become yet another footnote in the long list of ultimately unsuccessful bright ideas of which the history of American lower-income housing policy seems largely made.

The term "inclusionary housing program" and its counterpart, the "inclusionary zoning ordinance," have been present for a number of years at the margin of the planning vocabulary. When the term was initially used, it was often used to describe generically any concerted undertaking by a suburban municipality to foster affordable housing, by whatever means,[1] in direct contrast to the term "exclusionary zoning," which had come into prominence shortly before. While this usage is still found, the current usage, which is that of this book, is more narrow and more specific. Similarly, while the terms "inclusionary housing program" and "inclusionary zoning ordinance" are sometimes used in a manner which suggests that they are interchangeable, they are not. They do, however, as defined below, bear a close and important relationship to one another.

An *inclusionary zoning ordinance* will be defined as a zoning scheme under which prospective developers are required by a municipality or county to provide, as a condition of approval, or alternatively, are given incentives to provide, low- and moderate-income housing as a part of, or in conjunction with, their proposed development projects.

An *inclusionary housing program* is a program designed to bring about housing affordable to low- and moderate-income households in a community, using a variety of programs and activities, but relying principally for its implementation on an inclusionary zoning ordinance. An inclusionary zoning ordinance or the equivalent is a necessary condition for an inclusionary housing program; it is not, except in the unusual case, likely to be sufficient in itself for the resulting effort to be considered a legitimate program.

The crucial element in the foregoing is that under an inclusionary housing program, the provision of housing for lower-income households becomes part and parcel of the overall residential development of the community, constructed as a direct outcome of the construction of more expensive housing, and in some cases, even as an outcome of nonresidential development. This stands in marked contrast to previous practice, in which suburban low- and moderate-income housing development could only be constructed, if at all, as a separate entity, often isolated and ghettoized.

Given the history of American housing policy and social realities, it is readily apparent that the goal of inclusionary housing programs — the integration of lower-income housing into the growth and development of American suburbia[2] — is an ambitious one, which some might characterize as quixotic. While it is too soon to determine whether that is or is not the case, there has been enough experience to justify, indeed dictate, a thorough examination and evaluation. The purpose of this book is to conduct such an examination, which will look into not only the fundamental issues of law, policy, and economics raised by these programs, but will go beyond those questions to investigate the experience of inclusionary housing programs around the United States, and the practical and technical problems that have arisen through that experience.

This chapter, however, will seek to accomplish no more than a definition and description. After a discussion of the roots of the inclusionary housing approach and the considerations that have made it a major issue in housing and land use policy, the balance of the chapter is devoted to an effort to identify and describe the salient features of inclusionary housing programs, which are examined in more detail in subsequent chapters.

Why Inclusionary Housing?

Inasmuch as inclusionary housing policies and programs are a response to failures, real or perceived, in the previous conduct of American housing policies and programs, it is necessary first to examine those policies in order to identify and evaluate the basis on which the movement toward establishing inclusionary housing programs rests. Such an examination is made all the more important by virtue of the radical, or at least unprecedented nature of inclusionary housing in the context of more traditional American housing and land use policies. Such a dramatic departure from those traditional norms suggests a deep dissatisfaction with those policies, and a search for fundamentally new directions.

The movement toward inclusionary housing policies can be seen as an intersection of three separate concerns: First, the attempt of American housing policy to serve ambitious social policy goals, and the failure to achieve those goals; second, the national challenge to the practices of exclusionary zoning — a challenge both legal and political in nature; and third, economic trends reducing the affordability and availability of housing to the moderate- and middle-income population as well as to the poor during the past decade.

While housing policies at all levels of government as well as zoning, exclusionary or otherwise, go back in an unbroken thread to the 1920s and 1930s, the specific political, legal, social, and economic factors that have brought housing policy to its present state and prompted the undertaking of inclusionary housing programs are in essence a product of the past fifteen years since the late 1960s. During that period, whether by virtue of sustained economic expansion, progressive political thinking, or the chastening effect of widespread urban rioting, the United States committed itself to an ambitious social agenda, not least of which was the housing policy commitment embodied in the Housing Act of 1968. Whatever efforts may be made by the Reagan administration to reverse the trends, or redefine the national social policy agenda, the events of the 1960s defined sound social policy for the United States, in certain key regards, in a manner that has persisted remarkably to the present.

Housing Policy

Although the Housing Act of 1949 established the national ''goal of a decent home and a suitable living environment for every American family,''[3] neither at that time nor for nearly twenty years to come did Congress feel compelled to take any significant steps toward that goal. Indeed, the 1949 Housing Act was largely devoted to initiating the urban renewal program, which in the final analysis, is today widely held to have done significantly more harm than good to that goal.[4] This changed dramatically during the 1960s. The Department of Housing & Urban Development was established in 1965, and in 1968 Congress enacted the first legislation since the New Deal era which committed the federal government to provide the resources for a major program of construction and rehabilitation of housing for low- and moderate-income households, the Section 236 and Section 235 programs.[5] As a result of these programs, and the successor Section 8 programs, the production of federally subsidized housing units (both new construction and rehabilitation) swelled to nearly 500,000 by 1971, and after a decline and transitional period, returned to a level over 400,000 per year in 1979.[6]

More important than the number of units, however, was the spirit of the 1968 act, as embodied in its opening statement:

> The Congress finds that this goal [of the 1949 act] has not been fully realized for many of the Nation's lower income families; that this is a matter of grave national concern; and that there exists in the public and private sectors of the economy the resources and capabilities necessary to the full realization of this goal.[7]

A sense of urgency in meeting the housing needs of less affluent Americans became a part of the national consciousness, a sense of urgency to which the various commission reports and studies which followed the riots of the late 1960s contributed. Studies and publications on the subject of housing appeared in which the word "crisis" became more and more prominent.[8] From 1968 onward, efforts with varying degrees of success to meet the housing goals of the 1949 and 1968 acts were a significant part of the annual congressional agenda, and took up an increasing part of the federal domestic budget. Simultaneously, and perhaps inevitably, the fact that poor housing conditions, and of particular importance, extensive urban areas in which poor housing, poverty, and racial segregation coexisted, persisted throughout this period was an ongoing policy concern and an ongoing source of frustration to those involved in both making and executing policy in this area.[9]

The above conclusion points to a second goal of national housing policy, more complex and controversial both in framing and execution, which is that of fostering both racial and socioeconomic integration in housing. The provision of racially and socioeconomically integrated communities is widely held to be an important goal, not only for the poor and members of racial minorities alone, but for the society as a whole.[10] Furthermore, not only is racial discrimination clearly against the law, although nonetheless widely practiced, but the goal of socioeconomic integration has been embodied in federal policy in the Housing and Community Development Act of 1974.[11] In most parts of the United States, of course, the close relationship between racial and socioeconomic integration is so obvious as to hardly deserve comment — a relationship which has been recognized consistently by the conservative federal judiciary.[12]

During the last fifteen years, there have been hundreds, if not thousands, of efforts by community organizations, housing sponsors, and developers to foster integration through the use of federal housing programs — in particular Sections 235, 236, and subsequently, Section 8. Of these, only a small fraction were successful in the limited sense of bringing a group of housing units into being, often only as a result of litigation or of enormous effort expended over a considerable number of years. Furthermore, in many cases while the housing project may have integrated a community to some degree, in the statistical sense, it may have also turned into a suburban enclave of a low-income or minority population in which integration was more symbolic than real. Although there are few, if any, suburban low-income housing projects about which one could reasonably argue that it would have been better if they had never been built (which is by no means the case with regard to *urban* low-income housing projects), the fact remains that results often fell well short of sponsors' expectations.

There is little or no evidence, furthermore, that these efforts have had in the aggregate any meaningful impact on racial or socioeconomic segregation. During the 1970s, for example, in almost all cases the economic disparity between central cities and their suburban rings widened, the cities becoming poorer and the suburbs more affluent, at least in relative terms. Although the Department of Housing & Urban Development stepped into the picture in 1977, setting aside Section 8 subsidy funds for suburban communities willing to participate in Areawide Housing Opportunity Plans (AHOPs),[13] this too had little more than a marginal effect. The combination of the nearly inexorable workings of economic trends, once set in motion, coupled with the underlying values and attitudes of large parts of American society, have to date largely neutralized this entire aspect of American housing policy.

The above perceived failures and frustrations pale, however, by comparison with that experienced during the period following 1980, as the Reagan administration effectively eliminated over a period of less than three years any meaningful federal role in the production of new housing for low- and moderate-income households. It has long been recognized that with isolated and typically sporadic exceptions, neither state nor local government was capable of providing funding for housing programs in any manner capable of replacing the lost federal funds.[14] The loss of federal funds for new housing construction in the early 1980s was a significant factor in the growth of inclusionary housing programs; while some such programs initiated during the 1980s were seen as means of utilizing federal subsidies more effectively for socioeconomic integration,[15] by the early 1980s consideration was being given to inclusionary housing programs as an *alternative* to federal subsidy programs. The implications of this are considerable, and wil be discussed in detail later.

The Challenge to Exclusionary Zoning

Exclusionary zoning can be simply defined as zoning that "has the effect of keeping out of a community racial minorities, lower-income residents, or additional population of any kind,"[16] over and above intrinsic constraints such as the irreducible cost of land or construction. An extensive literature has been published detailing the specific machinery of exclusionary zoning, ranging from formal zoning ordinance provisions such as large lot size requirements, minimum dwelling unit floor area requirements, and prohibitions on housing types such as garden apartments to a variety of informal mechanisms and arbitrary patterns of municipal land use regulatory behavior.

Exclusionary zoning has existed as long as zoning; the pioneer case used by the U.S. Supreme Court to establish the constitutionality of zoning, *Euclid v. Ambler*, dealt with the exclusion of apartments from a residential district in a suburb of Cleveland, Ohio. Similarly, cases dealing with various of the zoning techniques that have come to be subsumed under the exclusionary zoning rubric have been brought to various state courts regularly since the 1920s. Numerous prescient judges, often in dissent, have pointed out the manner in which the techniques at issue were used to exclude "undesirable" populations, most notably the trial judge reversed by the Supreme Court in *Euclid*:

> The purpose to be accomplished is really to regulate the mode of living of persons who may hereafter inhabit it. In the last analysis, the result to be accomplished is to classify the population and segregate them according to their income or situation in life.[17]

This notwithstanding, the concept of exclusionary zoning as an issue to be challenged by litigation, political pressure, or otherwise, over and above specific zoning techniques or barriers, is a product of the 1960s and 1970s. This was to a large degree an outgrowth of the new focus not only by lawyers, but by planners, academics, and many public officials on zoning as a major factor in preventing the achievement of housing opportunity goals and the realization of national housing policies.[18]

While it would be beyond the scope of this book to attempt to trace the complex linkages between the exclusionary zoning challenge and the other social and political movements of the time, while simply noting its roots in the civil rights movement, it is clear that the challenge emerged in force quite suddenly in the late 1960s, at which time not only were numerous lawsuits filed,[19] but the issue was granted significant recognition at the political level in a number of states as well.[20] This is also the point at which the most important initial scholarly publication on the subject appeared.[21]

From this beginning, during the course of the 1970s a number of outcomes emerged. First, the focus of action shifted sharply from the federal to the state courts, as the federal courts — most notably in *Boraas v. Belle Terre* and *Warth v. Seldin* — adopted a posture essentially antagonistic to those who sought to challenge exclusionary zoning ordinances, except under the extremely narrow circumstances provided for in *Arlington Heights*. The state courts by comparison — most notably in New Jersey but in other states such as Pennsylvania, New York, and California — during the same period demonstrated a readiness to confront the issue in broader fashion. Second, despite frequent legal victories, the tangible outcomes in terms of units of low- and moderate-income housing produced as a result of these victories were painfully limited. The number and complexity of the intervening steps between a court decision and the actual construction of low- and moderate-income housing not only created major practical difficulties for plaintiffs, but offered a recalcitrant municipal defendant innumerable opportunities to prevent construction from taking place.

The difficulties were compounded by the variety of interests, often at conflict, involved in such litigation and by the varying perspectives adopted by different jurisdictions. In Pennsylvania, it became relatively easy for an offended builder to obtain affirmative relief in the form of a grant of building permits by the court, but the Pennsylvania doctrine, as it emerged in the 1970s, appeared almost entirely preoccupied with ensuring a variety of building *types* in each community, with little sensitivity to the issues of racial or socioeconomic integration, or to planning issues for that matter. In any event, the success of a single builder in obtaining permits for a single project, often with little regard to its merits, did not provide for any long-term reassessment of the land use scheme or for long-term provision of housing opportunities in the affected municipality.

In New Jersey, by comparison, the courts showed considerable sensitivity to broad housing and planning issues, but until 1983 were strongly disinclined to award any form of affirmative relief to a builder, except under the most unusual or extreme circumstances. Coupled with the unwillingness of the municipalities which had lost exclusionary zoning suits to undertake any affirmative programs in response to the court decisions, and in many cases, their readiness to obstruct those decisions, the likelihood of significant affordable housing production taking place as a result appeared more and more remote. Furthermore, as plaintiffs became more sophisticated about economic realities, they realized that simply eliminating exclusionary zoning barriers was not, in itself, necessarily a means to creation of affordable housing. If a municipality, for example, adopted an ordinance in which substantial land areas were zoned without exclusionary restrictions for housing types such as apartments and townhouses, but the market demand in the community for such housing at high price levels was substantial, it was unlikely that any of that land would ever become available for the construction of inexpensive housing.[22]

This reality was brought home in the case involving Mahwah Township, an affluent suburban community in northern New Jersey, in which an ordinance (adopted subsequent to the filing of an exclusionary zoning suit, but prior to the trial) designated substantial acreage for planned residential developments at gross densities of 4 and 6 units per acre, without egregious exclusionary standards or constraints. Trial testimony established that land in these districts was in the process of being developed with townhouses planned to sell, for the most part, at prices in excess of $100,000.

This was the first exclusionary zoning case, to the author's knowledge, where the thrust of the plaintiff's case was that compliance with the standards set forth in the New Jersey Supreme Court's 1975 *Mount Laurel* decision dictated the adoption of an inclusionary program by the municipality:

> In restructuring a zoning ordinance to comply with *Mount Laurel* and *Madison*, however, a municipality must take into account the context in which the ordinance will be implemented. Profit and market factors must be recognized and considered. *It is the duty of the municipality to ensure that construction of a sufficient supply of least cost housing will actually take place*, given the realities of the marketplace.[23] [Author's emphasis]

While this argument did not prevail at the trial court, it was adopted by the New Jersey Supreme Court in the 1983 case known as *Mount Laurel II*.[24] In this decision, which will be discussed in detail later, the court held that adoption of an inclusionary housing program would be expected, if not explicitly required, of any municipality subject to the obligation to provide for its fair share of regional low- and moderate-income housing needs.

By 1983 the proposition that municipalities had some responsibility to provide for a variety of housing needs, including those of low- and moderate-income households, was widely accepted, although arguably honored more in rhetoric than reality. Furthermore, among those involved with efforts to make that responsibility a reality, it had become clear that zoning, by its nature, cannot be socioeconomically neutral. The objective typical of early exclusionary zoning litigation of seeking a neutral, non-exclusionary ordinance, in the expectation that housing affordable to all would inevitably flow as a result, was unrealistic. The effect of any zoning provision is inextricably interwoven with the economic forces affecting its time and place. Thus, advocates of affordable housing or of socioeconomic integration realized that zoning and land use controls would have to be converted into affirmative instruments if their objectives were to be realized.

Trends in Housing Affordability

While public agencies were grappling with means to use public funds to create housing opportunities and the courts were seeking, with varying degrees of success, to resolve exclusionary zoning controversies, a fundamental change was taking place in the relationship of the average American household to the housing market — a change characterized by various official bodies as a "housing cost crisis"[25] or an "affordability problem."[26] While conventionally produced and financed housing had always been beyond the reach of the poor or near-poor, during the 1970s such housing moved further and further away from the grasp of large parts of the non-poor population, the American middle class.

The problem, in essence, was a combination of two factors. During the 1970s, house prices rose at a substantially faster rate than incomes. Second, beginning in the late 1970s, and particularly in the early 1980s, mortgage interest rates rose, compounding the effect of the price increases. For example, in 1965 a household earning the national median income would have been able to purchase a new home selling at the national median house price at an annual cost of 24 percent of their income for mortgage payments, property taxes, and insurance. By 1978, the median income household would have had to spend 36 percent of their income in order to buy a house at the median price. With only a modest change in the price/income ratio, but reflecting the change in the available mortgage interest rate, by 1981 the same household would have had to spend 50 percent of their gross income for the same house.[27] Put differently, if one holds the percentage of income to be used for mortgage payments, taxes and insurance at 28 percent,[28] one finds that in 1965, the median household could afford a house selling for 117 percent of the median new house price; by 1978 that household could afford a house selling for 75 percent of the median, and by 1981, only 56 percent of the median. In essence, the household that in 1965 had a choice of housing from among the substantial majority of new units on the market, was limited to a relatively small number by 1978, and was more or less completely locked out of the market by 1981.

There are many reasons for the affordability problem. Interest rates rise and fall for reasons having little if anything to do with the housing industry, which is a passive beneficiary or victim of national and international economic forces.[29] The cost of housing units, however, is more likely to be influenced by factors internal to the housing and development environment; there is a respectable body of opinion that argues that a substantial part of the increase is a function of the increase in growth regulation, much of it prompted by environmental concerns, real or otherwise, during the 1970s.[30] Given the nature of the concerns that prompt local government to seek to control growth, it is logical that the areas in which such controls are most stringent are often areas in which demand pressures are particularly strong — most notably in suburban areas around San Francisco and Los Angeles. In such areas, the juxtaposition of strong demand pressures and strong growth controls can be expected to have a mutually reinforcing effect on the price of housing; one indication of this is that house prices (new and existing) increased by 205 percent from 1970 to 1978 in southern California, while increasing by (only) 120 percent during the same period nationally.[31]

While affordability is a national problem to some degree, it is clear that it varies significantly from one part of the United States to another in its severity and in the number or percentage of area households affected. Since the same factors that are likely to trigger new house price increases in excess of the national average are also likely to push up the price of existing house resales, whatever utility the "trickle-down" theory may have in less impacted areas will be least in the areas of greatest demand and growth pressure. A host of informal observations suggests that such areas are concentrated most heavily in the northeastern United States, within the Boston-Washington corridor, and on the West Coast. Although other growth areas are hardly free of affordability problems, it would appear that such factors as a more open regulatory climate, ready availability of inexpensive land, and the existence of large unincorporated areas in which development can take place tend to mitigate the severity of these problems in large parts of the South and Southwest.

One effect of the "housing cost crisis" was to enlist in some parts of the country members of the middle class on the side of those seeking change. As Frieden writes:

> In the 1960's the victims of suburban exclusion were mainly poor people, a small and powerless minority. They are still victims of it in the 1970's. But now there are many more victims than before. Middle-income America, in addition to the poor, is now bearing the costs of suburban growth policies.[32]

The significance of this enlistment, as it were, in providing the impetus for the development of inclusionary housing programs cannot be overstated. In particular, in California the political constituency came into being to make possible the enactment of inclusionary zoning ordinances without reference to court challenges, real or imaginary. This same constituency, coupled with that of builders and developers thwarted by the imposition of increasingly stringent growth controls and development constraints, led to the enactment of a body of state legislation in California in 1980 far more extensive in the degree to which it set forth the local responsibility to foster low- and moderate-income housing and in its encouragement of inclusionary housing programs than has ever been enacted, or even seriously entertained, in any other state. One question that arises, however, is whether these activities have significantly benefited the low- and moderate-income population, as traditionally defined. As will be discussed, the terms "low income'' and ''moderate income'' have become subject to substantial redefinition and manipulation in the course of events.

Thus, by the early 1980s both a legal and a political climate had been established in which inclusionary housing programs — i.e., the use of local government land use regulatory powers to foster housing affordable to a less affluent population — logically followed from the perceived needs of a substantial part of the population coupled with the growing perception by both lawyers and planners that local land use regulations represented an appropriate, indeed, *the* appropriate, means by which those needs should be addressed. This is not to suggest that anything remotely akin to a national consensus had come into being in support of inclusionary housing programs. Both the concept itself, as well as many of its specific manifestations and elements, were the subject of severe disagreement on a wide variety of grounds, some trivial, but others thoughtful and significant. Such opposition was particularly apparent in those cases where observers perceived such programs as being the means whereby government could shift the responsibility for problems, often of its own making, off the public sector and onto the private sector to the development and homebuilding industry. That notwithstanding, the spread of inclusionary housing and zoning programs by the early 1980s was such that it was necessary to recognize the subject as one of the major land use issues of the decade. This was already the case prior to 1983 when the *Mount Laurel II* decision, coming from perhaps the nation's leading state court on land use matters, brought it to a central place in all serious discussion about future national housing and land use policy.

What is an Inclusionary Housing Program?

Throughout the various twists and turns of American housing policy, housing for lower-income households has been built almost entirely in the inner city, of which it is a well-known and distinctive feature. Suburban developments of low- and moderate-income housing have been few and far between, other than developments for lower-income senior citizens,[33] and where built, have often ended up as isolated, ghettoized enclaves. The only other previously available alternative for low- and moderate-income housing in suburban areas was through programs such as the Section 8 Existing Housing program, under which individual lower-income households were given federal assistance to enable them to rent apartments in already existing privately owned buildings — a program whose impact was extremely limited for a variety of reasons.[34]

In contrast, as was set forth at the beginning of this chapter, the fundamental approach of inclusionary housing programs is to make development of lower-income housing an integral part of other development taking place in the community, by setting forth either mandatory conditions or voluntary objectives for the inclusion of low- and moderate-income housing in prospective market-rate developments, coupled with incentives designed to facilitate the achievement of these conditions or objectives.

A typical inclusionary zoning ordinance will set forth a minimum number of percentage of units to be provided in a given residential development affordable to households at a specific income level, generally defined as a percentage of the median income of the area. For example, under the Orange County, California, ordinance, 25 percent of all units in developments to which the ordinance applies must be affordable to households earning less than 120 percent of the Orange County median income.[35] The ordinance further breaks down the 25 percent according to a formula which varies on the basis of whether public (federal, state or local) subsidies are available to the development (see Exhibit 1).

EXHIBIT 1

Units to be Affordable to Households Earning:	If Public Subsidies Available	Subsidies Not Available
below 80% of median	10%	0%
80% to 100% of median	10%	15%
100% to 120% of median	5%	10%

Source: Schwartz, Johnston & Burtraw, *Local Government Initiatives for Affordable Housing: An Evaluation of Inclusionary Housing Programs in California* (1981), p. 24

Ordinances have been enacted, however, with requirements that as many as 40 percent of all units be low- and moderate-income housing, and as few as 5 percent. While most ordinances require that low- and moderate-income housing units be located within the development, there are programs under which a developer may locate those units on a separate site, as a separate, unrelated development, or may pay a fee to the minicipality or to some other entity in lieu of building the units required by the ordinance.

In many ordinances, some form of incentive is provided by the county or municipality to the developer in return for the provision of low- and moderate-income housing. Under present California state law, a municipality is required to offer incentives to any developer providing at least 25 percent of the total units in any housing development for persons and families of low- or moderate-income.[36] In the case of Orange County, incentives include a "density bonus," modifications of development standards such as parking requirements, expedited development processing, allocation of Community Development Block Grant funds received by the county to write down project costs, and issuing of tax-exempt revenue bonds in order to make below-market interest rate mortgages to buyers at the low- and moderate-income housing units in the development.

The most fundamental features of an inclusionary housing program, therefore, are the inclusion of low- and moderate-income housing units within the fabric of private market residential development in the community, and the affirmative participation of local government in the process through the provision of various bonuses or incentives facilitating the provision of low- and moderate-income housing. The balance of this chapter will attempt to describe further elements which are central to the understanding of the concept, and to the framing of a responsible inclusionary program.

Voluntary or Mandatory Inclusion

The inclusionary programs undertaken to date fall into two camps based on a fundamental dichotomy. In some programs, the inclusion of low- and moderate-income units is provided as a voluntary option, for which some incentive is offered but which a developer is free to accept or reject; in others, it is a mandatory condition of development. The typical incentive offered under voluntary inclusionary plans is an increase in density, called a density bonus. In one of the more generous such plans, that of East Brunswick, New Jersey, a developer building in a zone in which the maximum density by right is set at 5 dwelling units per acre can increase that density to a maximum of 8 units per acre through the provision of low- and moderate-income housing. The low- and moderate-income units are allowed in excess of the ''by right'' density, and the developer is further allowed one additional conventional unit for each low- and moderate-income unit provided. For example, on a 100-acre tract, a developer by building 150 low- and moderate-income units is allowed to build an additional 150 market units over and above the 500 units allowed ''by right,'' for a grand total of 650 market units.[37] In addition, the township provides the developer with expedited processing and facilitates applications for federal and state housing subsidies.[38]

The East Brunswick program has yielded a not insignificant number of moderate-income, although no low-income, units — largely through the use of federal subsidy programs. It is, however, unusual in the scope of the incentives that it offers developers to provide low- and moderate-income units. The East Brunswick experience notwithstanding, most voluntary programs have not produced low- and moderate-income housing; one commentator reviewing the California experiences states unequivocally:

> No planning official we interviewed was aware of a situation in which density bonuses, fast track processing, or other incentives were sufficient inducement to produce low or moderate cost housing in the absence of

other programs and policies. Although a firm conclusion may be prema-
ture, it seems reasonable to regard incentives as a necessary accompani-
ment to . . . mandatory inclusionary programs.[39]

In essence, if federal subsidy funds are available which are more or less adequate
in themselves to make development of low- and moderate-income housing economically feasible, a voluntary density bonus may be an appealing means of
overcoming the typical developer's reluctance to participate in a federal program
or to incorporate such units in a development. If public subsidies are not available, it is unlikely that most developers will be adequately motivated by any
available incentive to undertake the efforts needed to provide low- and moderate-income housing without outside subsidy.

Under a mandatory program, of course, the burden is on the developer to arrive at a means whereby the required low- and moderate-income units can be
produced, utilizing such incentives and subsidies as may be available. If housing
subsidies are available, so much the better; their absence, however, does not re-
lieve the developer of the responsibility under a mandatory inclusionary ordinance. As a result, a mandatory program is unequivocally more effective as a
technique of generating low- and moderate-income housing. In the process,
however, it raises a number of issues of law and public policy, which are discussed in detail in the following chapter. Nevertheless, the fact remains clear that
in the current environment, no land use strategy heavily dependent on the availability of federal or other subsidies has any real capability of increasing the stock
of low- and moderate-income housing, and mandatory inclusionary programs
must be given more consideration and taken far more seriously than voluntary
programs offering incentives for the construction of low- and moderate-income
housing.

Determining Who is to Benefit

The term "low- and moderate-income housing" has been used as a general
phrase descriptive of the units that are to be created through the establishment of
inclusionary housing programs. This term, however, is subject to widely varying
interpretation. To begin, there may be wide variation in the sense in which terms
such as "low income" or "moderate income" are used; furthermore, there is
even wider variation in the determination of what housing, at what prices, and
under what conditions, may be affordable to a population of a given income
level.

A major question underlying much of the variation is one of policy: who is to
benefit from the program being established? Only occasionally is the social policy motivation made explicit. The New Jersey Supreme Court, in its *Mount
Laurel II* decision, made its priorities explicit by using uncharacteristically un-

ambiguous language: "If sound planning of an area allows the rich and middle class to live there, it must also realistically and practically allow the poor."[40] For purposes of implementing the decision, the court characterized the population to be served and toward whom inclusionary housing programs should be directed as follows:

> "Moderate income families" are those whose incomes are no greater than 80 percent and no less than 50 percent of the median income of the area, with adjustments for smaller and larger families. "Low income families" are those whose incomes do not exceed 50 percent of the median income of the area, with adjustments for smaller and larger families.[41]

In order to emphasize its point that it was not seeking through this decision to benefit the middle class rather than the poor, the court distinguished its characterization of these income ranges from the terminology used by HUD, which characterizes the above groups as "low income" and "very low income" respectively.

By comparison, the Orange County ordinance described earlier provides that beneficiaries may be those whose incomes are as high as 120 percent of the area median income and, where subsidy funds are unavailable, allows the inclusionary requirement to be met by providing units affordable to a segment of the population, *the least affluent of whom earn more than the most affluent member of the New Jersey Supreme Court's target population*. Although not set forth as such, it would appear to be the case that the political objectives of the Orange County program dictate as much, if not more, emphasis on meeting the housing needs of middle class households priced out of the marketplace by rampant housing cost inflation as on meeting the housing needs of the poor or near-poor. This is typical of many, if not most, of the inclusionary housing programs established within California jurisdictions.[42]

Establishment of the area median income for each area (which is generally a Standard Metropolitan Statistical Area, or SMSA) between the decennial census years is generally made by HUD, which undertakes an annual estimating process in order to adjust eligibility standards for the housing projects under its supervision. In Orange County, for example, early in 1983 the HUD median gross family income figure was $29,900. As a result, households with incomes up to $36,000 could qualify for low- and moderate-income housing under the Orange County inclusionary ordinance. Within the state of New Jersey, HUD median income figures ranged from a low of $21,800 (Cape May County), to a high of $33,100 (Hunterdon County). In the Newark SMSA, the largest SMSA in the state, the maximum income for a family of four to be considered "moderate income" by the definition of the New Jersey Supreme Court in 1983 was $25,200.[43]

An issue related to that of setting the income limits for the beneficiaries of in-clusionary housing programs is that of setting other eligibility criteria for occupancy of these units — particularly criteria having to do with prior residency or employment within the community. The issue of prior local residency as a condition for the occupancy of low- and moderate-income housing has been a constant bone of contention throughout the history of subsidized housing development in suburban areas. Such restrictions, either formally or *de facto*, have frequently been imposed by suburban governments as a condition of approval of a subsidized housing project, in violation of HUD regulations, as well as the spirit if not the letter of federal law.[44]

At least one inclusionary zoning ordinance — that of the town of Lewisboro, New York — establishes selection priorities in excruciating detail for occupancy of units created through the inclusionary program. Eight broad priority categories are established, and within each, various subcategories. The first priority category is "Town of Lewisboro municipal employees"; within that category, applicants are then to be ranked according to the following subcategories:

> Residents of the town of Lewisboro
> Cumulative length of service
> Cumulative length of residence
> Date of application
> Lottery

The ordinance further provides for "special priority" within each category for families displaced by governmental action, families of which the head is 62 years or older, and families of which the head is handicapped.[45] It is unclear whether a scheme of this nature would be sustained in the event of a serious court challenge, particularly in view of the rationale of *Berenson v. New Castle*, the leading New York State exclusionary zoning case.[46]

It takes little sophistication to appreciate that such priorities are set at least in part for reasons having to do with racial fears and prejudices, particularly when the suburban community is a largely white community within a manageable distance from a core city with a large minority population. Ironically, in the absence of an effective affirmative marketing program in which information on suburban low- and moderate-income housing opportunities is made available to urban residents in useable form, the simple factors of access to information and proximity tend to dictate that most such suburban developments will be largely occupied by residents of the immediate area, without any formal setting of priorities.

It is clear that these issues have major policy implications. In both income ceilings and residency requirements, the programmatic choices reflect the fundamental policy question of *whom does the community seek to have benefit from the program*? The political pressure for affordable housing by less advantaged members of the middle class — young couples, divorced mothers with children, senior citizens — is far more compelling in the typical suburban jurisdiction than is the demand for better housing and better access to suburban jobs by the residents of the inner city. It is not surprising that a review of inclusionary programs, particularly in California, suggests that the former is far more often treated as the target population than the latter; indeed, only in New Jersey, where the state supreme court has set clear ground rules, is this pattern likely to be consistently different.

Providing Bonuses and Incentives

It is generally recognized that the developer participating in an inclusionary housing program, whether voluntary or mandatory, should be offered incentives to foster his participation or at least to deflect criticism and discourage the charge that the program is economically ruinous to the participating developer. Leaving aside for the moment the question of the actual economic consequences, a further justification for the provision of incentives is as a recognition that the impetus for inclusionary programs stems from public policy objectives, and not from a need that developers right wrongs that they have somehow committed. As noted briefly earlier, incentives can take a variety of forms, including most notably the provision of density bonuses, expedited processing, waiver of fees or charges, and preferential access to housing subsidy funds of various sorts.

The notion of the "density bonus" is particularly significant, since it frequently appears to be a central element intrinsic to the entire inclusionary housing approach. Strictly speaking, a density bonus applies only to voluntary programs. A dictionary defines a bonus as "something given . . . in addition to the usual or expected."[47] Since under a mandatory inclusionary program the provision of low- and moderate-income units is clearly "usual and expected" in the context of the ordinance, there cannot be a bonus as such associated with the program. Density bonuses, when incorporated in a mandatory inclusionary ordinance (except if, for example, the bonus were offered as an incentive to produce more than the minimum required number of low- and moderate-income units), are simply a semantic hustle. It can be, however, a convenient accounting fiction for purposes of allocating the costs associated with providing the low- and moderate-income units in a development.

The same is true, to a degree, of other municipal incentives having to do with fees, exactions, and the time associated with the processing of development applications. It is generally recognized that the fees and exactions associated with new residential development in many communities are patently excessive, and that the length of time required by most municipalities to process development applications from initial application to final approval is inordinate.[48] In that context, the provision of "incentives" under an inclusionary program in this sphere is really a matter of providing a *quid pro quo*; in return for providing low- and moderate-income housing, the developer will not be forced to subject himself to delays and exactions which both he and the municipal officials well know to be unreasonable.

Indeed, the question logically arises that if the exactions and delays are acknowledged to be unreasonable in the case of a developer building low- and moderate-income housing units, why are they not equally unreasonable in the case of any developer proposing a *bona fide* residential development? In some cases there may be a legitimate distinction. A particular exaction (such as the dedication of land, or the making of a payment in lieu of dedication of land for park purposes) may in itself be sound public policy. It does, nonetheless, impose a potentially significant cost on a development, which makes the objective of providing low- and moderate-income housing more difficult. The waiver may, therefore, be appropriate, and by imposing the full burden on the developers not participating in the inclusionary housing program, provide a means whereby certain of the costs associated with the program may be more equitably distributed. Leaving aside the legal issues involved, this may be reasonable public policy. The fact remains that not all exactions, and certainly not unreasonable delays in processing, can be similarly justified.

A similar argument can be made in the case of density bonuses. Euclidian zoning dictates that the establishment of density standards should reflect the most appropriate use of land from the physical standpoint. In the East Brunswick example given earlier, for example, if 8 units per acre is an appropriate density of development for the site, should it not be so established by right? If 5 units per acre (the density allowed by right) is appropriate from a land use standpoint, is not allowing the density to be increased so drastically irresponsible? At a minimum, such variations arguably impede the process of rational planning for the expansion of infrastructure and community facilities to a given area.

The above argument should not be taken as seriously as it is taken by some commentators, since it is well known that density choices are by their nature highly arbitrary and subject to a variety of policy inputs other than those of physical capacity, and in any event, the notion that there is a single "proper" density or intensity of land use for each parcel in a community has long since been acknowledged to be absurd. Nonetheless, leaving aside the lack of mathematical perfection in this area, the question of inconsistency does arise and should not be totally disregarded.

In the remaining area, that of preferential access to housing subsidies, there can be little serious quarrel. If a municipality has determined that its public policy approach to meeting low- and moderate-income housing needs will be through means of an inclusionary program, it is arguably obligated to seek out whatever subsidies may be available in order to offer them to developers participating in the program. Even in the absence of massive federal subsidy programs for new construction such as the now defunct Section 8 program, available subsidies may be of crucial importance in determining who will have access to the "low and moderate income" units provided, a fact recognized by the provisions of the Orange County inclusionary zoning ordinance described earlier. Federal funds under the Community Development Block Grant program can be used in a number of ways, such as for land acquisition or writedown or the provision of infrastructure, that directly benefit potential tenants or buyers; tax-exempt mortgage financing for the purchasers of housing units created through inclusionary programs can often make a major difference in the affordability of those units.

Leaving aside for a moment the questions and policy issues touched upon briefly above, the rationale that lies behind any or all "bonuses" or "incentives" is central to the concept of inclusionary housing: *if a developer is to be expected to provide low- and moderate-income housing, the municipality making that demand must ensure, to the degree feasible, that the circumstances under which he is to develop are conducive to that goal.* Land development standards must be such that a cost-efficient, economical product can be constructed, and costs extraneous to the needs of the development itself must be minimized, including the costs of delay. Finally, whether through utilization of outside subsidy funds or through the resources of the municipality itself, every reasonable effort should be made to assist the developer in bearing the costs associated with the development and increasing the affordability of the units produced. An ordinance or program which simply imposes an inclusionary requirement on a developer without any municipal *quid pro quo* is an act of irresponsibility on the part of the municipality. Such ordinances, upon investigation, rarely turn out to have been motivated by the objective of meeting low- and moderate-income housing needs.

Who Benefits II: Creating and Maintaining
Low- and Moderate-Income Occupancy

Once units are built and priced in a manner making them affordable to low- and moderate-income households, a host of issues arises with regard to ensuring first, that they are initially occupied by households in the putative beneficiary class; and second, that they continue to be so occupied over an extended period — if not by the same household, then by a household similarly economically situated.

The process by which units created through inclusionary housing programs are marketed, in particular some of the circus-like lotteries conducted in connection with inclusionary programs in California, has been noted. A major issue, to which there is no simple answer, is that these programs by their nature produce significant benefits for a small percentage of the potential beneficiary population and no benefit to the majority of that population, thereby dictating in each case that the competition for those benefits will be strong.[49] This is compounded by the fact that a large part of the units produced in these programs are located in elite or "premium" communities such as Orange County, California, or Montgomery County, Maryland, thus heightening the competition.

Ironically, by setting ceilings on what a household can earn and still qualify for such units, a potential marketability problem can be created. For example, if the ceiling income for a particular project is X, and a household earning that ceiling income can afford a unit selling for 2X, the developer placing units on the market at a price of 2X may well find few, if any, takers. Since no one earning less than X can afford the unit, and no one earning more than X can legally qualify, the universe of households who can both afford the unit and qualify (those earning precisely X) is likely to be too small to provide a market. Although there is no mathematical formula that can be consistently applied, it is clear that the actual prices of low- and moderate-income units will have to be pegged substantially below the ceiling price dictated by the language of the ordinance governing the development.

The question of maintaining units as low- and moderate-income housing over an extended period is more complex and important enough to justify devoting a chapter to the subject. A few comments here, however, are in order. By its nature, an inclusionary housing program — particularly in a premium community — will provide its beneficiaries with units likely to sell for prices well below the market price for that unit in that community. Given that and given the transient nature of much of the American population, in the absence of controls designed to prevent such an outcome, a large number of these units are likely to be resold within a short period to more affluent households at market prices, thereby providing the initial low- and moderate-income buyer with a windfall, and permanently removing the unit from the stock available to low- and moderate-income households. While such an outcome is not bad for the initial buyer — now the seller — of the unit, it tends at a minimum to exacerbate the problem of disproportionate benefit to a small part of the potential beneficiary population, and to raise a variety of public policy considerations.

The most frequent response by policy makers framing inclusionary housing programs is the adoption of rent controls for rental units and resale controls for owner-occupied units. There is little controversy associated with the former, other than that associated with rent control generally within the society — indeed, public agencies providing housing subsidies or below-market mortgage financing routinely exercise control over the rents charged in projects so assisted, for the duration of the financing or other subsidy.[50] The subject of controls on the sale of units is more complex, but of great importance, inasmuch as a significant part of the housing produced under inclusionary programs is and will continue to be sales housing. The reasons for this are complex, and are discussed in detail later.

Leaving aside the legal issues they raise, resale controls raise policy issues about the nature of homeownership and the significance of appreciation in the bundle of goods known collectively as "home ownership." Resale controls typically control either or both of these elements: the appreciation of house value, by setting the price at which the unit can be sold; and the transfer of property, by limiting or dictating the party or parties to which the unit can be sold. Typically, a formula will be established to determine the selling price — a formula which may take into consideration changes in the consumer price index, the value of improvements made by the owner, and so forth.[51] A program may further provide that a public agency, such as a housing authority, have the right of first refusal to purchase the unit at the formula price, or have the right to nominate buyers from a pre-screened list of qualified households. Alternatively, the seller may be able to sell the unit on the open market, but pass on the difference between the market price and the formula price, if any, to the housing agency which will use the funds to subsidize another unit elsewhere for a qualified household.

The permutations of such a practice are almost infinite, and each community either tailors a control scheme to its needs or chooses to do without. Any such scheme, however, must walk a narrow tightrope between fostering the public policy of continued low- and moderate-income benefit and undermining the public policy, widely held, of encouraging home ownership. It would appear likely that if the controls are too stringent and too confining of the owner, the "ownership" of the unit may come to be perceived as a sham, with potentially deleterious social effects.

An American Phenomenon

It is worth noting that although the objectives of an inclusionary housing policy are widely shared by planners and policy-makers in the industrialized nations, the specific approach characterized as an inclusionary housing program is largely an American phenomenon. Policies designed to promote economic and demographic integration have been encouraged by a number of governments: Israel undertook to create a planned demographic mix between new immigrants, typically of lower income, and veteran Israelis in a number of planned new communities;[52] the city of Paris has adopted plans and policies to maintain the historic economic mix in "gentrifying" older areas through the construction and rehabilitation of housing for lower-income households;[53] and Canada has actively fostered economic integration in a planned community in Vancouver, British Columbia.[54] These are merely a few examples of what is a widespread housing policy objective throughout the industrialized world.

With the limited exception of the Vancouver development, the inclusionary objectives of other countries are achieved through more direct public sector intervention in the financing and production of housing than in the United States. The city of Paris, for example, seeks to ensure continued low- and moderate-income occupancy of historic areas through the acquisition and rehabilitation of buildings, under public or nonprofit auspices, for lower-income occupancy in areas such as the Marais and Beaubourg.[55] In the Israeli new towns, the great majority of the units for people of varying economic levels were built under governmental or quasi-governmental programs.[56] It would appear that public policy in most European countries is supportive of more direct, ongoing public intervention in the housing market than is the case in this country.[57] In such a climate, a delegation to the private sector to the extent implicit in the inclusionary housing program approach could be seen as a failure on government's part to carry out its responsibilities. This is particularly the case in those countries in which a clear political distinction is made between the private sector and the "social sector" which must be protected from the vagaries of the private marketplace. In the United States, by comparison, even in the heyday of federal housing programs, the dominant ideology consistently maintained that the provision of housing was a private sector responsibility, to be only supplemented by public resources.

One project which combines elements from both American and European approaches was the False Creek planned community in Vancouver. The False Creek area was a large tract of vacant and underutilized land in Vancouver which was the subject of a systematic planning and development effort to create a "new town in town" beginning in the late 1960s, and designed eventually to accommodate a population of 30,000. Starting with the premise that,

> communities which offer little social and physical diversity are unhealthy [and] people living in them have limited access to the wide range of values, habits and beliefs which are the essential ingredients of urban living,[58]

the False Creek planners decided that the project should have an economic mix reflecting that of the Greater Vancouver area. That was translated in 1976 dollars (Canadian) to a mix of one-third of the households earning under $11,700; one-third between $11,700 and $18,600; and one-third over $18,600.[59] The economic mix target was coupled with a demographic mix target to ensure a mixture of young and old, and small and large families.

Achievement of the income mix objective was exceptionally difficult and resulted in the creation of a variety of new and creative approaches, including a program for "controlled leasehold condominiums" combining some of the features of a mortgage buydown and a lease-purchase structure.[60] An internal subsidy was also incorporated into the project — by applying a different ground rent to each type of housing being developed, "higher income households would, in effect, subsidize lower income ones."[61] The ground leases were structured so that they could be renegotiated at ten-year intervals to reflect changing economic conditions.

The last example comes closest to the American model of the inclusionary housing program. Still, the "inclusionary" element of the overall project is clearly subordinated to intense public sector involvement and intervention in making housing available to lower-income households through a variety of national and provincial programs and resouces. The False Creek project is closer in its underlying philosophy and *modus operandi* to the European model than the American one.

In conclusion, this chapter has attempted first, to set forth some of the circumstances by which inclusionary housing programs have come to be a major element in American housing and land use policy; and second, to provide a brief overview of the concept known as an inclusionary housing program, along with some initial discussion of the major elements of such programs and the policy issues raised by each element. In the following chapter, the author attempts to explore the implications of inclusionary housing programs in terms of the law and public policy considerations.

NOTES

1. It is in this generic sense that the term is used in the first major work on this subject, Herbert M. Franklin, David Falk & Arthur J. Levin, *In-Zoning: A Guide for Policy-Makers on Inclusionary Land Use Programs* (Washington D.C.: The Potomac Institute, 1974).

2. While the principal thrust of inclusionary housing programs has been suburban, it is by no means limited to suburban communities. Substantial inclusionary efforts, either in planning or under way, have been or are being carried out in such cities as Los Angeles, San Francisco, and New York City. As will be discussed later, however, economic constraints are likely to preclude serious consideration of inclusionary programs in all but the atypical central city.

3. Housing Act of 1949, P.L. 171, 81st Congress, 63 Stat. 413; 42 U.S.C. 1441.

4. See Nathan Glazer, "The Bias of American Housing Policy," in Jon Pynoos, Robert Schafer & Chester W. Hartman, eds., *Housing Urban America* (Chicago: Aldine, 1973); see especially Chapter 8 in Charles Abrams, *The City is the Frontier* (New York: Harper & Row, 1965).

5. These programs provided a federally funded interest rate subsidy, so that the effective interest rate on the mortgage as paid by the homeowner or tenant was 1 percent, with federal funds making up the difference between 1 percent and the actual market rate. The Section 235 program provided mortgage financing to individual homebuyers, and the Section 236 program provided financing to the developers of rental housing projects.

6. See George Sternlieb & James W. Hughes, "Housing in the United States: An Overview," in Sternlieb & Hughes, eds., *America's Housing: Prospects and Problems* (New Brunswick, N.J.: Center for Urban Policy Research, 1980), pp. 1-92. By comparison, during the period from 1948 through 1966, public housing starts averaged only 26,000 per year. The only other new construction program during that period, the Section 221(d)3 below market mortgage program, yielded a total of 48,000 new units from 1962 through 1966, or under 10,000 per year. See *Progress Report on Federal Housing Programs*, U.S. GPO (1967).

7. P.L. 90-448, 82 Stat. 476; 12 U.S.C. 1701t.

8. Including one by the author, who was principal author of a report entitled *The Housing Crisis in New Jersey*, issued by the New Jersey Department of Community Affairs in 1970.

9. There is a respectable body of opinion which holds both that American *housing* policy, as such,

has been substantially more successful than for which it is given credit; and, second, that the problems as they are manifest are largely not housing problems, but other social problems of which housing deficiencies are largely a symptom. This is possible, although debatable. What is apparent, however, is that whatever the merits of the issue, these deficiencies are generally perceived as a failure of housing policy.

10. See in particular Anthony Downs, *Opening Up the Suburbs* (New Haven, Ct: Yale University Press, 1973), for an excellent statement of this position.

11. P.L. 93-383, 88 Stat. 633; 42 U.S.C. Sec. 5301.

12. There is an extensive line of federal cases in which housing sponsors seeking to develop subsidized housing in more affluent suburban areas have prevailed, largely on the basis of the link between racial and socioeconomic integration, under the provisions of Title 8 of the Fair Housing Act; see, in particular, *Metropolitan Housing Development Corp. v. Village of Arlington Heights*, 429 U.S. 252 (1977), and *United States v. City of Black Jack*, 508 F.2d 1179 (1974), cert. den. 422 U.S. 1042 (1975).

13. See Mary Brooks et al., *Housing Choice* (New York: Suburban Action Institute, 1980), pp. 250-257. It should be noted that the amount of funding resources allocated by HUD for the purpose of fostering such integration was never more than minimal.

14. Generally speaking, state housing agencies had become during the 1970s largely conduits for federal housing funds. In many cases state housing finance agencies provided the mortgage financing (through tax-exempt bond sales) needed to utilize Sec. 236 and Sec. 8 subsidies; when those subsidy programs ended, these state agencies found themselves essentially without a useful role to play in housing policy.

15. The Los Angeles, California, inclusionary ordinance, adopted in 1974, was entirely designed to be realized through the use of federal housing subsidy programs; see Thomas Eleven, "Inclusionary Ordinances — Policy and Legal Issues in Requiring Private Developers to Build Low Cost Housing," 21 *UCLA Law Review* 1432, at 1446 (1974).

16. Brooks, *Housing Choice*, p. 264.

17. 297 F. 307 at 316 (N.D. Ohio 1924).

18. See e.g., the "Douglas Commission," *Report of the National Commission on Urban Problems* (Washington, D.C.: U.S. Government Printing Office, 1968), pp. 211 et seq.

19. Nearly all of the "first generation" civil rights-oriented cases were filed in federal court, a reflection of the preference of civil rights lawyers for federal courts based on their earlier experiences in the civil rights movement. Major cases included *SASSO v. City of Union City*, 424 F.2d 291; *Kennedy Park Homes Ass'n v. City of Lackawanna*, 318 F.Supp. 669, aff'd F-2d 108; and *Parkview Heights Corp. v. City of Black Jack*, 335 F.Supp. 899. Note as well that the important New Jersey cases of *Mount Laurel* and *Madison* were filed at roughly the same time.

20. Most notably, the enactment of the Urban Development Corporation legislation in New York State, with a provision allowing that agency to override local zoning (1968) (the provision was repealed in 1973); the Massachusetts Zoning Appeal Law, known widely as the "anti-snob zoning law," enacted in 1969; and the call for similar legislation, although unsuccessful, by New Jersey Governor Cahill in 1970.

21. Most notably, Lawrence Sager, "Tight Little Islands: Exclusionary Zoning, Equal Protection, and the Indigent," 21 *Stanford Law Review* 767 (1969); and Linda & Paul Davidoff, "Opening the Suburbs: Toward Inclusionary Land Use Controls," 22 *Syracuse Law Review* 509 (1971).

22. Ironically, this is likely to be the case even if substantially more land is zoned for higher density development than that which the marketplace can realistically absorb in the near future. Since as long as there is any market at all for land so zoned each landowner will have some expectation that his/her parcel will be sought by a developer, no landowner has any incentive to reduce his/her price below that obtained by other landowners.

23. Plaintiff-Appellants' Brief on Appeal (Richard F. Bellman, Esq,) p. 35, in *Urban League of Essex County et al. v. Township of Mahwah*, Appellate Division, Docket No. A-3004-178.

24. *Southern Burlington County NAACP et al. v. Township of Mount Laurel* 92 NJ 158, 456 A.2d 390.

25. *Final Report of the Task Force on Housing Costs*, U.S. Department of Housing & Urban Development (Washington, DC, 1978).

26. *Homeownership: The Changing Relationship of Costs and Incomes and Possible Federal Roles,* Congressional Budget Office (Washington, DC, 1977).
   27.

Year	Median Price	Median Income	[Mortgage] Rate	Property Tax Rate	Insurance
1965	$20,000	$ 6,957	6%	1.40%	0.4%
1978	55,600	17,640	10%	1.66%	0.4%
1981	68,900	22,388	15.5%	1.66%	0.4%

Data on 1965 median price and income from Sternlieb & Hughes, "Housing: An Overview," p. 86; 1978 and 1981 median price and income from *Statistical Abstract of the United States 1982-1983,* U.S. Bureau of the Census (1983); mortgage interest and property tax rates for 1965 and 1978 (rounded), cited in Richard Muth, "Condominium Conversions and the 'Housing Crisis'," in M. Bruce Johnson, ed., *Resolving the Housing Crisis* (San Francisco, Ca.: Pacific Institute, 1982). 1981 mortgage interest rate estimate by author. The calculations are based on a 90 percent mortgage for a 30-year term.
   28. This is the underwriting standard used by the Federal National Mortgage Association (FNMA). When utilities and maintenance are added, the typical family spending 28 percent of gross income for mortgage, taxes, and insurance will spend 35 to 40 percent of gross income for all shelter costs. It is recognized, of course, that many households spend more than that for shelter.
   29. There have been periods where national economic policy was, at least in part, oriented to maintaining a flow of relatively low interest funds into the home mortgage market. This is no longer the case.
   30. See in particular Bernard Frieden, *The Environmental Protection Hustle* (Cambridge, MA.: 1979).
   31. Southern California Council of Governments, *Regional Housing Element* (1979), p. 15. National estimate made by author from data in Sternlieb & Hughes, "Housing: An Overview," pp. 43-45.
   32. Frieden, *Environmental Protection Hustle,* p. 167.
   33. During the second half of the 1970s, a substantial number of senior citizen housing projects were built in suburban communities under the Section 8 New Construction program, often approved by communities that had previously rejected or were subsequently to turn down proposals for family housing. The history of this process and the near-total failure of efforts, despite the language of the Housing and Community Development Act of 1974, to maintain some balance in the use of resources in this area, is complex and distressing.
   34. Agencies administering this program have found, on a number of occasions, that it is impossible to utilize the federal funds that they are allocated, largely for one or more of three reasons: (1) community opposition; (2) unwillingness of landlords to participate in the program; and (3) unavailability of apartments whose market rent (before the subsidies) is under the ceiling rents set by the federal government for participation in the program. Based on statements to date from officials in the Reagan administration, nothing in the proposed housing voucher program would in any way overcome any of the above problems.
   35. Described in Seymour I. Schwartz, Robert A. Johnston & Dallas Burtraw, *Local Government Initiatives for Affordable Housing: An Evaluation of Inclusionary Housing Programs in California* (Davis, CA: Institute of Governmental Affairs and Institute of Ecology, 1981), p. 24. In 1983 the median income in Orange County was $29,900.
   36. California Government Code, Title 7 (Planning and Land Use), Chapter 4.3, Section 65915.
   37. East Brunswick Land Use Ordinance, Sec. 132-41(c).
   38. "East Brunswick Planner Prepares Mount Laurel Defense," New Brunswick *Home News,* February 20, 1983.
   39. Schwartz, Johnston & Burtraw, *Local Government Initiatives,* p. 12.

40. 92 NJ at 211.
41. Ibid., note 8 at 221.
42. See chapter eight, section A.
43. Area Economist, Newark Area Office, U.S. Department of Housing & Urban Development. Median Income Figures effective 3/1/83. It should be noted that the Area Office of HUD also promulgates figures setting forth income limits adjusted by family size, consistent with the definition of the New Jersey Supreme Court in *Mount Laurel II*. Assuming that HUD figures were to be applied directly, which is a reasonable approach in light of that decision, one would obtain the following income ceilings in the Newark SMSA (*Mount Laurel II* terminology):

	Moderate Income	Low Income
1 person	$17,650	$11,450
2 persons	20,150	13,100
3 persons	22,700	14,700
4 persons	25,200	16,350
5 persons	26,750	17,650
6 persons	28,350	18,950
7 persons	29,900	20,250

44. See *Shapiro v. Thompson*, 394 U.S. 618 (1969), invalidating a one-year residence requirement for public welfare payments; and *Cole v. Housing Authority of City of Newport*, 435 F.2d 807 (1st Cit. 1970) invalidating a two-year residence requirement for access to a public housing project. These decisions do not, however, invalidate residency requirements, as such, as long as no *length* of residence criterion is used.
45. Town of Lewisboro, New York, *Land Use Ordinance*, Sec. 324.165; and Housing & Community Development Committee, Town of Lewisboro, "Additional Selection Priorities," March 25, 1980.
46. 38 NY 2d 102, 378 NYS 2d 672, 341 NE 2d 236 (1975).
47. *American Heritage Dictionary of the English Language* (New York, N.Y., 1969).
48. See U.S. Department of Housing & Urban Development, *Affordable Housing: How Local Regulatory Improvements Can Help* (Washington, D.C.: 1982). There is an extensive literature on this subject.
49. This is true, unfortunately, of nearly all housing subsidy efforts in the United States, and is hardly unique to inclusionary housing programs.
50. Both the U.S. Department of Housing & Urban Development and at least one state agency, the New Jersey Housing Finance Agency, have won court battles establishing that their regulations preempt local and rent control ordinances, largely in order to protect their financial investment from what could be potentially irresponsible (at least in the sense of having no financial responsibility for the project in question) local restrictions. See *Overlook Terrace v. Rent Levelling Board of West New York*, 72 NJ 451 (1976).
51. A model formula is provided in Schwartz, Johnston & Burtraw, *Local Government Initiatives*, Appendix B, pp. 66-70.
52. Erika Spiegel, *New Towns in Israel: Urban and Regional Planning and Developments* (New York: Praeger, 1967); Erik Cohen, "Development Towns — The Social Dynamics of 'Planted' Communities in Israel," in S.N. Eisenstadt, Rivkah Bar Yosef, and Chaim Adler, eds., *Integration and Development in Israel* (Jerusalem: Israel Universities Press, 1979).
53. L'Atelier Parisien D'Urbanisme (APUR), *Schema Directeur D'Amenagement et D'Urbanisme de la Ville de Paris* (Paris: Paris Projet, 1980), especially pp. 68-73.
54. Ruth Rodger, *Creating a Livable Inner City Community: Vancouver's Experience* (Vancouver, B.C.: False Creek Development Group, 1976). The author would like to thank Marilyn Lennon, of Lennon Associates, Atlantic City, New Jersey, for bringing this exceptional project and document to his attention.
55. *Schema Directeur*, pp. 132-134.

56. Spiegel, *Israel*, pp. 67-73.

57. See, generally, E. Jay Howenstine, *Attacking Housing Costs: Foreign Policies and Strategies* (New Brunswick, N.J.: Center for Urban Policy Research, 1983).

58. Rodger, *Creating a Livable Inner City*, p. 8.

59. Ibid., p. 25.

60. Ibid., p. 26.

61. Ibid., p. 26.

2

Inclusionary Housing Programs and Public Policy

In the course of the preceding discussion it was made clear that the inclusionary housing programs, as defined and described, raise a variety of legal, public policy, and economic issues, many of which are far from trivial. It is appropriate that a discussion of these policy and legal issues precede the discussion of the functional details of inclusionary housing programs, to which the greater part of this volume is devoted. During the course of this chapter it is hoped that at least some of the issues raised may be resolved; in the case of other issues, where merit arguably lies to some degree on both sides, their resolution will depend more on the philosophical or ideological position of the reader than on any ability of the author to establish the truth or falsehood of one proposition or another.

Establishing a Legal Basis for Inclusionary Housing Programs

A threshold issue is whether inclusionary housing programs are indeed legal, either in terms of the available statutory law or in terms of the United States Constitution. Although the case law on the subject is surprisingly limited in view of the many programs and ordinances in existence and the seriousness of the issues raised, it appears that initial answers to this threshold legal question may nonetheless be available.

As with any complex land use issue, particularly one which represents such a significant departure from past practice, there are many legal or quasi legal points that can be raised on the subject. The purpose of this section is not to conduct an exhaustive examination of all such issues, many of which have already generated a substantial body of commentary.[1] In this section the three issues considered to be of most significance are reviewed. These are first, the issue of whether such ordinances are *ultra vires* in that they exceed the scope of the zoning power or the power delegated to local government; second, whether they can be considered a taking, in the constitutional sense; and finally, whether and to what degree such ordinances are subject to the laws governing exactions — that is, the costs that may be imposed by municipalities on developers and their developments. These issues are introduced by a discussion of the leading cases on the subject, those of Virginia and New Jersey.

The Cases: DeGroff and Mount Laurel II

There have been two resolutions of the legality of inclusionary housing programs or zoning ordinances by state supreme courts up to now — one in Virginia, in which such ordinances were found to be both *ultra vires* as well as violative of the Virginia State Constitution; and the other in New Jersey, where such ordinances were found to be not only legal, but all but mandated by the New Jersey State Constitution. This rather remarkable dichotomy is worthy of serious exploration.

The Virginia case, *Board of Supervisors of Fairfax County el al. v. DeGroff Enterprises, Inc. et al*,[2] decided in 1973, dealt with a challenge to an inclusionary ordinance in an affluent suburb of Washington D.C., in which developers were required to rent or sell 15 percent of the units in developments of 50 or more units to low- and moderate-income households, defined on the basis of eligibility for public housing or for the Section 235 and 236 programs, respectively.[3] The ordinance was invalidated by the Virginia Supreme Court in a stark, two-page opinion on the following grounds:

> The amendment in establishing maximum rental and sale prices for 15% of the units in the development, exceeds the authority granted by the enabling act to the local governing body because it is socio-economic zoning and attempts to control the compensation for the use of land and the improvements thereon.
>
> Of greater importance, however, is that the amendment requires that the developer or owner rent or sell 15% of the dwelling units in the development to persons of low or moderate income at rental or sale prices not fixed by a free market. Such a scheme violates the guarantee set forth in Section 11 of Article 1 of the Constitution of Virginia, 1971, that no property will be taken or damaged for public purposes without just compensation.[4]

It must be noted before commenting on the *DeGroff* decision that it is not given great weight by most commentators. One leading writer on planning and zoning characterized it as "almost uniquely lacking in legal reasoning or rationale."[5] The first argument, that the ordinance is *ultra vires* in that it deals with "socio-economic" rather than purely physical zoning, is patently absurd. This argument was dashed in blunt terms in *Mount Laurel II*:

> It is nonsense to single out inclusionary zoning (providing a reasonable opportunity for the construction of lower income housing) and label it "socio-economic" if that is meant to imply that other aspects of zoning are not. Detached single family residential zones, highrise multi-family zones of any kind, factory zones, "clean" research and development zones, recreational, open space, conservation, and agricultural zones, regional shopping mall zones, indeed practically any significant kind of zoning now used, has a substantial socio-economic impact, and in some cases, a socio-economic motivation. It would be ironic if inclusionary zoning to encourage the construction of lower income housing were ruled beyond the power of a municipality because it is "socio-economic" when its need has arisen from the socio-economic zoning of the past that excluded it.[6]

The point need not be further belabored.[7] The taking issue — of far more consequence — will be discussed below in this chapter.

The New Jersey case, *Southern Burlington County NAACP et al. v. Township of Mount Laurel*,[8] reached the opposite conclusion. It should be stressed that this case, *Mount Laurel II*, came as the culmination of a long series of New Jersey decisions clearly cognizant of the socioeconomic nature of zoning and land use controls and establishing the appropriate role of the courts in dealing with that reality.

Mount Laurel II, in fact, represented the second round of the initial *Mount Laurel* case, which had been tried in 1972 and decided by the New Jersey Supreme Court in 1975. That 1975 decision was at the time, and continues to be, the strongest statement on the obligation of local government to provide lower-income housing opportunities by any state supreme court. The specific issue of a mandatory inclusionary zoning ordinance was, in fact, treated in an earlier unreported trial court opinion, *Uxbridge Associates v. Township of Cherry Hill* in 1980.[9] In this decision the trial judge upheld an ordinance requiring that 5 percent of all units constructed in a high-density multifamily residential zone be "low or middle income housing units." The court disposed quickly of the *ultra vires* argument from *DeGroff*, and found that there had been no taking. With regard to the taking issue, however, the court relied heavily on a conclusion that any hardship had been largely self-inflicted, by virtue of the failure of the plaintiff to make any effort to seek federal or other subsidies, which arguably might have mitigated any economic harm that he was suffering. While this was, therefore, a relatively narrow ruling, it presaged the direction that would soon be taken by the New Jersey Supreme Court.

The fundamental *Mount Laurel* doctrine is that each municipality subject to the doctrine must provide a "realistic opportunity" through its land use controls to provide for its fair share of regional housing need.[10] A major purpose of *Mount Laurel II* was to set down means by which it would be ensured, to the degree possible, that this opportunity would indeed be "realistic," pointing out that "whether the opportunity is 'realistic' will depend on whether there is in fact a likelihood — to the extent economic conditions allow — that the lower income housing will actually be constructed."[11] Given the evidence, which is discussed in some detail in the opinion, that "neutral" ordinances are unlikely to accomplish this goal, the court points out:

> Therefore, unless removal of restrictive barriers will, without more, afford a realistic opportunity for the construction of the municipality's fair share of the region's lower income housing need, affirmative measures will be required.[12]

and:

> In many cases, the only way for courts to ensure that municipalities with fair share obligations do not, directly or indirectly, hinder the construction of lower income housing is to require affirmative measures encouraging the construction of such housing.[13]

After an extensive discussion in which the municipal obligation to make possible the use of federal and state subsidy programs by local developers (through filing applications, adopting appropriate resolutions, and granting tax abatement) is made clear, the decision turns to inclusionary zoning devices. Voluntary programs (referred to as "incentive zoning") are discussed briefly, and citing the work of Fox & Davis,[14] the court notes that "those municipalities that relied exclusively on such programs were not very successful in actually providing lower income housing."[15] The court then states:

> A more effective inclusionary device that municipalities *must* use if they cannot otherwise meet their fair share obligations is the mandatory set-aside.[16] [emphasis added]

It is clear from the discussion leading up to this point, which has been very briefly summarized above, that the court expects the above conclusion to be reached in most, if not all, circumstances.

The court then establishes two practical conditions to govern such inclusionary programs: first, that "where practical, a municipality should use mandatory set-asides even where subsidies are not available;"[17] and second, dwelling units *must* (emphasis in original) be maintained, through appropriate means, affordable to lower-income households over an extended length of time.[18] No set number of years during which time resale or rental controls must be in effect, however, is set forth.

The legal findings, in the strict sense, in that part of the decision dealing with mandatory inclusionary programs, are not extensive. As noted above, the issue of "socio-economic" zoning is dealt with in unequivocal, even barbed, terms. The taking issue is dealt with in a more perfunctory manner, in a footnote, as follows:

> As for confiscation, the builder who undertakes a project that includes a mandatory set-aside voluntarily assumes that financial burden, if there is any, of that condition. There may well be no "subsidy" in the sense of either the landlord or other tenants bearing some burden for the benefit of the lower income units: those units may be priced low not because someone else is subsidizing the price, but because of realistic considerations of cost, amenities and therefore underlying values.[19]

While it is true that in some cases there may well be no subsidy from the developer, or from others bearing the burden, it is likely that in many cases there will be; indeed, the restricted definition that the court adopted for "low and moderate income households" comes close to dictating that such a subsidy will be necessary, particularly with regard to the "low income" units. This is not to suggest that the question cannot be resolved; simply, that it has more dimensions than suggested in the opinion. It is very likely, however, that Justice Wilentz, the author of the opinion, is well aware of the dimensions of the issue; perhaps, in an opinion already 270 pages long, he felt it unnecessary to add further to the already extensive literature on the taking issue.

One additional New Jersey case should be noted — one which is cited with approval by the court in *Mount Laurel II* — the decision by the appellate division of New Jersey Superior Court in *In The Matter of Egg Harbor Associates*.[20] This decision upheld the authority of the New Jersey Department of Environmental Protection to impose a permit condition under the Coastal Area Facilities Review Act (CAFRA) requiring that developments meeting certain other conditions must provide 10 percent of their units as moderate-income housing, and 10 percent as low-income housing.[21] Aside from a question of statutory construction, the decision hinged largely on the determination of the circumstances under which an economic return to a developer may be limited in the interests of public policy objectives. As such, the court found that the public policy objective of providing low- and moderate-income housing, particularly in the context of the increased need for such housing triggered by the development of casinos in Atlantic City, justified a limitation on return that was not "excessive," and that with regard to that concern, plaintiffs had made no case that the limitation was excessive, nor had made any effort to do so.[22]

In conclusion, the New Jersey courts have found, in contrast to the Virginia Supreme Court in *DeGroff*, that neither the *ultra vires* question nor the taking issue stand as impediments to the enactment of inclusionary ordinances as elements in an inclusionary housing program.

Inclusionary Ordinances and the Taking Issue

The Fifth Amendment to the United States Constitution provides that private property "shall not be taken for public use without just compensation." From that sentence and its counterparts in the fifty state constitutions has developed an extensive body of law on the subject of "taking," not limited, clearly, to the physical taking of property by a public agency, but extending to the restriction on its use and the diminution of its value in the interest of a public use or public purpose. This argument, in conjunction with the *ultra vires* issue, was used by the Virginia Supreme Court in *DeGroff* to invalidate the Fairfax County inclusionary zoning ordinance.

It is hard to determine the basis on which the Virginia court arrived at that conclusion, since it appears to fly in the face of other state and federal case law.[23] To begin, it should be clearly understood that despite some folk beliefs to the contrary, the law in the United States does not ensure the owner of property any particular level of return from that property, and certainly no right to the pecuniary "highest and best use" of the property. A good statement of the fundamental doctrine in this area was made by the New York Court of Appeals in *Golden v. Planning Board of Town of Ramapo*:[24]

> *The fact that* [an] ordinance limits the use of, and may depreciate the value of the property will not render it unconstitutional, however, unless it can be shown that the measure is either unreasonable in terms of necessity or the diminution in value is such as to be tantamount to a confiscation.[25]

The case dealt with a "timed-growth" ordinance which had the effect of severely limiting all development in substantial parts of the town for periods as long as eighteen years. It was, as can be inferred from the above, sustained by the New York Court of Appeals.

This position was supported by the United States Supreme Court in a 1980 decision, *Donald W. Agins v. City of Tiburon*,[26] in which an ordinance severely limiting development on a particularly valuable parcel was upheld in view of the public interest in protecting "the residents of Tiburon from the ill effects of urbanization."[27] Although the purpose of the ordinance was other than that discussed here, the fundamental holding was that seemingly drastic limitations on use or value can be justified, if a compelling public purpose is present.

The New Jersey courts have upheld similar restrictions in the public interest on a number of occasions. In *New Jersey Association of Health Care Facilities v. Finley*,[28] the New Jersey Supreme Court upheld a Department of Health regulation that required all nursing homes in the state to make a reasonable number of beds available to indigent patients, stating:

> Restrictions on the use of property, if in furtherance of a valid governmental purpose, serve the public interest and are considered a proper exercise of the police power even though they may result in some economic disadvantage.[29]

The court further noted that if the effect of this regulation were to require nursing homes to "increase their rates to private patients to offset the net cost of maintaining indigent patients,"[30] no legal problems were posed by such an outcome, as long as it was not excessive.

The above brief survey is meant to be illustrative, rather than definitive. It does, however, suggest a clear basis for evaluation of inclusionary zoning ordinances from this perspective. Specifically, if the public purpose underlying the ordinance is sufficiently compelling and if the restrictions are reasonable and not confiscatory, the taking issue, *pace* Virginia, is substantially resolved. That the provision of housing affordable to low- and moderate-income households meets the public purpose test is so well established as to need no further discussion. It is, therefore, appropriate to turn to the question of a reasonable use or return.

While the notion of reasonable use has not been quantified in the land use area to the degree that it has in other areas, such as public utility regulation or rent control, the general standard is as given in the language cited from *Golden v. Ramapo*. This is a comfortable standard for the regulator, and as Agins learned, a difficult one for the individual being regulated to challenge. As long as there is *a use* of some economic worth, the property in the eyes of most courts is not likely to be considered subject to the taking issue.

In its application to an inclusionary zoning ordinance, a series of relatively straightforward tests are in order to provide reasonable assurance that such an ordinance falls clearly within constitutional bounds.

(1) *Does the proposed ordinance, as a part of an overall inclusionary housing program, appear on its face to make possible economically feasible development?* Based on a reasonable level of economic analysis and thoughtful consideration, it should be at least facially indicated that the provision of the required number and type of low- and moderate-income housing units either requires no loss on the developer's part; or alternatively, that the loss is modest enough so that the development, taken as a whole, retains its economic feasibility. By "economic feasibility," it is meant that there is enough potential return from undertaking the development that a rational and efficient developer could reasonably be expected to undertake it.[31]

The question of whether it is appropriate to expect a developer to lose money on the low- and moderate-income units is not without interest; the points of interest, however, have to do with economic fairness or perhaps appropriateness; they are not legal considerations. As this author understands the law, the tests of reasonable return and use are meaningful from the legal standpoint only as they affect the development taken as a whole.

(2) *Does the developer have the opportunity, based on specific circumstances, to seek modification of the inclusionary provisions; or is there an alternate land use for the parcel that can be utilized by the developer?* There are factual circumstances affecting a development parcel that may not be anticipated by the regulatory body and which may affect the economic feasibility of carrying out an inclusionary program in the precise manner, or to the precise degree, required by the ordinance. Fairness dictates that a developer should have the opportunity to present such circumstances to a body that is empowered to modify the conditions governing the proposed development, on the basis of appropriate findings, rather than force the matter into the never-never world of zoning litigation.[32] Such a body — typically the municipal planning board or governing body — could modify the ordinance provisions, retain the provisions as set forth but provide additional incentives or waivers to balance the apparent hardships, or retain the provisions as set forth without modification, at which time the developer would have the option of moving forward, litigating, or abandoning the project. The outcome of the appeal process would vary; the point is that there should be a process.

The alternative is that there be other permitted uses for the parcel. Such other uses, however, must be carefully determined so that the municipality does not inadvertently build in a disincentive to use of the inclusionary housing program. This is the weakness of the voluntary inclusionary program: If a developer can build the same type of housing without including low- and moderate-income housing at an only slightly lower density than that permitted under the inclusionary program, his choice is usually clear. Imagine, however, if an ordinance were adopted allowing multifamily development at ten units per acre with a substantial inclusionary requirement, and the alternate use, if one were desired, were single family residential development on large lots[33] — a developer might well find that residual return from developing at a higher density, even after absorbing any losses from the low- and moderate-income housing, would outweigh the return from large lot, single family development.

(3) *Does the proposed ordinance invidiously discriminate against any group of developers or landowners?* An ordinance which contained, for example, two multifamily zones of similar character, differentiated solely by the fact that in one zone, low- and moderate-income housing was required as a condition of development, and in the other zone it was not, would be subject to challenge. In other cases, the test is likely to be whether there is a rational relationship between the land use distinction made in the ordinance and the public purpose that the or-

dinance seeks to achieve. To require, for example, the developer of a shopping center to include a given number of low-income housing units in the shopping center is likely to be, in most cases, an absurdity; the absence of such a requirement in that zone is unlikely to be considered discrimination from the perspective of an apartment developer subject to an inclusionary requirement in another part of the community. Alternatively, the shopping center developer could be required to provide low- and moderate-income housing units elsewhere, or make a payment to some appropriate body in lieu of building the required housing units. This subject raises other issues, which are discussed in chapter seven.

In conclusion, it appears likely that a carefully drafted inclusionary zoning ordinance, particularly when it is coupled with appropriate regulatory and financial *quid pro quos* will withstand a taking challenge. This does not mean, however, that the economic issues raised by inclusionary housing programs are trivial — on the contrary, as will be discussed in detail. They are not, however, significant *legal* issues, except where they are made so by unreasonable or irresponsible regulatory behavior.

Inclusionary Housing Programs as an Exaction

Although the issue has never been the subject of a court decision other than a passing mention in the *Egg Harbor Associates* case, the question of whether a requirement that developers provide low- and moderate-income housing meets the standards set in case law for subdivision exactions has been a topic of considerable concern on the part of writers and commentators on the subject of inclusionary housing programs.[34] Subdivision exactions are those requirements imposed by a community on a developer to provide land for public facilities (such as schools or parks), to construct such facilities, to make off-site improvements, or to pay fees to the municipality in lieu of providing land or constructing facilities. Case law has consistently held that for such an exaction to be legal, there must be a relationship between the nature and extent of the exaction and the facility needs generated by the residents in the development itself, although the precision with which that relationship must be established has become substantially weaker in recent years.[35] Commentators have found this test either a significant impediment to the imposition of inclusionary zoning ordinances,[36] or in their desire to overcome the impediment, have constructed elaborate but unconvincing arguments that there is indeed a relationship between the provision of low- and moderate-income housing and the needs generated by the development within which the low- and moderate-income housing is to be provided.[37]

All of this argument, however, when applied to inclusionary zoning ordinances, has a highly academic flavor about it. The inclusionary zoning ordinance is not an exaction; it is a form of zoning district, as the New Jersey Supreme

Court noted in *Mount Laurel II*, drawing a comparison to its 1976 *Weymouth* decision upholding a zoning ordinance which allowed mobile homes limited to the elderly as a permitted use.[38] The use designation was one that integrated both the physical (mobile homes) and the socioeconomic (elderly residents) categories. As the court further noted, and as all serious planners and land use lawyers are well aware, the socioeconomic dimension is implicitly present in all district standards that appear in a zoning ordinance.

In the case of an inclusionary zoning ordinance, the use designation is similarly inclusive; it is for a use that encompasses within it (among other things) a certain amount of low- and moderate-income housing. The low- and moderate-income housing does not stand outside the use definition; it is part and parcel of it. As it was put in *Mount Laurel II*:

> The rationale of *Weymouth* could, under appropriate circumstances, sustain a zoning ordinance that restricted a particular district exclusively for mobile homes for the elderly (the actual restriction allowed other uses). If that is permissible, then the comparable special need of lower income families for housing, and its impact on the general welfare, could justify a district limited to such use and certainly one of lesser restriction that requires only that multi-family housing within a district *include* such use (the equivalent of a mandatory set-aside).[39]

In short, the imposition of an inclusionary zoning ordinance is a use of the police power in order to serve the general welfare — and in New Jersey an explicit constitutional obligation — by setting specific standards to govern the nature of the development that will take place in certain districts. It is not an exaction, which is by nature external to the use permitted in the zoning district.[40] A more complex issue is whether the alterntives of off-site development or the payment of fees in lieu of low- and moderate-income housing development fall into the category of exactions. This will be discussed in chapter seven.

Inclusionary Housing Programs and Housing Policy

The legal issues raised by the inclusionary zoning concept and the resulting housing programs are for the most part relatively straightforward. The social and public policy issues raised by the concept are more complex and, unfortunately, not amenable to being resolved with any finality by any external body, be it legislative or judicial. Two central issues which must be addressed are first, how inclusionary programs comport with a sound and rational housing policy; and second, how to approach the questions of racial and economic integration that such programs raise. These two areas are discussed in the balance of this chapter.

A third area, that of the distribution of economic costs and benefits associated with the implementation of an inclusionary housing program, is presented in the following chapter, where it can be discussed in the context of other related economic issues.

It is nearly a truism to note that the outcome of a public policy assessment is largely defined by the position that one brings to the assessment, which in turn largely defines the analytical perspective that one adopts. Certainly, at a minimum, such an assessment can be carried out from either of two radically different perspectives: an ideal perspective, in which the program or idea under consideration is matched against a Platonic ideal of sound policy; and a more pragmatic perspective, in which the program is examined in light of alternative solutions that may be available given the confines of the present and the constraints of social, political, and economic realities.

The drawbacks of both approaches, as well as their uses, are apparent. Since any program which has reached the point of actually being carried out will inevitably be the product of compromises dictated by an imperfect world, its weaknesses and limitations will inevitably be emphasized by any comparison to an ideal policy. It is, therefore, an excellent technique to adopt if one's objective is to demonstrate the futility, or, at least, inadequacy of a proposed course of action. Alternatively, too great a pragmatism leads the analyst or planner into accepting more compromises than are truly necessary, even with reality at its harshest, and may easily result in a policy being advocated, not because of its outstanding merits, but because of the lack of imagination or energy of the advocate.

The underlying proposition of this study, as has been noted, is that inclusionary housing programs represent a sound and desirable public policy direction, albeit one not entirely without its problems and difficulties. For that reason, as well as by virtue of the author's predilections, this discussion tends to stress the pragmatic, rather than the ideal perspective. It will attempt, however, at the same time, to keep at least some of the larger policy considerations in sight.

The relationship of inclusionary programs to a rational housing policy is a good illustration of the dichotomy of perspective noted above. Programs can be evaluated both with regard to their effect on the dynamics of the housing market as it functions, generally speaking, in the United States in the 1980s, or by comparison to an ideal model of housing policy. One such ideal policy that appears on a number of occasions in the literature — a policy to which inclusionary programs are unfavorably compared — is that of an increase in transfer payments to lower-income households, in order to enable them to compete more effectively for housing of good quality in the private market.[41] Not only is that alternative, however, while appealing, seriously flawed, but only a passionate believer would concede such a policy any chance of being enacted in a manner and at a level capable of making a significant difference in the housing market in the foreseeable future.[42] In any event, such choices have as much if not more to do with the ideology with which one perceives the housing market as with the workings of that market itself.

While drawing comparisons with an idealized alternative policy is simplistic, the underlying question, which is that of the nature of a sound policy for meeting the housing needs of less affluent Americans, is not; the issue, however, given that such a policy will by necessity have many features and many dimensions, is first, whether there is a legitimate place for inclusionary housing programs in such a policy, and if so, where that place can be found.

Inclusionary Programs and the Housing Market

A more immediate question can be raised with regard to the place of inclusionary housing programs within the housing market as presently constituted; namely, its place within a private marketplace, however regulated and constrained. It has been argued that private market machinery already provides adequate means of meeting the housing needs of lower-income households, so that in the long run the imposition of an inclusionary requirement on that machinery works against meeting those needs. This argument is grounded in the weight and interpretation one gives to the filtering process. The argument can be roughly summarized as follows: The housing needs of less affluent households in the United States have historically been appropriately met through the filtering process.[43] Such households buy or rent older units as they filter down from the more affluent, and it is therefore more appropriate as well as more economically efficient to construct new units largely or entirely for the more affluent share of the market. Furthermore, by interfering with that process, new construction for less affluent households is not only inefficient, but arguably diminishes housing opportunities for lower-income households by reducing the amount of filtering taking place.

The latter argument — that inclusionary programs reduce the amount of filtering and, therefore, the overall amount of housing available to lower-income households — appears to be predicated entirely on the proposition that an inclusionary program will result in a reduction in the absolute number of more expensive units constructed in the market area in which an inclusionary housing program has been put into place. This, in turn, appears unlikely, except perhaps in those rare cases where a municipality imposes a more or less arbitrary growth quota on housing production, within which an inclusionary program results in lower-income units displacing more expensive units. Otherwise, the demand for the more expensive units should result in their number not being significantly curtailed by the construction of adjacent or nearby lower-income units. In any event, since the need for filtered-down units is, presumably, reduced by the number of new lower-income units constructed, the amount of filtering *relative to the need therefor*, would only be affected if the inclusionary program resulted in a decline in production of expensive housing greater than the increment of lower-income housing resulting from the inclusionary program. Such an outcome appears extremely unlikely, under any plausible body of circumstances.

The above notwithstanding, there is little doubt that filtering, if it could be counted on to work as efficiently as market theory would suggest, would be a more efficient means of providing housing for lower-income households than extensively subsidized new construction. It is not difficult to define what a perfect filtering process should be capable of achieving. The process should be capable of providing nearly all households with housing,[44] meeting reasonable but minimum standards of quality at a price that is not burdensome to the less affluent households. Furthermore, the geographic distribution of such units should bear a reasonable relationship to the availability of goods and services, and the patterns of economic growth and employment opportunity in society as a whole.

In practice, the efficiency of the process falls far short of the above. While there is no question that the process *exists* and provides a substantial amount of used housing to the marketplace, it does not do so in a manner which argues for reliance on filtering as the exclusive or even the principal means of providing for lower-income housing needs. It is generally acknowledged that units deteriorate physically as they reach the lower levels of the filtering chain, so that the housing alternatives available to the lower-income population contain a disproportionately large share of substandard housing. While there is some evidence to suggest that this problem has been ameliorated in recent years, and that the percentage of lower-income households living in seriously substandard housing has declined — as has, to some degree, the percentage of households living in seriously overcrowded conditions[45] — this improvement has been accompanied by a significant increase in the housing cost burden on lower-income households. By 1976, 50 percent of renter households in central cities were spending 25 percent or more of gross household income for rent, a substantial increase from earlier years, and a substantially higher level than in suburban or rural areas.[46] This problem is arguably one to which a program of transfer payments, or a "demand-side" housing policy, could be directed. A question at that point would be whether such a policy would result in further inflation of rents rather than a reduction in effective housing costs to the lower-income population.

The problem of excessive cost burden, however, is not the most serious imperfection in the working of the filtering process. More serious is the increasing geographic and economic fragmentation of the housing market, and the resulting segregation of the lower-income population into an isolated, limited segment of the housing market. To begin, it should be noted that not all housing filters down. Although this is generally acknowledged, the extent is often not appreciated. In areas of strong housing demand, existing housing appreciates, often at levels comparable to or greater than new housing. As a result, the price of existing housing does not decline consistently relative to new housing, and in many cases can be more expensive than new housing. Exhibit 1 compares the cost of new and existing housing in the United States:

EXHIBIT 1
Median Sales Price of New and Existing
Single Family Houses in the United States 1981

	Existing	New	Ratio
Northeast	$63,700	$76,000	0.83 to 1
North Central	54,300	65,900	0.82 to 1
South	64,400	64,400	1.00 to 1
West	96,200	77,800	1.24 to 1

Source: New house sales from U.S. Bureau of the Census; Existing house sales from National Association of Realtors.

In the South, the median price of existing homes is comparable to that of new homes, and in the West, it is substantially greater than the price of new homes. These are, of course, the two geographic regions in the United States experiencing the greatest economic growth, and by extension, the greatest amount of in-migration.[47] It would appear extremely likely that in areas of substantial housing demand, where in-migration has been triggered by employment or other opportunities, proportionately less housing is likely to filter down to the lower-income population. Furthermore, since such in-migration is likely to be heavily concentrated in the moderate- and middle-income population, thereby creating a massive demand "bulge" in that area, it is unlikely that filtering (resulting from construction of new housing for the upper-income population) will be capable of responding both to their need for housing as well as that of the indigenous moderate- and lower-income population. It can be reasonably argued that in areas of strong demand and population growth, where the demand is substantially greater than that generated by indigenous needs and replacement, the failure to generate new construction *at a minimum* for the middle- or moderate-income population, will result in substantial negative impact on the lower-income population in the area, either in the form of displacement or deterioration of housing conditions. Many of the areas in which inclusionary housing programs have been promoted, such as Orange County, California, meet this description.

Regional disparities such as those shown in Exhibit 1 are exacerbated within regions. A significant phenomenon of the 1970s, as noted by a number of commentators, was the increasing economic gap between central cities and the suburban balance of metropolitan areas. Despite the media glorification of the "return to the cities," during the course of the decade the cities became substantially poorer relative to their suburban surroundings. A significant correlative of this was that urban housing, gentrification notwithstanding, became a progressively greater repository of lower-income households, and a progressively greater concentration of the less expensive housing stock of a region. A study of existing house sales in 1979 in the northeastern New Jersey region, which included a major part of the greater New York area, found that within the suburban part of that region, only 11 percent of the sales were affordable by normal standards, to households earning less than the regional median income.[48] By contrast, within the urban core of that region, 55 percent of all sales were affordable to households earning less than the regional median income. Put differently, while the urban core accounted for only 13 percent of all house sales in the region, it accounted for 43 percent of all sales affordable to households earning less than the regional median income.

Filtering may provide a moderate income household the opportunity to buy a house meeting minimum quality standards, at a price not hopelessly out of the household's reach, in Newark, New Jersey, or in Cleveland, Ohio. Filtering will provide no such opportunities to that household in the suburbs of Newark, where the overwhelming majority of regional employment growth has taken place during the past decade, or in the comparable regional growth areas of southern California. Excessive reliance on filtering as the means by which housing will be provided to less affluent households reinforces existing disparities between urban and suburban areas and between areas of economic growth and stagnation, both on a national scale and within the different regions of the United States. If the exacerbation of these disparities is considered contrary to sound social policy, then sound policy cannot rely beyond a certain limited point on filtering as the means of providing low- and moderate-income housing.

Furthermore, as was noted briefly above, sustaining economic growth arguably requires the production of *new* housing, if not for the poor, at least for households earning at and about the median income for the region. Since the normal income distribution of a population centers around the median, the ability of filtering under nongrowth circumstances to meet all lower-income housing needs is doubtful. As noted above, economic growth triggers significant in-migration concentrated in the moderate- and middle-income brackets. It is unlikely in the extreme that the same growth processes will trigger enough new construction of expensive housing to generate meaningful filtering, since no comparable explosive growth is taking place among the wealthy, and since the price of existing housing is being bid up by the upward economic mobility of the population. If new affordable housing cannot be built within the economic growth area, people will seek to build such housing as close as possible to that area; failing that, the absence of such housing can act as a brake on the continued economic growth of the area.

In these areas where the filtering process has been so severely impeded by the demand pressures associated with growth and inmigration, it is likely that the appreciation of the existing stock prevents more than limited movement down the filtering chain. Under such circumstances, the construction of affordable housing, by shortening the chain, carries with it at least some greater potential of eventually benefiting the low-income population than does the construction of expensive housing. The fact remains, however, that in these areas it is unlikely that any housing program which does not involve a substantial measure of some form of subsidy will benefit that last population.[49]

Inclusionary Programs and Integration

The policy objectives of racial and economic integration are an extreme case of the divergence of rhetoric and reality; while a public policy commitment to such integration — particularly racial — has been a part of the national rhetoric at least in recent years, reality has continued to move toward persistent separation. Although one can argue that there has been some increased racial integration through middle-class suburbanization, the scale of such integration is modest by comparison to the continued segregation of the majority of black households.[50] The problem is exacerbated by the close relationship between racial and economic segregation. Given the continuing economic disparities between the non-Hispanic white population on the one hand, and the black and Hispanic populations on the other, the relationship is a strong, and in all probability, an abiding one.   .

It does not necessarily follow from the apparent intractability of present reality that the underlying objective of fostering integration be abandoned. There are compelling arguments in support of that objective. The most straightforward lies in the needs of the less affluent population itself; confinement to inner city ghettos places such people at an increasing disadvantage in terms of access to employment opportunities and to societal goods and services, and locks them into an environment in which the opportunity for upward mobility and escape is increasingly limited. Anthony Downs has provided a "checklist" of benefits from suburban integration:

1. Better access to expanding suburban job opportunities for workers in low and moderate income households — especially the unemployed.
2. Greater opportunities for such households to upgrade themselves by moving into middle-income neighborhoods thereby escaping from crisis ghetto conditions.
3. Higher quality public schooling for children from low-income households who could attend schools dominated by children from middle-income households.
4. Greater opportunity for the nation to reach its officially adopted goals

for producing improved housing for low- and moderate-income households.

5. Fairer geographic distribution of the fiscal and social costs of dealing
   with metropolitan area poverty.

6. Less possibility of major conflicts in the future caused by confrontations
   between two spatially separate and unequal societies in metropolitan
   areas.

7. Greater possibilities of improving adverse conditions in crisis ghetto
   areas without displacing urban decay to adjacent neighborhoods.[51]

Many writers, including Downs, have noted, however, that the various purposes
to be served by integration tend to suggest different levels or degrees of economic
integration. The first, access to jobs and services, is really a product of *commu-
nitywide* integration; as long as the lower-income population is distributed in a
similar manner relative to those jobs and services as the more affluent population, the objective would appear to be served even if the communities remain
largely segregated at the neighborhood level. Other objectives, particularly those
in which social or personal interaction are an element, require what could be
termed a finer "grain" of integration.

These same writers have pointed out that the finer the grain, the more problematic efforts to foster racial and economic integration are likely to be.[52] Within
a hierarchy of community, neighborhood, and block, it has been argued that as
the area becomes smaller, the benefits of integration become more speculative,
and the costs associated with fostering integration greater. At the finer grain, a
further issue appears to be that of the extent of the difference between the groups
being integrated; the greater the difference, the more problematic and less potentially beneficial it would appear the integration is likely to be.[53]

There is no doubt that the proponents of inclusionary housing programs must
take these questions very much to heart in the framing and execution of the programs; it is debatable, Ellickson and others notwithstanding, whether they are really policy issues or technical issues. The threshold policy issue is whether racial
and economic integration, as a general proposition without regard to the level or
form that integration will take as a practical consequence, should be an objective
of housing policy. Although that proposition is not universally accepted, it is
widely enough accepted both as an article of faith and a proposition of law, and is
well enough grounded in reasonable public purpose (even if one accepts many of
Downs' arguments with reservations) that it can be considered a sound, even
fundamental, proposition. Given that, one must then ask how, *within the available means at hand*, can one foster integration? It would be difficult to argue, for
example, that if the only available means dictated that integration would take
place at a small scale neighborhood level, that one should forego the opportunity
in view of the potential problems involved.

At this stage in American housing policy, one sees few vehicles capable of fostering meaningful residential integration unrelated to inclusionary housing programs. It has already been noted that programs such as the Section 8 Existing Housing program, in which low-income households are given subsidies in order to be able to afford existing private market housing, have been structured in such a way that few real housing options outside the inner city become available to program participants. While it might be possible to design a housing voucher program in such a way that it could foster integration, such a program appears remote at present.[54] The programs that subsidized new construction of low- and moderate-income housing, such as Section 236 and Section 8 New Construction, provided a trickle of racial and economic integration, but are now history.

If it is indeed the case that inclusionary housing programs are the best, perhaps even the only, currently available means by which residential integration can be actively fostered,[55] then the issues do indeed become technical rather than policy issues. That does not mean that they are trivial issues. The questions of scale of integration have significant bearing on determining the size of projects in which low- and moderate-income units are to be included; the circumstances under which units should be provided within the development or in another location (off-site); the site planning most appropriate for developments which include low- and moderate-income housing; and many more. In framing answers to such questions, policy issues invariably arise: Should a site be laid out in order to encourage social interaction between households of different economic levels, or discourage such interaction? Depending on the specific circumstances, either objective might be appropriate. In view of some of the foregoing discussion, one consideration that might be relevant would be the extent of the economic gap between the two populations within the development.[56]

One final point should be made in order to place the discussion of economic integration in context. The difficulties of integration that have been discussed above are difficulties only in the context of serious integration goals. Many of the inclusionary housing programs that have been enacted, by virtue of their definition of the target population to benefit from the "low- and moderate-income" housing units, avoid both the problems as well as the broad societal benefits that can potentially arise from a more meaningful effort at economic integration. The inclusionary program enacted in Lewisboro, New York, and described elsewhere is an example of such a program which minimizes the risk to the community at the cost of minimizing the potential benefit to the region as a whole, as well as to the community. The New Jersey experience of the next few years, given the strict standards set down by the court in *Mount Laurel II*, is likely to be a more stringent test of economic integration efforts than most of the inclusionary programs undertaken to date.

Toward a Rational Lower-Income Housing Program

We have argued that it is both unreasonable and tendentious to compare inclusionary housing programs against an idealized model of a rational policy of meeting lower-income housing needs. It is appropriate, however, to examine briefly the contours that such a policy might exhibit, in order to determine whether inclusionary housing programs have a significant role to play, in the unlikely event that such a rational body of lower-income housing policies is ever adopted, or seriously entertained. This policy, however, would not be a simplistic income, or "demand-side" policy, as has been suggested in some of the more polemical literature on the subject. While increases in transfer payments may be appropriate, as is greater and more effective reliance on the existing housing stock, a broad view must recognize first, that housing needs and their solutions do differ and at times significantly from one part of the country to another; and second, that housing policy must serve goals that go beyond simply providing a minimally acceptable unit *somewhere* for those in need.

It must be recognized that the majority of lower-income housing needs can and should be met through more sensible use of the existing housing stock. As noted earlier, a relatively small minority of lower-income households live in units that are either overcrowded, by the standard definition, or lack fundamental facilities such as indoor plumbing, hot water, and central heating. The great majority live in housing that is either physically sound at present, or can be made physically sound at costs substantially less than those associated with new construction.

A major part of the problem is an income problem. Not only do many lower-income households pay a disproportionate share of their income for shelter, but, even so, they cannot as a rule pay enough to support either necessary rehabilitation or a level of ongoing maintenance capable of sustaining reasonable housing quality. Whether the income supplement that is needed to improve the quality of this part of the housing stock should take the form of a housing-specific payment, such as the Section 8 existing housing certificate, or a direct transfer payment increasing the low-income household's income, is a matter on which there is considerable disagreement. Much of the disagreement is predicated on the uncertainty of the housing effects of direct transfer payments. The experimental evidence is ambiguous, but in some cases is at least suggestive that low-income households would not use such transfer payments to increase the quality of their housing, but to reduce the share of total income devoted to shelter costs. This, of course, raises a philosophical issue, about which Hagman has commented:

> There are two kinds of egalitarians in the world, those who are willing to redistribute money and let the recipient spend it as he or she will (the negative income tax advocates) and those who will redistribute only if the recipient will spend it as the donor prefers . . . of these in-kind redistributors, housers are among the worst.[57]

It is not difficult to sympathize with this position, but there are practical arguments as well for in-kind distribution, inasmuch as the purpose of housing-linked payments is not solely to improve the quality of housing for the direct recipient of the payment, but to increase generally the stability and survivability of the older housing stock, by establishing an economic underpinning for rehabilitation and improved maintenance.

Such an objective requires an increase in income for the owners of property occupied by lower-income tenants. Contrary to some popular speculation, the ownership of rental buildings occupied by lower-income households is rarely an economically viable proposition, as attested by the hundreds of thousands of inner city apartments that have been abandoned during the past decades. Common sense dictates that rather than allow abandonment to take place, at which time units must either be rehabilitated from scratch at costs approaching those of new construction or be demolished, a means be found to provide the necessary economic incentives for ongoing maintenance and relatively inexpensive rehabilitation.

In most, although not all, parts of the United States a policy organized around the above propositions would provide sound housing units for the majority of lower-income households. There are extensive geographical areas, however, in which this may not be the case. As discussed previously, in areas where substantial economic development is taking place, thereby generating large-scale in-migration, construction of new housing for moderate-income and arguably for low-income households is essential to provide all such households with decent housing opportunities. Other areas may require new construction as well, particularly if economic constraints have resulted in the accelerated erosion of the existing housing stock in an area.

Even in areas in which the quality of existing units is adequate, a policy organized around the propositions of maintenance and modest rehabilitation of the existing housing stock would fail to reflect other considerations of importance which are closely interwoven with the provision of housing. These include increasing access to employment opportunities, fostering racial and economic integration, and promoting the upgrading and improvement of existing neighborhoods.

Of these three considerations, only the last is principally directed to urban areas. Much of the existing urban housing stock is located in areas which if the stock is to be maintained, require improvement on a scale greater than the rehabilitation of the existing buildings. This is particularly the case in communities in which there has been substantial abandonment and in which the texture of the neighborhood has been largely, if not entirely, lost. There are many such circumstances, even leaving aside the stereotypical "bombed out" areas, in which new construction, either as infill or on a larger scale, can be a significant factor in maintaining or restoring neighborhood quality, and by extension, the existing housing stock.[58] A fundamental proposition which underlies this comment is that the construction of new lower-income housing in urban areas should come about only when that construction, in a particular location, serves a clear purpose over and above the provision of additional housing units. Although the problems of the cities are legion, a quantitative shortage of units, as such, does not appear to be a major problem.

The other considerations strongly argue for a suburban strategy for development of new housing units for lower-income households in locations that will improve access to job opportunities and increase racial and economic integration. Those objectives are not likely to be served through the filtering process, since that process as it tends to operate throughout the United States maintains the patterns of *de facto* segregation that result in lower-income households being disproportionately concentrated in inner city areas. For such a strategy to be meaningful as well as realistic, it must be grounded in two basic propositions, both at variance with past practice in the area of new construction for lower-income households. First, the production of such housing must be targeted rather than distributed randomly or on a pure "first come, first served" basis; and second, it must be designed and carried out in as cost efficient a manner as possible. Ideally, any federal subsidies should be limited to that modest amount still needed to make a unit affordable to a lower-income household after all available economies and internal subsidies have been obtained.

The allocation of federal subsidy funds for new construction, both under the recent Section 8 program and the earlier Section 236 program, have been characterized by policies which followed the path of least resistance. The customary practice has been to finance those projects which presented the fewest problems, technical or political, and which could be built with the least delay, other than those delays intrinsic to the funding process itself. While this was understandable, given the bureaucratic pressures for production totals and the nature of the process which dictated discrete and highly visible projects, it resulted in substantially less than optimal allocation of the available resources. A disproportionately large percentage of units built were concentrated in inner city areas, and of those built in suburban areas, the overwhelming majority were earmarked exclusively for senior citizen occupancy. A case in point is Suffolk County (Long Island), New York, an archetypal suburban area. By 1980, of a total of 1826 units constructed under the Section 8 new construction and substantial rehabilitation programs, 1651 or 90 percent were exclusively for senior citizen occupancy.[59]

As important as it is that units be targeted according to some rational strategy, rather than the path of least resistance, it is equally important that any such program be demonstrably cost efficient. This has clearly not been the case with recent programs for new construction of lower-income housing units. Indeed, the great and arguably excessive costs associated with such programs, particularly the Section 8 program, were instrumental in the political movement away from new construction by the Reagan administration, and the inability of those programs' defenders to mount a successful case for their retention. This has been a function both of the cumulative cost impact of multiyear subsidy contracts, which represent a sort of "time bomb" in the federal treasury, and of the per unit costs associated with Section 8 projects themselves. By the early 1980s costs of $60,000 per unit in Section 8 projects, particularly senior citizen projects, were the rule rather than the exception. Periodically, a project in which costs — for whatever reason — had risen to nearly $100,000 per unit would be featured in the media.[60] As a result of these costs, the annual subsidy needed to make the units affordable to low-income households increased dramatically; furthermore, a very large part of that subsidy — often as much as 40 percent — was directly attributable to costs which were in excess of the cost of comparable conventional housing, thereby being expended with no direct benefit to the low-income household occupying the units.

A large part of the cost disparity between subsidized housing and conventional housing is found in "Davis-Bacon"[61] or similar requirements that dictate that workers on subsidized housing are paid union scale in an industry where, at least with regard to lowrise or "stick" housing, the labor force is not unionized and is paid wages which, while hardly penurious, are between one-half and two-thirds union scale.[62] The problem goes substantially beyond that, however. In essence, the combination of Davis-Bacon requirements, cost certification requirements, the delays and timetables of federal or state processing, and the like have created a two-tier housing industry. Nearly all subsidized housing projects are built by firms specializing in that work, who have adapted to or internalized the government requirements and standards, and who, stripped of any marketplace incentives, operate on the assumption that whatever *maximum* prices, costs, or rent levels are established by the federal government become in short order the *minimum* costs as well. As a result, one typically finds on subsidized housing projects, particularly garden apartments or townhouse projects, that construction costs are 40 percent to 50 percent higher, and the length of time of construction is often twice as long as a comparable conventional project.

As a result, construction costs are inflated, the cost of construction financing (which is a function of time of construction) increases, and a variety of additional costs, such as fees and professional services — many of which are linked to construction cost — are added far in excess of comparable costs in conventional projects. Not only are developers and builders freed of marketplace constraints, but no similar constraints affect the public agencies financing the units, except when pressure from the public or from Congress results in cost containment efforts, which by their nature are as likely to be arbitrary as the excesses that prompted them.[63]

The excessive costs associated with federally subsidized housing are intimately related to and inseparable from the policy of constructing such housing as discrete, separate projects — a policy which has been a part of the statutory and regulatory scheme of federal and state housing programs since their inception. It would be inherently far more cost effective to design subsidy programs so that they "piggyback" on the conventional development process if that could be done in a manner that would not seriously interfere with the flexibility that a conventional developer has in his private business relationships — a flexibility which is crucial to obtaining cost savings. That, in turn, would dictate that the emphasis be on results, rather than process. Establishing lengthy and burdensome application and review procedures, which in some cases take a year and a half or more from application to groundbreaking, is inimical to a cost effective approach. As long as a developer can produce a unit to rent or sell at the lowest available cost and agrees to provide that unit to a low- or moderate-income household under appropriate conditions, it should be no concern of the agency providing the subsidy how he has accomplished that feat.

Over and above the social benefits of integration, linking housing subsidies to inclusionary housing programs represents arguably the most effective way of ensuring that new construction will be cost efficient. In essence, the inclusionary housing program, properly designed and implemented, imposes a stringent cost discipline on the developer building under such a program. Since in order to meet the requirements of the program, he must rent or sell units at a price generally below the going market level for the units, any rational developer will seek to maximize all available cost savings on those units, far beyond the normal level of marketplace discipline. Similarily, such incentives or *quids pro quo* that the municipality or county is providing, as is appropriate in an inclusionary housing program, will further reduce the cost of the units. It should be readily feasible to design a housing subsidy program linked to inclusionary housing programs which will maximize the cost efficiency with which the public funds are used and ensure that every dollar of those public funds is directly linked to a shelter cost reduction for a low- or moderate-income household.

By so doing, goals other than cost efficiency are served as well. Public funds can be effectively targeted to foster racial and economic integration, in furtherance of the objectives of the 1974 Housing and Community Development Act, and indeed, to foster a wider range of integration than is likely to take place through inclusionary programs operating without such subsidies. Priority in the use of available funds can be given to developments in communities which also foster access by lower-income households to suburban job opportunities and in areas of particular employment growth. In short, there would appear to be a synergistic relationship potentially available between inclusionary housing programs and a rational use of public funds to subsidize the construction of new housing for low- and moderate-income households.

This does not necessarily mean that use of such subsidy funds should be limited to developments constructed under inclusionary housing programs. Outside

New Jersey and California, there is no legal mandate under which municipalities must consider, let alone adopt, such ordinances. It would be patently unreasonable to impose such a limitation in areas where there is no mandate, if a showing can be made that the same goals can be achieved in other ways. Given the historical suburban resistance to low- and moderate-income housing, it would be absurd to establish any more barriers than are inherently present. The fact remains, however, that in many cases it will be far more feasible to achieve the appropriate policy goals through inclusionary housing programs than in their absence. It would therefore be potentially desirable to design the housing subsidy programs and other programs such as the Community Development Block Grant program (or its future equivalent) to provide incentives to suburban municipalities — particularly those in areas of major employment growth — to implement inclusionary housing programs.

The above discussion has focused on broad policy considerations and directions, and has tended to pass lightly over the many technical problems likely to be associated with designing and implementing a program that represents such a fundamental departure from past practice. This is an effort for another time and place. The discussion has established, however, that not only is the fostering of inclusionary housing programs not inimical to sound housing policy, but that such programs have a potentially significant role in the context of a rational national housing policy. In that context it is now appropriate to turn to the economic forces and factors governing inclusionary housing programs.

NOTES

1. See, in addition to Kleven, "Inclusionary Ordinances"; John Baade, "Required Low-Income Housing in Residential Developments: Constitutional Challenges to a Community Imposed Quota," 16 *Arizona Law Review* 439 (1974); Charles Pazar, "Constitutional Barriers to the Enactment of Moderately Priced Dwelling Unit Ordinances in New Jersey," 10 *Rutgers-Camden Law Review* 253 (1979); Richard Fishman, ed., *Housing for All Under Law* (Cambridge, MA: Ballinger, 1978).
2. 214 Va. 235, 198 SE.2d 600.
3. A detailed description of the Fairfax County ordinance is given in Kleven, "Inclusionary Ordinances," pp. 1439-1442. It should be noted that this ordinance waived the inclusionary requirement if HUD subsidies were not available "for reasons other than costs." If the subsidies were unavailable because of high costs, the developers were required to subsidize the units to enable them to be sold within the price limitations. Ibid., at 1441. This somewhat arbitrary provision may have influenced the court's position; it is impossible to tell, however, from the decision.
4. 198 SE.2d at 602.
5. Norman Williams, *American Land Planning Law* (Chicago: Callaghan & Co., 1975), Vol. 3, p. 77.
6. 92 NJ at 272-273.
7. Although the "socio-economic" zoning issue is absurd, in the eyes of all writers who have commented upon this decision, there may be substance in certain cases to the argument that an inclusionary ordinance may exceed the scope of delegated zoning authority, under a particular body of state statutes and case law. This is suggested by Fishman, *Housing for All*, as applying to Virginia. If there are any other states to which this argument applies other than Virginia, however, it is not likely to be a large number.
8. 92 N.J. 158, 456 A.2d 390. Although the case is known as *Mount Laurel II* in deference to the

great significance of the initial *Mount Laurel* decision, it is a consolidated decision dealing with six separate exclusionary zoning cases, one of which was the *Mahwah* case discussed in chapter 1.

9. Superior Court of New Jersey, Law Division — Camden County, Docket No. L-47571-77 (decided, January 11, 1980). This case was not appealed.

10. In the 1975 opinion, this obligation had been placed on "developing" municipalities, an evanescent concept which triggered a spate of poorly reasoned and irresponsible judicial decisions and substantial critical comment; see Buchsbaum, Peter, "The Irrelevance of the 'Developing Municipality' Concept," in Jerome G. Rose & Robert Rothman, eds., *After Mount Laurel: The New Suburban Zoning* (New Brunswick, NJ: Center for Urban Policy Research, 1977). This definition was discarded by the court in *Mount Laurel II*, which substituted for it a reliance on the growth districts in the New Jersey State Development Guide Plan, thereby providing a straightforward, relatively objective standard.

11. 92 NJ at 221-222.

12. Ibid., at 261.

13. Ibid., fn 26 at 262.

14. Gregory Fox & Barbara Davis, "Density Bonus Zoning to Provide Low and Moderate Cost Housing," 3 *Hastings Constitutional Law Quarterly* 1015 (1977).

15. 92 NJ at 267.

16. Ibid.

17. Ibid., at 268.

18. Ibid., at 269.

19. Ibid., fn 29 at 267-268.

20. 185 N.J. Super 507. Affirmed, New Jersey Supreme Court, 94 N.J. 358 (1983).

21. New Jersey Department of Environmental Protection, Division of Coastal Resources, *Rules of Coastal Resource and Development Policies: Affordable Housing Policy*, N.J.A.C.7:7E-7.2.

22. 185 N.J. Super at 523. Specifically, the applicant waived his opportunity for a plenary review board hearing, prior to pursuing his appeal to the Appellate Division of Superior Court.

23. One can only speculate as to the reasoning, inasmuch as the decision arrives at the conclusion that there was a taking without discussion or analysis. The arguably arbitrary feature of the ordinance in question was noted, see note 2, *supra*. One can speculate that the language of the Virginia Constitution, e.g., "no property will be taken *or damaged* for public purposes" may have had a bearing. A detailed investigation of Virginia case law, however, is beyond the scope of this book.

24. 30 N.Y. 2d.359 (1972).

25. 30 N.Y. 2d. at 382.

26. 447 US 255, 65 L Ed 2d 106 (1980).

27. 447 US at 261. This opinion is characterized by a gratuitous anti-development or anti-people approach to land use regulation. Such a posture by the United States Supreme Court, which reached its apex in *Boraas v. Belle Terre*, goes back at least as far as *Euclid v. Ambler*, with its characterization of apartments as "parasites."

28. 83 NJ 67, 415 A.2d 1147 (1980).

29. Ibid., at 1154.

30. Ibid., at 1155.

31. Inefficiency, or — as will be discussed below — the lack of the requisite creativity and flexibility that are needed to solve the economic problems created by inclusionary housing programs, are no excuse, nor are they a legal argument. See *Hutton Park Gardens et al. v. Town Council of the Town of West Orange et al.*, 68 NJ 543 (1975).

32. Again, this is analogous to rent control case law requiring the opportunity to prove hardship, and having proven hardship, obtain a commensurate rent increase. See *Helmsley et al., v. Borough of Fort Lee et al.* 78 NJ 200 (1978). One commentator, Baade, note 1, suggests that the availability of federal or similar housing subsidies is the threshold test of whether development under an inclusionary zoning ordinance is economically feasible. This is not the case, as discussed in chapter three.

33. If the purpose of having an underlying use is to provide an "escape hatch" for the developer, it must not be arbitrary or unreasonable in its own right. Zoning for large lot single family development, where imposed on clearly unsuitable parcels, has been found by state courts to be confiscatory; see *Schere v. Freehold*, 119 NJ Super. 433 (1972), cert. den. 62 NJ 69 (1972).

34. See Kleven, "Inclusionary Ordinances," pp. 1493-1500; Pazar, "Constitutional Barriers," pp. 269-272; J. Benjamin Gailey, "Municipal Regulation of Housing Costs and Supply," 4 *Zoning and Planning Law Report* 105 (Feb. 1981) pp. 109-110; Linda J. Bozung, "Inclusionary Housing: Experience Under a Model Program," 6 *Zoning & Planning Law Report* 89 (Jan. 1983), pp. 93-94.

35. The most frequently cited expression of the classic, narrow view of exactions is contained in *Pioneer Trust & Savings Bank v. Village of Mount Prospect*, 22 Ill.2d 375, (1961) which struck down an ordinance requiring dedication of land for school and park purposes as not being "specifically and uniquely attributable" to that development. Since then, a broader test has become acceptable; see *Associated Home Builders, Inc. v. City of Walnut Creek*, 4 Cal. 3rd 633, 484 P2d 606 (1971). Although courts in many states have recognized that the line between the needs of the development and those of the community cannot always be firmly drawn, they have consistently held that there must be *some* reasonable measure of benefit to the development.

36. E.g., Gailey, "Municipal Regulation of Housing Costs."

37. See Bozung, "Inclusionary Housing," p. 94. "When a developer builds a conventionally priced project, a need is created by the residents of that project for services (grocery, drug store, cleaners, etc.) that traditionally employ individuals who are paid only low and moderate incomes. It is not unreasonable to require that developer who created the need for employees within that income range to provide proximate affordable housing for them." This argument would strain the "rational nexus" text beyond even the most liberal construction, particularly in view of the miniscule numbers of low- and moderate-income households that would be derived from any rigorous economic application of that argument.

38. *Taxpayers Ass'n of Weymouth Twp. v. Weymouth Township*, 71 NJ 249 (1976).

39. 92 NJ at 272.

40. This is not to suggest that a rational subdivision ordinance will not distinguish between different development types, housing types, etc., in the extent and nature of the exactions it imposes, but that the exaction is never intrinsic to the development itself.

41. See Robert Ellickson, "The Irony of 'Inclusionary' Zoning," in Bruce Johnson, ed., *Resolving the Housing Crisis* (San Francisco: Pacific Institute for Public Policy Research, 1982); Ward Connerly & Associates, *The Implications of Inclusionary Housing Programs* (Sacramento: California Building Industry Association, 1979); and Donald Hagman, "Taking Care of One's Own: Bootstrapping Low and Moderate Income Housing by Local Government," in *Urban Law & Policy*, Vol. 5, No. 2 (June 1982).

42. While a housing voucher program has been discussed in Washington for many years and is at present the only substantial element in the proposed housing policy of the Reagan administration, that administration's statements on the proposal make clear that it would be so penurious, and so narrowly conceived, as to have no more than a minimal impact on housing needs if enacted.

43. Ellickson, "Irony of 'Inclusionary' Zoning," pp. 149-151; Connerly, *Implications of Inclusionary Housing Programs*, pp. 49-51.

44. Even the most dedicated free market advocates are likely to acknowledge that there is a minimum income below which filtering cannot work; e.g., that income at which a family cannot afford to pay the rent needed to cover exclusively the operation and maintenance of a fully amortized unit. Such families need subsidy, by any standard or frame of reference.

45. Sternlieb & Hughes, *America's Housing*, pp. 28, 64. As the authors note, the decline in overcrowding has little if anything to do with improvements to the housing stock, and almost everything to do with the steady decline in average household size.

46. Ibid., p. 85. Certain population groups are particularly severely affected. Senior citizen households, for example, spent an average of 30 percent (husband-wife couples) to 38 percent (single individuals) of gross income for rent; female-headed families spent an average of 36 percent of gross income for rent.

47. Between 1975 and 1979, the South and the West each had a *net* in-migration of approximately 1 million; during the same period, the Northeast and North Central regions each had a net *out*-migration of roughly 1 million. U.S. Bureau of Census, *Geographical Mobility: March 1975 to March 1979* (Series P-20, No. 353, August 1980).

48. The analysis was for Bergen, Essex, Hudson, Hunterdon, Middlesex, Morris, Passaic, Somerset, and Union Counties in New Jersey. The core area was considered to be Hudson County

and the cities of Newark, East Orange, Paterson, and Elizabeth. Since the data were only available n aggregated form, the range from $0 to $39,999 was considered affordable to households at the area median income or below. Data were from New Jersey Division of Taxation *Average Assessment/ Sales Ratio in New Jersey by Taxing District - Property Class* (1980).

49. A further issue within the general purview of the market is that of the effect of regulation. t has been argued, notably by Bernard Frieden, "The Exclusionary Effect of Growth Controls," in M. Bruce Johnson, ed., *Resolving the Housing Crisis*, that were it not for regulatory constraints, there would be less, and perhaps no, need for inclusionary programs. This is undoubtedly true to a degree but it appears largely immaterial. American land use practice is not about to return to a laissez-fair state of nature. The panoply of 1970s regulations, growth management plans, controls, environmental statements, and the like, shorn, one hopes, of the more egregious abuses, must be considered a given in the future framing of housing policies.

50. From 1970 to 1979, the percentage of black population in the suburban parts of metropolitan areas in the United States rose from 4.6 percent to 5.8 percent, an arguably significant increase; U.S. Bureau of the Census, *Population Profile of the United States, 1979* (Series P-20, No. 350, 1980). Massive disparities exist, however, within most suburban areas. See also Robert W. Lake, *The New Suburbanites: Race and Housing* (New Brunswick, NJ: Center for Urban Policy Research, 1981).

51. Anthony Downs, *Opening Up the Suburbs: An Urban Strategy for America* (New Haven, CT: Yale University Press, 1973) p. 26.

52. See Downs, *Opening Up the Suburbs*, pp. 87-102, 109-111; Herbert J. Gans, "The Balanced Community: Homogeneity or Heterogeneity in Residential Areas?" in Pynoos, Schafer & Hartman, eds. *Housing Urban America*; also, Herbert J. Gans, *The Levittowners* (New York: Columbia U. Press, 1967); Ellickson, "Irony of 'Inclusionary' Zoning," pp. 160-164.

53. See Gans, "The Balanced Community;" also discusson with John Nolon, executive director of the Center for Community Development & Preservation, Tarrytown, N.Y. (1983).

54. Leaving aside the particular circumstances of the Reagan administration, it appears likely that any such program would have to incorporate incentives to encourage use of housing in integrated communities; incentives would be necessary, at a minimum, in view of the fact that such housing is likely to be considerably more expensive than inner city housing.

55. Whatever claims are made for the free market by its advocates, such as Ellickson, no one appears to argue that it is capable, under any remotely plausible set of circumstances of fostering economic integration in suburban America.

56. It should be noted that the economic gap between different sections of some large scale planned developments, prompted not by any formal inclusionary requirements but by an effort to increase market absorption by simultaneously appealing to as wide a spectrum of buyers as possible, is often substantial. The most expensive units can easily sell for 2 to 3 times the cost of the least expensive units. Units are almost invariably clustered, however, in relatively homogenous subareas within such developments.

57. Hagman, "Bootstrapping Low and Moderate Income Housing," p. 8.

58. Determining under what circumstances this is appropriate and when it is not is a delicate balancing task in what is likely to be a highly politically charged environment. Clearly, deterioration and abandonment can reach a point, and have, in many communities, where the level of investment required to restore a neighborhood, particularly in view of the small and diminishing number of people served, makes such investment highly debatable.

59. Suffolk County, Office of the County Executive, *Housing Report* (1980), p. 95. Neither of the two non-senior citizen projects involved new construction.

60. For example, Whitman Park Homes, Philadelphia, or Taino Towers, New York City.

61. 40 U.S.C. 276a; see also Housing Act of 1937, as amended, Sec. 212(a). This provision was enacted during the Depression, as a means of preventing the payment of starvation wages on federally-supported public works projects. The need for such protection has arguably passed.

62. An important distinction must be made between low-rise (garden apartments and townhouses, up to three stories) and high-rise (four or more stories) construction. The former are constructed using a wooden frame, and are, with rare exceptions, the domain of non-union contractors around the United States. The latter are constructed with either steel or concrete structural systems, and are, in most areas, constructed by union labor, whatever the financing involved. High-rise housing, however, represents only a very small proportion of American residential construction.

63. An example of such a cost-inflating practice was that adopted by the New Jersey Housing Finance Agency, which over a period of nearly ten years, until withdrawn under duress from the U.S. Department of Housing & Urban Development, imposed "recommended" minimum floor area requirements substantially in excess of any statutory or formal requirement. The rationale was, in essence, that since it was possible to build larger units and stay within the federal cost ceilings, why not?

3

The Economics of
Inclusionary Housing Programs
I: Housing Costs and
Housing Affordability

Any program which seeks to intervene on behalf of public policy goals in the private marketplace will lead to a variety of planned or unplanned economic consequences. The nature of those consequences will depend, in turn, on the underlying objective conditions governing each market, and on the behavior of the various actors who participate in that market. In the case of housing, significant actors include builders and developers, landowners selling land for development, and the purchasers or tenants of the housing built by the developer. The relationship between a body of objective conditions and the ensuing behavior by the actors is often complex and uncertain; not only are housing market conditions widely variable, often uncertain, and frequently not clearly established until after the fact, but the behavior of principal actors is likely to be influenced both by irrationality and by their lack of complete information.

The purpose of this and the following chapter is to trace these relationships, in order to identify the economic parameters that govern the implementation of inclusionary housing programs under a variety of conditions. This should make it possible to establish the degree to which the underlying propositions on which inclusionary housing programs are grounded do or do not meet reasonable standards of economic fairness and responsibility. To that end, the initial section of this chapter is devoted to an exploration of the manipulability of housing costs; given that the underlying premise of inclusionary housing programs is to manipulate the economics of private housing production in order to produce less expensive housing units, any assessment of their economic consequences must be grounded in a thorough examination of the extent to which such manipulation can realistically take place. The balance of the chapter places these cost considerations in the context of the goals that inclusionary housing programs seek to achieve, that is, providing housing units affordable to low- and moderate-income households.

Chapter four assesses the role of the housing market and its circular relationship to inclusionary housing programs and concludes with an evaluation of the fairness and soundness of the underlying economic propositions on which inclusionary housing programs are grounded.

The Manipulability of Housing Costs

Popular perceptions of the degree to which systematic efforts can bring about significant reduction in housing costs tend to oscillate wildly from a resigned fatalism to a naive belief in magical nostrums such as manufactured or modular housing. While industrialized processes and systems, whatever their real merits, contain no magic, there is substantially more flexibility to many components of housing cost than is apparent not only to the general public, but to many active participants in the development and homebuilding industries. Being able to take advantage of whatever flexibility may exist is of crucial importance to the success of an inclusionary housing program. To the degree that inclusionary programs can provide housing affordable to low- and moderate-income households through maximizing economy and efficiency — rather than through internal or external subsidization — such programs will be more effective and more widely acceptable.

This point is worth some emphasis. The object of an inclusionary housing program is to produce housing that is less expensive than that otherwise available in the marketplace. In order to do so, ways must be found to reduce its cost and make it affordable to the households to which it is to be targeted. There are a limited number of ways in which it can be done; if costs are not to be reduced by maximizing economy and efficiency, they must be reduced through subsidy. Subsidy can take two forms: either public subsidy or a subsidy by the developer, which may be borne by the developer, the initial landowner, or the buyers of the more expensive units. Public subsidies are in extremely short supply; although there are some limited resources available to defray the costs associated with inclusionary housing programs, they are, at present, negligible by comparison to the amount that would be required if such programs were to be entirely dependent on public subsidy.

Leaving aside questions of economic morality, the extent to which a developer will subsidize low- and moderate-income housing, or pass that subsidy on to homebuyers, is severely limited by the marketplace. Only so much subsidy can be provided until the economic feasibility or profitability of the project is impaired, and the developer decides that the project should not be undertaken. For an inclusionary housing program to insist on any developer subsidy that places the profitability of a project in jeopardy is self-defeating.

Given the inherent limitations on both public and private subsidies as a means of creating low- and moderate-income housing, it becomes essential that the greatest possible cost reduction be obtained through maximizing the economy and efficiency of the housing development process. By so doing, some inclusionary housing programs may work with no subsidy, with developers' profits comparable to conventional development.[1] In the majority of cases, most probably some subsidy will be required. The degree to which costs can be reduced through maximizing economy and efficiency, however, is such that the subsidy required will be modest and not beyond the reasonable means of the public and private sectors, even under current adverse conditions.

As will be discussed below, the process of reducing costs through maximizing economy and efficiency is a joint undertaking between the developer and the municipality. The regulatory standards and procedures of the typical municipality or county in the United States are riddled with features which generate additional costs which must be borne by developers, often with little or no commensurate benefit to the public. For inclusionary programs to work, the municipality must be aware of these cost-generating features and must resist the natural tendency to seek the maximum possible concessions from each developer seeking to build in the community.

Opportunities to reduce housing costs can be found by reducing first costs — or the development cost — of housing produced under an inclusionary housing program, or by reducing the carrying costs to the buyer or tenant of the unit once the initial costs have been set. Sometimes there are trade-offs between the two, which for the most part tend to be resolved in favor of reducing first costs, rather than what have been termed "life cycle" costs.[2]

The diversity of elements that go into the development cost of a housing unit is such that a separate discussion of each is appropriate. The principal cost categories are the following:

- Land
- Site Improvements and Site Preparation
- Off-site Improvements, if any
- Construction (bricks & mortar)
- Interest and Financing Costs
- Fees, Permits, Processing & Miscellaneous Costs

The cost of land is a special case in which marketplace factors cannot be separated from technical ones — it will be discussed later. The purpose of the discussion of the remaining factors is not, it should be stressed, to provide a "cookbook" with which to determine the actual costs of specific housing projects, but rather to suggest the extent to which flexibility exists and on what basis, and the manner in which either developers or local officials can take advantage of such flexibility to reduce housing costs and make inclusionary housing programs work.

Site Improvements

Site improvements and site preparation are the cluster of related activities that must take place on a building site in order for housing meeting contemporary standards of livability to be built. The principal elements begin with the preparation of the site itself (grading, clearing, brush and tree removal, etc.) and include the provision of streets and sidewalks, sewer and water lines, utility lines and connections, as well as amenities such as landscaping and recreational or community facilities. The cost incurred by developers for site improvements is in many cases substantially greater than that which could result from a more efficient scheme and from development standards limited to more realistic health and safety requirements.

Given the nature of the principal site improvement components, their cost in nearly all cases is directly proportional to the number of feet that each component must be extended. Five hundred linear feet of a given type of sewer pipe will cost five times the cost of 100 feet. The same is true for roads, curbs, gutters, wiring, etc. The cost of site preparation is equally affected by the square footage of the area to be prepared. The more a given number of units can be clustered or concentrated within a site, the more economical the provision of site improvements and services is likely to be.

A case study by the National Association of Home Builders demonstrated that simply clustering a given number of units more effectively on a given site, with no increase in density, would lead to a reduction in site improvement costs of more than one-third compared to conventional subdivision of the site — from $6367 per unit to $4222 per unit.[3] If density is increased within a generally efficient site development scheme, an even greater effect on the cost of site improvements is achieved. An extensive study, carried out some years ago by the Real Estate Research Corporation under the auspices of a cluster of federal agencies, described in detail the effect of increasing density and varying housing type on the cost per dwelling unit of site improvements. Exhibit 1, adapted from *The Costs of Sprawl*, shows the cost *per unit* of various site improvement components as a percentage of the cost of that improvement in a conventional subdivision.[4]

EXHIBIT 1
Comparison of Per-Unit Cost
of Various Site Improvements
by Housing Type and Density Increase
(expressed as percentage of conventional subdivision costs)

	Conventional Subdivision	Cluster Subdiv.	Cluster Townhouse	Garden Apart.	Highrise Apart.
Streets	100%	86%	69%	48%	26%
Sewers	100	66	42	25	15
Drainage	100	67	45	29	18
Water	100	66	43	30	18
Gas & Electric	100	58	37	26	15
Hookups, parking & landscaping	100	83	43	24	19
Total Site Improvements	100	76	50	53	20

Note: Costs are expressed as a percentage of that component in a conventional subdivision. For example, the cost of providing sewers for a garden apartment is 25 percent of the cost of providing sewers for a unit in a conventional subdivision.
Source: Adapted by author from data in *The Costs of Sprawl.*

The point is straightforward. Site improvements can be minimized by providing both a high *gross* density, i.e., the total number of units permitted on the site as a whole; and by allowing higher *net* density, i.e., the number of units that can be concentrated within those parts of the site used for development. In essence, clustering simply increases the net density, without affecting gross density. But by raising both to reasonably high levels, commensurate with sound planning and livability considerations, substantial site improvement savings can be obtained.

The subject of density increases which would maximize the efficiency of construction and site improvements is capable of generating considerable controversy. Many municipalities, particularly those which perceive themselves as having a distinct rural or small-town character, are reluctant to allow development at efficient densities. Although there are a variety of site planning and landscaping techniques which allow development at high density to be incorporated into such communities, local officials tend to lack confidence both in their own ability to impose and enforce appropriate development standards as well as in the ability of local developers to utilize those techniques.

Beyond that, acceptable densities appear to have more to do with socially acceptable norms than with environmental or planning criteria. Density standards for development in suburban communities in California, for example, are consistently higher than in comparable communities in the Northeast; garden apartment developments are built in affluent southern California suburbs at densities of 20 to 40 units per gross acre, while a proposal to develop at densities of 12 to 15 units per acre will be considered excessive in most Eastern suburbs. In a similar vein, densities for single-family subdivisions of six to eight or more units per acre will be acceptable in shoreline communities in the Northeast, as an extension of the economic dictates of a limited land supply, while anything in excess of two or three units per acre will be anathema ten miles to the west.

Inasmuch as a higher density of development is likely to be a necessary condition of inexpensive housing, it is unlikely that an inclusionary housing program superimposed on a low-density zoning ordinance will be successful, unless accompanied by substantial public subsidies. The establishment of a successful program in many communities will demand at least some compromise with cherished notions of the density that is "suitable" for that community. The degree of compromise, in reality, may not be as great as some may believe. Indeed, much of the apparent increase in intensity of development resulting from multifamily construction is an artifact of the way in which density is measured, rather than a true increase in the intensity of the use of land. In many affluent communities, the typical new single-family dwelling unit will contain 2000 to 3000 square feet of floor area. A unit in an affordable housing development, on the other hand, may contain as little as 500 to 600 square feet, and the average for such a development is likely to be under 1000 square feet. By most objective indices of physical intensity, therefore, each expensive unit may well be equivalent to three or four low- or moderate-income housing units. Alternative development measures, such as floor area ratio or land use intensity, both of which have been used for a number of years by the Federal Housing Administration, would allow a municipality to make more responsible comparisons and regulate developments involving a wide variety of housing types more effectively.

Beyond the simple effect of density on site improvement costs, a second area — that of the standards required for site improvements — is significant. It is generally acknowledged that the standards for site improvements, embodied typically in the subdivision ordinance of each municipality, frequently exceed those which are necessary to meet health and safety standards, either by virtue of failure to consider technological improvements, insensitive application of "cookbook" standards in inappropriate situations, or deliberate intent to keep development costs high, analogous to exclusionary zoning.[5] Examples of such excessive standards and unreasonable provisions frequently cited in the literature include:[6]

- excessive pavement width and right-of-way requirements for streets unlikely to carry heavy traffic;
- excessive engineering and structural/material requirements for local streets;

- requirements for curbs and gutters where not necessary for physical or environmental reasons;
- requirements for sidewalks on both sides of a street where not required by volume of pedestrian traffic;
- parking space requirements in excess of reasonable vehicle projections, given the character of the units to be constructed;
- requirements for elaborate drainage systems, where the character of the terrain and the development permit natural drainage systems, such as swales.

Modification of such standards, where appropriate, can substantially reduce site improvement costs with no negative effect on the community or its citizens. In this area, as in all aspects of development cost, it is patently unreasonable for a municipality to impose any costs not strictly necessary on a developer on whom the municipality has also imposed a requirement to produce low- and moderate-income housing.

Off-site Improvements

There is no disagreement regarding the scope, generally speaking, of *on*-site improvements, as discussed above. The issues and the areas of potential cost reduction lie in maximizing the efficiency of systems such as on-site streets, sewer lines, and the like that are generally acknowledged to be necessary. The picture is utterly otherwise with regard to *off*-site improvements, which are those improvements either outside the site boundaries, or designed to meet the needs (in whole or part) of users other than the residents of the proposed development, imposed by a municipality on a developer as a condition of approval. This is, in essence, the same as the term "exactions" as it was used in the previous chapter. As was noted there, the law governing such requirements, particularly in California, has broadened to the point where municipalities can require major undertakings by developers bearing at most a tangential relationship to the development under consideration. Furthermore, in addition to those exactions clearly permitted by the law, a vast underground body of exactions or impositions has come into being. Under circumstances resembling extortion, because of the far greater cost and delay of challenging, and if necessary, litigating those impositions, developers have agreed to provide improvements or facilities which cannot legally be imposed by the municipality.

Such requirements vary widely in the nature and extent of their relationship to the needs of the development and its future residents. In some cases, such as when a development is proposed some distance from the nearest sewer extension, an off-site improvement in the form of extending the line is necessary for the development. There is little question about the legitimacy of requiring such an extension in most cases, although the courts in New Jersey have held that where such an extension will benefit other sites as well, the developer must be required to pay for only his pro rata share of the cost of the improvement.[7]

In other cases, such as the dedication of a park site, there is still arguably some clear benefit to the residents of the development from the facility being required. It is frequently the case, however, that municipalities require fees, often substantial ones,[8] from developers in lieu of providing land for park facilities. As a general rule, these funds are placed in the overall park and recreation budget, rather than being earmarked for the benefit of the residents of the development. This is a common practice in New York and California, and has been upheld by the California courts on the general supposition that the development generates additional burdens on the municipal park system generally.[9] In other cases, however, such as where a developer has been required to improve a highway or intersection a considerable distance from the development, the connection may be minimal, and highly debatable.

Requirements which go beyond a reasonable connection to the needs generated by the development and its prospective residents represent a clearcut effort to divert expenditures off the general public or the tax base, and onto the developer. This has become particularly common in California since the passage of Proposition 13, which has placed substantial obstacles before municipalities seeking to increase budgets or taxes. These impositions raise substantial questions of fairness, particularly in view of the fact that the residents of the development will be paying full taxes, which by the nature of rising housing costs are in most cases likely to be substantially more per household than paid by the rest of the municipal population. They are also clearly incompatible with the objective of making inclusionary housing programs work.[10]

Whatever justification a municipality may have in extracting such expenditures from developers, the imposition of any costs over and above those directly attributable to the needs of the residents of the development is inconsistent with the need to reduce costs to the degree possible, which is in turn central to the objective of inclusionary housing programs. To the degree that a municipality customarily imposes such costs, reason dictates that they should be waived in the case of developers producing low- and moderate-income housing under an inclusionary housing program. Indeed, as has been done in a number of communities with federal funds provided under the Community Development Block Grant program, a municipality should consider assisting the developer by defraying some of the costs associated with the needs of the development itself, particularly if development requires substantial investments such as sewer or road extensions to the site.

Finally, it is not difficult to distinguish the practice of exactions from the requirements of the inclusionary housing program itself. It is, fundamentally, a difference in the nature of the public purpose involved. In essence, exactions, when carried beyond certain modest limits, are a means by which the residents of a community get a developer to pay for benefits *to them*, which they are unwilling to support through taxing themselves. In the great majority of cases, there is no real question of hardship, except to the degree that a normal citizen considers any increase in tax burden a hardship. While there may be no immorality to it, in that the developer presumably makes a rational choice whether or not to build under those conditions, it is of a fundamentally different order of public good from the provision of low- and moderate-income housing. As such, it is only reasonable to expect a municipality to restrain itself from imposing such exactions on developers providing low- and moderate-income housing under inclusionary housing programs.

Construction Costs

Construction costs, which typically represent from one-half to two-thirds of the finished cost of a housing unit, can be reduced significantly through a combination of two factors: *the size of the unit*, and *the cost per square foot of building the unit*. By producing a smaller and more efficiently constructed unit, significant cost savings can be obtained.

The single largest source of savings in the total housing cost of a conventional suburban housing project is likely to be found in reducing the size of the individual housing units. As a result of a combination of market tendencies and public regulation, the size of the typical newly constructed unit has increased steadily since the end of World War II, although the trend appears to have crested in 1979 and diminished slightly since then. In 1979, the median square footage of newly constructed single family homes in the United States was 1645 square feet.[11] In typical affluent suburbs, it is rare that a new house (even a new townhouse) is constructed with less than 2000 square feet of floor area. Market demand for larger units, at least among those who can afford such units, is combined with municipal zoning ordinance provisions defining the minimum floor area of permitted dwelling units. Such regulations have been typically cumulative with the lot size standards of the ordinance; in other words, the larger the minimum lot size, the larger the minimum floor area requirements — a clear manifestation of the fiscal or socioeconomic intent of such ordinances. While such ordinances have a checkered legal history, they are still widely present around the suburban communities of the United States.[12]

From 1979 to 1980, the median size of new single family houses declined from 1645 square feet to 1550 square feet, a reflection of the affordability pressures on the housing market as well as the increase in the cost of energy, both dictating a more efficient product from the marketplace. This reflects a growing degree of interest within the homebuilding industry in providing "affordable housing," which generally means reduced floor areas. "Smaller is smarter" was the headline in a recent trade publication on affordable housing.[13] There is considerable

EXHIBIT 2
Efficient Floor Plans from Princeton University's *Planning & Design Workbook for Community Participation*

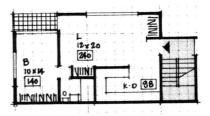

1-Bedroom Units
522 Sq. Ft.

540 Sq. Ft.

600 Sq. Ft.

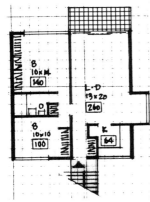

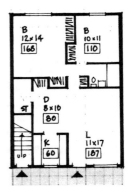

2-Bedroom Units
628 Sq. Ft.

650 Sq. Ft.

750 Sq. Ft.

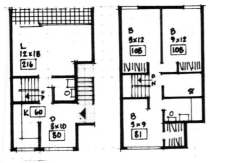

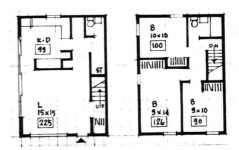

3-Bedroom Units
880 Sq. Ft.

935 Sq. Ft.

room in which to reduce the size of housing units; the floor plans illustrated in Exhibit 2 demonstrate the feasibility of providing functional housing within square footages substantially smaller than is customary in almost all American development.[14] These square footages fall within the following ranges:

- One bedroom units   — 522 to 600 square feet
- Two bedroom units   — 628 to 750 square feet
- Three bedroom units   — 880 to 935 square feet

The plans are far from representing the absolute minimum floor area within which a unit meeting basic functional requirements can be accommodated; that minimum would be 10 percent to 20 percent less than the lower end of the above range.

Even in the context of ''affordable housing'' developers are reluctant to reduce the floor area of units as much as would appear feasible, partly, one assumes, out of fear of impairing the marketability of the units, and partly from inertia. A development in Orange County, California, for example, constructed under that county's inclusionary housing program, provided units ranging from 720 square feet for a one-bedroom unit, to 1250 square feet for a three-bedroom flat, substantially higher than the above ranges. Even these square footages, however, were substantially below the norm in Orange County, particularly in the area in which this project was built. Typical new houses are exceptionally large in that area, which may be a way of compensating for the higher-than-average density of development that is also typical of the area.[15]

Developers participating in inclusionary housing programs are likely to reduce floor areas, as well as seek other economies, only to the degree that they are necessary to achieve the affordability goals established by the ordinance. The Orange County ordinance, as has been noted, sets the income range for the beneficiaries of the program relatively high, certainly by comparison with the standard established by the New Jersey Supreme Court. If the developers of the Orange County projects had been required to make their units affordable to low- and moderate-income households as defined in New Jersey, it is not unlikely that they would have further reduced the square footage in the units that they produced.

In any event, it is extremely unlikely that smaller units, if attractively designed in attractive surroundings, will have any difficulty selling or renting in the context of inclusionary housing programs, given the degree to which their price is likely to be lower than that customary in the area. Even outside of the context of inclusionary programs, planned developments in New Jersey have successfully marketed condominium developments in which one-bedroom units contain 575 square feet, and two-bedroom flats, 750.[16]

The foregoing discussion of reducing floor areas has focused entirely on those floor space reductions that are achievable *within the framework of established and traditional patterns of occupancy and market preferences.* As such, they represent options that should be available to almost any builder operating in almost any environment within the United States. It should be noted, however, that a substantial and growing body of more creative and nontraditional alternatives are coming into being, whereby even smaller units can be constructed, or more people decently housed in less floor space. One example, which represents the recognition of a pattern of living that has existed for many years in urban areas, is the construction of apartments or houses to be shared by unrelated individuals, couples, or families. A typical sharing apartment would provide two separate master bedrooms, each with its own bathroom and dressing area, linked by a single common kitchen, dining area and living room. Since such a unit will have a total square footage of 850 to 900 square feet, each "household" utilizes only 425 to 450 square feet, substantially less than a normal one-bedroom apartment.

Another approach is to make radically downsized units more livable by designing downsized furniture for the units, as well as creating multiple and more flexible uses for interior spaces. A creative approach to a 375-square foot apartment was exhibited in *Housing* magazine.[17] Such units, however, are likely to incur, at least initially, some measure of market resistance, given American traditions about space and livability. Certain parts of the country, such as those where outdoor living is more feasible or those where small apartments are already more widely acceptable, could be exceptions to this rule.

If reducing the number of square feet in a dwelling unit is the first step to cost reduction, reducing the price per square foot is the second. The disparity between the per square foot costs obtained by different builders or by using different building systems within the same geographic area is great, even after high-rise construction, which utilizes a fundamentally different building technology, is eliminated from the comparison. Within a single area, the cost of different projects using the same basic building system, "stick building," can range from $22 to $45 per square foot.

The difference has to do both with the nature of the project and the nature of the developer. Although the basic building system may be the same in an expensive single family house as in a modest townhouse, the former will typically use far more expensive finishing materials, fixtures, and other treatments, and will contain a much greater variety of dimension and angle, resulting in substantially greater labor costs in the installation of floors, sheetrock, and the like. The most inexpensive units are built to a standard module which is consistent in turn with standard factory dimensions for mass-produced components, thereby reducing both the material cost and the labor cost associated with installation. The latter may become not only a function of time savings, but of less need for highly skilled and more highly paid construction craftsmen.

The greatest economies are obtained, however, not only by constructing the most economical building, but by those developers who have developed management and scheduling systems designed to maximize the efficiency of their labor force and to produce a large volume of housing units in a short period of time.[18] Such efficiency in building, which can be said to have originated shortly after World War II with William Levitt on Long Island, New York, has resulted in a rationalization of the homebuilding industry in many areas in a manner comparable to that of the growing manufactured housing industry. The efficient approach to building yields savings through a number of means: a more efficient use of construction manpower, a reduction in the time of construction, and a reduction in the cost of materials. Reducing the time of construction saves money both in reducing the amount of construction interest that must be paid, and in reducing the builder's overhead during construction. Material savings are obtained through volume purchasing, which under most circumstances results in discount prices, and in a reduction in the amount of inventory that must be carried for a given construction project. Typically, some efficient builders utilize elements of manufacturing technology, assembling building components such as wall sections or roof trusses off-site, or in a shed erected adjacent to the construction site. It would appear that this group of highly efficient builders produces a given product, when building at significant volume, at prices between 15 percent and 25 percent below those achieved by more "traditional" small-volume builders producing a comparable project.

Manufactured housing achieves its savings largely in the same way as efficient on-site builders. The use by site builders of manufactured components has been noted above; a 1981 survey found that 28 percent of all builders use at least some manufactured components, many of which they manufacture themselves.[19] In the same survey, 11 percent of the builders, all of whom had built 51 units or more during the past year, used some form of manufactured home units.

Manufactured housing, with rare exceptions, is technologically little or no different today from conventional low-rise or "stick" building. While certain technological innovations have emerged in the field of high-rise construction through manufactured housing, by the mid-1980s no new technology was in sight that could compare to conventional stick construction — appropriately rationalized — for cost economy, flexibility of building product, and ability to respond to diverse consumer needs and performances. As a result, by the 1980s most of the "space age" notions that had been part of Operation Breakthrough, HUD Secretary Romney's effort to transform the building industry in the late 1960s, had been abandoned. The successful manufactured housing builders in the United States, with a handful of exceptions,[20] were those who used a factory to build a housing unit substantially similar to a site-built "stick" unit. Cost savings were obtained essentially in the same manner as those obtained by efficient site builders, rather than through any innovations or technology.

As a result, it is not surprising that the brick and mortar costs resulting from the use of manufactured housing systems tend to resemble very closely the costs obtained by efficient site builders for a comparable product, since the difference between the two is not that substantial. Indeed, it is likely that the cost of transportation, which is added to the cost of a manufactured unit, tends to balance out the residual site diseconomies of the builder. In any event, the differences are not significant.

Certain other differences should be noted. One major limitation of the efficient site builder is that his techniques are fully effective only when undertaking a large-scale project—one with, conservatively, over one hundred units under way on a single site. Since the economies of manufactured housing are obtained in the factory, there is no significant cost difference between a project of fifteen or five hundred units, thereby making manufactured housing arguably more cost-effective than conventional techniques for small projects, such as infill projects in urban or older suburban areas. Manufactured housing comes in a variety of forms which permit attaching and stacking of units, suitable for such areas. Such projects, however, are likely to be of relatively less importance to the success of inclusionary housing programs than are the larger developments, in which there is no significant cost advantage to manufactured housing.

A second consideration, which has to date worked against manufactured housing, particularly where suburban jurisdictions are becoming more sensitive to and sophisticated about design considerations, is the nearly total lack of design awareness or sensitivity in the manufactured housing industry. This is a serious liability in a period where even the less sophisticated site builders are coming to realize that "design sells," especially when it must compensate for smaller units on tighter sites. There is nothing intrinsic to the manufactured housing process, however, which makes better design impossible; it is likely that the remoteness of the project from the site or the end user creates an orientation to the lowest common denominator of design choices, and a lack of awareness of the significance of good design. Before manufactured housing is able to become a significant factor in the development of townhouses and apartments, particularly in suburban areas, it will have to demonstrate that it can compete aesthetically with site-built housing.

The end result of these efficiencies, whether applied in a factory or on-site, is that construction costs, as of 1982, can be as low as $26 to $28 per square foot for small, one-bedroom or efficiency units; and $22 to $24 per square foot for large, two- or three-bedroom units. The cost differential between the larger and smaller units arises from the common requirements in both for kitchen, bathroom, heating, and other systems, the cost of which must be distributed among a much smaller number of square feet in the smaller units, thus raising the cost of the unit on a per square foot basis. It should be clear that these costs, particularly for site builders, assume non-union labor on the building site. While many manufactured housing plants are unionized, although generally at industrial rather than higher building trade wage scales, it is doubtful that any efficient stick builder in the United States works with a unionized labor force

On this basis, the hard construction cost of a space-efficient one-bedroom unit can be as low as $15,000 to $16,000. A representative cost in 1982 for a three-bedroom townhouse produced by a manufactured housing firm, delivered and installed on-site, but exclusive of the cost of the slab on which it was placed, was $26,350 for an 1120-square-foot unit, or roughly $23.50 per square foot. As will be seen in the following section, construction costs at this level begin to make some of the low- and moderate-income housing goals that have been enunciated earlier appear achievable.

While there is no question that these costs can be achieved, they do not come about automatically. A developer of luxury homes or townhouses, accustomed to building at $40 to $50 per square foot, will not be able to build at $25 per square foot on another part of a project, simply because an inclusionary housing requirement has to be met. It is unlikely that such a developer will be able to build affordable low- and moderate-income housing at costs comparable to those obtained by an efficient large-volume builder experienced in producing such a project. A developer of luxury housing, in order to meet inclusionary housing goals without incurring substantial losses, may well seek to enter into some form of agreement with a volume builder of affordable housing, whereby the latter builds the units, or explores the option of manufactured housing — although the design deficiencies of that product, as noted above, act as a strong disincentive. Finally, the luxury housing developer, if permitted to do so under the inclusionary ordinance, may simply seek to "buy out" of the ordinance; in Orange County, such developers are allowed to buy credits from other developers who have earned those credits by building more than the minimum required number of affordable housing units in their developments. The value of each credit to the over-achieving developers is considerable, and has been estimated at $10,000 to $15,000.[21]

The Cost of Money

As was pointed out early in this book, a substantial part of the "affordability crisis" which with other factors can be said to have instigated the movement for inclusionary housing programs, had little or nothing to do with the cost of housing, but rather with the cost of money in the form of skyrocketing interest rates. Interest rates affect the affordability of housing in two ways: first, the direct and obvious effect on the monthly carrying cost to the buyer or renter; and second, through the cost of construction financing by increasing the total cost of the unit and the total amount which must be supported by the permanent long-term mortgage.

Leaving aside for a moment the overwhelmingly important factor of long-term mortgage interest rates, the effect of the cost of money on a developer and, by extension, on the cost of the house that developer can build is considerable. In some ways, the cost of construction financing is merely the tip of his particular financial iceberg. It becomes a direct cost, included in the cost of the unit; based on a construction interest rate of 18 percent (typical during the height of the interest rate crunch of 1981) and a project requiring financing for one year, the cost of the project is increased by 9 percent, a substantial amount.[22] At the same time, indirect factors include the length of time the developer's own money (which, typically, has been used to purchase the land and pay for the professional services and application fees) is tied up in the project, and the amount of money which can be made in areas other than residential development. The more attractive the alternatives, the more profit a developer will seek to make from a housing development in order to justify the venture and the assumption of risk associated with it. Speed of both processing and construction, therefore, takes on great significance in light of the cost of money, as does the project balance sheet itself.[23] An educated guess, which is all it can be, would suggest that a high interest rate environment adds 10 to 12 percent to the sales price of a given housing unit, compared to the price of the same unit with the same hard costs in a more modest interest rate climate. This increase is more or less evenly divided between the direct and the indirect costs described above.

The effects of long-term mortgage interest rates on housing affordability have

EXHIBIT 3
Effect of Changes in Mortgage Interest Rate
on the Affordability of a $50,000 House

Percent Interest Rate	Minimum Income Needed*	Ratio of House Price to Income	Minimum Income As Percentage of U.S. Median†
8	$18,323	2.73	96%
10	20,913	2.39	110
12	23,623	2.12	124
14	26,420	1.89	139
16	29,207	1.71	153
18	32,127	1.56	168

Notes: *Assumptions: (a) 90% mortgage (10% down payment) for 30-year term; (b) constant taxes and insurance cost; taxes @ 2.5% of equalized market value, and insurance at $250/year; (c) minimum qualifying income based on household spending 30% of gross income for mortgage, taxes, and insurance.
†Median household income (1981) was $19,074. U.S. Department of Commerce, Bureau of the Census, *Statistical Abstract of the United States 1982-1983*, p. 429.
Source: Analysis by author.

been well documented and have been alluded to in the first chapter of this volume. For purposes of illustration, Exhibit 3 shows the effect of interest rate changes on the affordability of a single house, based on a range from 8 percent to 18 percent — roughly the extreme points of interest rate fluctuation during the past decade. One point the exhibit makes well is the obsolete status of the maxim that a household can afford a house costing 2.5 times the household annual gross income. As the exhibit shows, given its basic assumptions, that ratio of house price to income is tenable only where the mortgage interest rate is well below 10 percent.

Another point well illustrated by the exhibit is the importance of even a modest decline in the mortgage rate to the housing industry, particularly once the rates have fallen to the 12 to 13 percent range as they did during the second half of 1982. Since the distribution of households by income tends to cluster around the median, when interest rates decline to that level each additional modest decline adds a significant number of households to the potential homebuying pool; conversely, even a modest increase above that level tends to eliminate a significant number.

Given the significance of interest rates, it is distressing that there are relatively few approaches, other than prayer, that can be used to have any more than a nominal effect on housing costs and housing affordability.[24] A few approaches will be discussed briefly here; further discussion, particularly with regard to the use of tax-exempt bond financing, follows in chapter five.

Many techniques are grounded on the supposition that a benefit is obtained by reducing costs in the short run and deferring the full impact of the interest rate until later. In view of the high mobility of American households, such approaches are often attractive. The most common is that known as the ''buydown,'' which is used widely by developers at times when high interest rates appear to be making their housing units unmarketable. A buydown is achieved by a developer paying the permanent mortgage lender an amount with which the lender reduces the amount of the mortgage payment required from the homebuyer for the first few years of mortgage payments, usually for two to four years. Thus the developer is held to be ''buying down'' the mortgage. The funds for the buydown are obtained by either reducing the profit margin on the unit, or if the developer believes that there is enough price flexibility in the market, increasing the price of the unit. The nature of the buydown dictates that if the price is increased by the amount of the buydown, the mortgage payments during the bought-down period will still be considerably less, since the increased cost of the unit is spread over the life of the mortgage, and the benefit of the buydown taken entirely up front.

A hypothetical case can illustrate this point. A homebuyer of a $50,000 house, putting 10 percent down, and financing the balance at 12 percent, will spend $5,587 per year in mortgage payments. Exhibit 3 will show that the minimum qualifying income under those circumstances is $23,623. In order to enhance the marketability of his unit, a developer may seek to buy the mortgage down on a three-year basis, so that the interest rate will be at 9¾ percent in the first year, rising gradually to 12 percent by the fourth year. That relatively modest rate of increase is conservative enough to allow many lenders as well as private mortgage insurance firms to qualify buyers on the basis of the first-year interest rate.

The cost of buying down the mortgage to that extent is roughly $1,840. If the developer increases his price to include the buydown, the resulting price will be approximately $51,900 (since the mortgage will now be larger, the buydown amount will increase as well). The first year payments on a mortgage of $46,710 (90 percent of $51,900) at a 9¾ percent interest rate will be $4,852, which is a savings of $735 over the "real" interest rate. At that price, a family can qualify for the unit with a total household income of $21,173. For this household, however, to be able to continue making their mortgage payments without difficulty as the interest rate rises each year, requires an annual increase in income of 6 to 8 percent.

Most so-called creative mortgage financing devices, in one manner or another, place the future at risk in order to create an affordability, sometimes forced, in the present. Certain types of variable rate mortgages — balloons, and the like — can create massive levels of uncertainty about the future, should the buyers remain in the unit long enough to be affected by these factors. Since the true cost of money is determined by factors far beyond the control of any local actor, the only way of reducing interest rates on a long-term basis relative to the going rate is through some form of subsidy. The most widespread such subsidy is the exemption from state and federal taxes on the interest paid on bonds issued by public bodies, known somewhat misleadingly as "municipal" bonds. Under the provisions of the Internal Revenue Code, public bodies properly authorized by state-enabling law can issue such tax-exempt bonds for the purpose of making loans to finance both rental and owner-occupied housing; specifically, both construction and long-term financing can be provided on a tax-exempt basis to the developers of rental housing, and permanent financing, or end loans, can be provided to the buyers of single family homes or condominiums. There are many restrictions on how funds raised through the sale of tax-exempt bonds can be used. With regard to sales housing,[25] end loans can be made only for units selling below certain area ceiling prices set by the Department of the Treasury, and (with the exception of certain inner-city or low-income areas) can be made available only to buyers who have not owned a home at any time during the preceding three years; in essence, first-time homebuyers.

While the restrictions on rental housing are less extensive, one key feature, which is a form of federally-mandated inclusionary housing program, is that any rental housing project financed through tax-exempt bonds must provide that 20 percent of the housing units in the project be affordable to, and occupied by, lower-income households. In this case, lower income is defined as equal to eligibility for the federal Section 8 program, or an income at or below 80 percent of the median income set by HUD for the area in question.[26]

Despite the restrictions, use of tax-exempt bond financing for housing development is widespread, since the tax-exempt feature allows mortgages to be provided at interest rates lower, and at times substantially lower, than from alternative sources. The savings thereby obtained have been characterized, although not without disagreement, as a subsidy from the federal Treasury in the form of tax revenues foregone on interest earnings. Whether it should be characterized as a subsidy or not, it is clear, however, that it is not highly efficient. For a variety of reasons, one of which may be an oversupply of municipal bonds relative to interested investors, or simply the risk perceived by investors in long-term fixed investments, the interest rate savings on tax-exempt bonds relative to taxable instruments or similar term in the market is substantially less than the extent of the tax foregone by the Treasury. In the middle of 1983, for example, 30-year tax-exempt revenue bonds issued for single family mortgages typically carried interest rates of 9¾ to 10 percent, resulting in mortgages some 50 basis points higher, or 10¼ to 10½ percent. At the same time, the conventional permanent single family mortgage rate was appropriately 13½ percent. If one assumes that the typical tax-exempt bond investor is in a 40 to 50 percent tax bracket, it follows that only one-quarter to one-third of the tax revenues foregone by the Treasury are passed on to the end user of the mortgage financing in the form of interest rate savings.[27]

Inefficiencies notwithstanding, it is the only tool short of direct subsidy from general tax revenues available to state and local government to reduce mortgage interest rates and is, as a result, widely used. Nearly every state in the United States has an agency, and in some cases more than one agency, statutorily authorized to sell bonds for the purpose of making mortgages; in many states, local agencies are authorized to sell tax-exempt housing bonds as well. In California, local governments (counties and cities) have broad general powers to do so; in New Jersey, counties, but not municipalities, may establish authorities to sell tax-exempt bonds for rental, but not sales, housing.

The use of tax-exempt bond financing can clearly enhance the effectiveness of an inclusionary housing program. Every reduction in interest rate can either substitute for a parallel reduction in actual housing cost, or given a constant housing cost, provide affordability for a still lower-income household. Orange County, California, indeed, sold a $100 million housing bond issue explicitly for the purpose of providing below-market financing for units to be constructed under its inclusionary program. While many jurisdictions with land use control powers do not have the power to issue tax-exempt housing revenue bonds, such as in New York and New Jersey, there are state agencies in those states as well as in almost all states empowered to do so. It is likely that with the active support and involvement of the municipality, these state agencies will entertain proposals either for special bond issues for a particular project or group of projects, or for earmarking a portion of the proceeds from a larger bond issue.[28]

A final source of subsidy, which in this case is clearly a subsidy without dispute and can be made available to defray a variety of housing-related costs, is the Community Development Block Grant (CDBG) program. Under this program a wide variety of municipalities and counties receive substantial federal funds, intended generally for the purpose of improving housing conditions for low- and moderate-income households. While CDBG funds cannot be used for housing construction *as such*, they can be used for a variety of related purposes, such as interest rate reduction, land acquisition, construction of off-site improvements, and the like. The Orange County program has incorporated the use of CDBG funds for off-site improvements into the package of incentives that is offered to participating developers. More detailed discussion of the ways in which such programs can be used to enhance an inclusionary zoning program, as well as other tools available to municipalities for that purpose, will be found in chapter five.

Before turning to the general issue of cost and affordability, further note should be made of the cost of time — an insidious factor that affects development costs in a variety of ways. The direct financial impact of construction time, by virtue of the cost of construction financing, has already been noted. The longer the construction period, the more the developer is at the mercy of inflationary increases in material costs as well as wage increases. It is interesting to note that during the past five years, builders have been able to reduce the average length of construction of their projects by 6 percent.[29]

Because construction periods, at least for efficient stick builders or builders using manufactured systems, are short — typically under three months — the length of time involved in processing the development proposal from application to permit is often considerably more than the construction period for the project. This has become particularly burdensome in many communities where extended review periods and delays have become the norm when dealing with residential, especially large-scale residential, projects.[30] Large residential projects are confronted not only with drawn-out reviews, but are required to go through extended, often duplicative, review processes with a number of separate agencies. Processing delays and complex review procedures increase housing costs in a number of ways. The longer the period between application and approval, the more the eventual development will be subjected to inflationary pressures. Similarly, because of the length of time in which the developer's money and energy are tied up, the greater the return he will require from the project, if it is ever built. Finally, the developer must tie up substantially more money in land contracts, professional service contracts, application fees, and the like.

It is therefore logical that fast-track, expedited, and simplified development processing is universally acknowledged to be a major factor in making affordable housing generally, and inclusionary housing programs specifically, workable. Such expedited processing is an element in the Orange County inclusionary program; furthermore, such a provision was embodied into a California statute which provides that "every city, county, or city and county shall . . . provide for coordination of review and decision making and the provision of information regarding the status of all applications and permits for residential developments, as required by such city, county, or city and county, by a single administrative entity."[31]

Maximizing the efficiency of the housing development process requires that the efficiency of the review process be similarly maximized. Ample precedents for highly efficient review and approval procedures exist in most parts of the United States, in the form of expedited procedures for approving non-residential industrial and office "rateables." Effective production of affordable housing dictates that appropriately defined residential developments get comparable treatment.

Housing Costs and Housing Affordability

The effort of manipulating housing costs is designed, of course, to create units that will be affordable to low- or moderate-income households, as that term may be defined in an inclusionary ordinance or program. Although crude rules of thumb may be useful, determining the price at which a unit is affordable to a household of a given income requires some careful sifting both of standards of affordability, and specific factual information regarding the community and the development. In all of this there is a pervasive tension: on the one hand, each program seeks to make housing affordable to as many households as possible; on the other, the program must always be conscious of the burden to the developer, and the limited degree to which costs can realistically be reduced. The crucial test of the soundness of a standard of affordability is one of common sense; i.e., that the definitions and standards can be applied in a realistic marketing program, and that their application results in genuine benefit to the intended beneficiary population.

Defining Affordability

For an extended period until the past decade, a comfortable rule of thumb widely applied was that households should not spend more than 25 percent of gross household income for all shelter costs. This rule of thumb was characterized by Downs as "The 'normal share' of income that society has traditionally defined as appropriate for housing."[32] Downs was writing in 1973. Since that time it has become apparent that "normal" or otherwise, larger and larger parts of the population were indeed spending more than that amount. From 1970 to 1978 the median rent paid by tenants, as a percentage of income, increased from 20 to 25 percent. Exhibit 4 shows the distribution of households by percentage of income spent for rent within the Newark SMSA, in 1977.

EXHIBIT 4
Distribution of Renter Households in the Newark SMSA
by Percentage of Income Devoted to Rent, 1977*

0 to 14 percent	16
15 to 24 percent	30
25 to 34 percent	17
35 percent or more	37
median percentage of income for rent	27

Note: *Excludes subsidized housing.
Source: *Annual Housing Survey*, 1977

Within the city of Newark proper, the median percentage of income spent for rent was 32 percent. It must be stressed that this increase is substantially more attributable to the impoverishment of the American tenant population than to any remarkable increase in rent levels; nationally, 73 percent of very low-income households (as defined by HUD) spend over 30 percent of their income for rent, compared to 24 percent of "low-income" households, and only 2 percent of the balance of the populations.[33]

That notwithstanding, the decision by HUD to increase its standard of affordability for tenants in federally-subsidized housing from 25 percent of income to 30 percent of income in 1981 was as much a recognition of these trends as an effort to economize on federal subsidies. After a flurry of indignation, this change has been accepted by most participants in the housing field. This standard, which is inclusive of utility costs, has now been widely adopted. Most *non*-low-income households, however, spend less than 30 percent of income for shelter. Many such families, therefore, may well be reluctant to move into better housing where their rent would increase to that level, preferring to remain in less desirable accommodations at lower cost.

In its practical application, since rents in newly developed housing are designed with rare exceptions to be exclusive of utilities, the calculation of the maximum rent level must be adjusted for a "utility allowance," which represents initially the best estimate of utility costs, and which is subsequently adjusted based on actual experience. Exhibit 5 applies such a formula to determine rents that will be affordable to households earning 80 percent of area median income, adjusted for family size, in the Newark, New Jersey SMSA. It will be noted that certain assumptions have been made regarding the relationship of household size to unit size, which have a significant impact on the derivation of ceiling rent.

EXHIBIT 5
Calculation of Ceiling Rent Levels Affordable to Households
Earning 80 Percent of Median Income in Newark, New Jersey SMSA

Unit Size	Household Size	Ceiling Income	Maximum Affordable Monthly Rent*	Utility Allowance	Ceiling Rent
1 BR	2	$20,150	$504	-60	$444
2 BR	3	$22,700	$568	-75	$493
3 BR	4	$25,200	$630	-90	$540

Note: *Based on 30 percent of income being devoted to shelter costs.
Source: Analysis by author.

Marketing considerations or simple common sense dictate that the actual rent or rent range will begin substantially below the ceiling figures given in the exhibit. A plausible rent range for the one-bedroom unit, for example, could run from $355 to $444 per month, the former being 80 percent of the latter.

The affordability picture applied to owner occupancy is more volatile than that affecting the rental market. Although most homeowner households spend under 25 percent of income for housing, having as a rule bought their homes some years previously, new home buyers are spending substantially higher amounts for housing. A survey by *Professional Builder* magazine found that the average first-time home buyer is willing to spend 32 percent of gross income for mortgage payments, taxes, and insurance.[34] This may be conservative, as a separate survey of home buyers conducted in October 1981 found that their average monthly payment represented nearly 36 percent of income, an increase from 24 percent for buyers in 1976.[35] As a result of this variability, no standard is universally accepted. Even in the same geographic area, different lenders may apply different standards, and the same lender will apply a different standard to different households, differentiating on the basis of such factors as number of dependents, level of competing debt, and a host of other idiosyncratic factors. The "normal" range, it if can be so characterized, would appear to run from around 28 percent to 35 percent. Since low- and moderate-income households will have less excess disposable income to begin with and obtain less benefit from homeowner tax deductions, it would be preferable to set the standard for units in an inclusionary housing program at or near the bottom of that range.

Carrying costs are a composite, as noted, of the mortgage payment, property taxes, and homeowner insurance. For condominiums it is customary to include the homeowner association payment, if any, within the ceiling. Utility costs, as well as owner-initiated maintenance costs, are generally considered to lie outside the ceiling. Establishing affordability, therefore, of a given housing unit requires determining the amount of taxes and insurance that will be paid. While insurance tends to vary little, given the price of the unit, property taxes vary widely within the United States from below 1 percent of market value in large parts of the south and southwest, to over 4 percent in northeastern urban areas. Data cited previously would suggest that the national average tends to fluctuate between 1½ percent and 2 percent.[36]

Given values for tax rates, insurance, amount of down payment, and mortgage interest rate and term, the process of relating house price to income becomes a simple algebraic procedure. First, it is necessary to determine the relationship between the sum of the three costs to the house price, as follows, using reasonable assumptions:

- Insurance is $40 per $10,000 house value; or .4 of 1 percent   0.4%
- Taxes are 2 percent of market value   2.0%
- Mortgage on 90 percent (10 percent down) at 13 percent for 30 years.
  .13342 (annual constant) ×.9   12.0%
- Sum of costs   14.4%

Any values for mortgage, taxes, and insurance can be substituted for those above. Based on the standard that 28 percent of income will be applied to these costs, if P represents house price, and I represents income, then:

$$.144P = .28I$$

If it is solved for a house price of $50,000 (P=$50,000), for example, one obtains:

$$.144(\$50,000) = .28(\$25,714)$$

A house costing $50,000, therefore, will be affordable to a household earning $25,714.

Assuming that these represent reasonable values, the exercise highlights the difficulty of making housing affordable to low- and moderate-income households, since as shown in the preceding table, the ceiling income for a moderate-income household (as defined by the New Jersey Supreme Court in *Mount Laurel II*) of four is $25,200. Such a household, using the same values, could afford a unit selling for no more than $49,000. Providing a reasonable range between the floor and the ceiling would dictate that housing units targeted to that population sell for no more than a price in the low- to mid-$40s.

It should be recognized that there are other approaches. One, which is patently unsound, is to adopt coefficients that "work," whatever their realistic plausibility. Such an approach might involve assuming that households will make a down payment of 20 percent or 25 percent, thereby significantly reducing the scale of the mortgage payment. While there are undoubtedly moderate-income households who can make such a down payment, it is likely that those will be either young couples with well-to-do parents who lend them the money, or senior cit - zens using the proceeds of a house sale for that purpose. It is doubtful, however, that the young working family or the single working parent with children typi- cally will have access to that large a down payment. A more reasonable assump- tion, therefore, is that the *representative* moderate-income family will be able to make a down payment of no more than 10 percent. Given that mortgage insur- ance is widely available to allow down payments as small as 5 percent, an argu- ment can be made that even the smaller number is preferable.

One returns to the commonsense test: Given the actual tax rates, and the mort- gage packages that are available, will representative households within the target income ranges be able to qualify for the units without it being an unreasonable burden? For the program to be soundly conceived, its planners must be able to answer that question unequivocally in the affirmative.

Exploring Costs

Based on the affordability approach adopted, it is a straightforward matter to work back to a house price that can reasonably be considered affordable by a household of a given income. One question which is particularly important and should be addressed before turning to some of the fundamental questions of the next chapter, is whether the house prices that result from the application of these formulas are at least potentially attainable, or whether massive subsidies will be necessary in order to carry out inclusionary housing programs for beneficiaries meeting relatively stringent definitions of low- or moderate-income.

EXHIBIT 6
Efficient Development Exercise

Part 1: Assumptions and Parameters
1. Development of 160 units in two-story stick garden apartment buildings at density of 16 units/acre
2. Land cost at $50,000 per acre
3. No off-site improvement costs
4. Unit mix within development of 80 one-bedroom apartments at 550 square feet (SF), 40 two-bedroom apartments at 750 SF, and 40 three-bedroom apartments at 950 SF.
5. Construction cost of $30/SF for one-bedroom units and $25/SF for two- and three- bedroom units. Since unit access will be from decks and exterior staircases, there are no hallways or other common areas.
6. Fees and other costs are typical of industry standards, with exception of marketing costs which have been reduced from 6% to 4% on assumption that lower cost units will require less extensive and expensive marketing efforts.

Part II: Development Pro Forma

Land (10 acres at $50,000/acre)		$ 500,000
Site improvements at $5000/unit		800,000
Landscaping, hookups, patios, and finishing at $2,500 per unit		400,000
SUBTOTAL		$1,700,000
Construction of units		3,020,000
Gen. requirements & overhead at 7% of construction		211,400
SUBTOTAL		$4,931,400
Architecture & engineering at 2.5% construction	$ 75,500	
Legal and consulting services	40,000	
Property taxes during construction	7,500	223,000
Warranty & Services (HOW)	80,000	
Fees, permits, misc. costs	20,000	
SUBTOTAL		$5,154,400
Construction financing at 12% for 9 months	$268,148	
Financing fees and contingency at 4%	238,354	
Marketing expense at 4%	238,354	804,444
Closing & title at 1%	59,588	
DEVELOPMENT COST		$5,958,844
PROFIT & RISK at 10%		595,884
TOTAL PROJECT COST		$6,554,728

Total project cost per square foot $6,544,728÷112,000	$ 58.52/SF

	One Bedroom	Two Bedroom	Three Bedroom
Unit cost on per-square-foot basis	$32,186	$43,890	$55,594
Unit cost—proposed pricing	$35,000	$42,500	$51,500

Source: Analysis by author.

It is difficult to present, even as an exercise, an estimate of the cost of producing a given unit without it either being criticized for being unrealistic in a particular location or under a particular set of specific circumstances, or it being accepted uncritically as a firm, replicable standard. Although the efficient development exercise (Exhibit 6) will, therefore, be misinterpreted or misused, it will be pursued nonetheless. The exercise is the development of a highly efficient condominium apartment development, at a moderately high density, assuming realistic but near-optimal coefficients for the different elements of development cost, but without any subsidy, either private or public. The numbers do not represent "hard" numbers, and should not be considered as such. They should be considered, rather, as estimates based on a composite of different projects constructed recently or under construction; or, alternatively, as estimates by developers of costs that *can* be achieved, in the absence of unreasonable fees or development standards. It is, therefore, not a specific project, but an exercise, for purposes of illustration.

Given the selling prices that are obtained in the final row of the efficient development exercise and using reasonable coefficients, the minimum income required for each unit can be estimated. In Exhibit 7, the assumption is that the ratio of 28 percent of income for these costs may not be exceeded, although some households, as has been noted, may be willing to pay more. In addition, since this is a high density multifamily development, and will most probably be organized as a condominium, a moderate homeowners' association fee has been added to the cost total.

Returning to the income figures for the Newark, New Jersey SMSA, one finds that depending on the household size associated with each unit, the unit either is affordable, or closely approaches affordability, to a moderate-income household as defined in *Mount Laurel II*. The ceiling income for a two-member moderate-income household, for example, is $20,150, which places the one-bedroom unit within the range. The two-bedroom unit falls within the range for a four-member household ($25,200), but not for a three-member household ($22,700). The three-bedroom unit only falls within the moderate-income range for a household of six members ($28,350), which it must be acknowledged is unreasonable, since there are few households in the housing market, generally speaking, with six or more members.

It is clear that a project of this sort would be successful in the context of the Orange County, California program, although it can be argued that the land cost assumption is unrealistic for that area, as may be the assumption that no off-site improvement costs would be incurred. The project would not, however, meet the *Mount Laurel II* standards in most parts of New Jersey, particularly given that the median income in the Newark SMSA is higher than that in most of the balance of the state. The exercise, however, made no assumptions about a variety of options which are likely to be available to both the developer and the municipality in which the project is to be constructed, not least of which would be tax-exempt bond financing for the units. If mortgage financing were available at 10½ percent, rather than the 13 percent rate used in the example, affordability would be much enhanced. The annual carrying cost of the two-bedroom unit, for example,

EXHIBIT 7
Affordability Analysis for Efficient Development Exercise

	One Bedroom	Two Bedroom	Three Bedroom
Selling Price	$35,000	$42,500	$51,500
10% down payment	(3,500)	(4,250)	(5,150)
Mortgage amount	$31,500	$38,250	$46,350
Annual Mortgage payment (30-year term at 13%)	4,200	5,100	6,180
Property Taxes at 1.6% of market value	560	680	824
Insurance	140	170	206
Homeowners' Association at $100/$10,000 value	350	425	515
Total Annual Expense	5,250	6,375	7,725
Minimum Income at 28 percent for Housing Expense	$18,750	$22,768	$27,590

Source: Analysis by author.

would be reduced by $900, making it affordable to a family earning under $20,000. This would include a substantial number of three-member moderate-income families. In the absence of any assumptions that could further reduce the cost of the unit — either development cost or carrying cost — the exercise suggests that ambitious inclusionary goals such as those enunciated by the New Jersey Supreme Court may be reachable, but remain uncertain. Less ambitious programs, which do not seek to reach as deeply into the low-income population, would appear to be substantially more easily achieved.

NOTES

1. This appears to be the case with some of the developers building under California inclusionary programs; see Schwartz, Johnston & Burtraw, *Local Government Initiatives*, p. 34.

2. In recent years, the practice of "life cycle costing," which is designed to evaluate trade-offs between reduced development costs and increased annual maintenance costs, or vice versa, has become common in the engineering profession. It has not, however, been widely used in homebuilding (despite some lip service to the idea), since a variety of pressures dictate keeping first costs down at the expense of future costs. Certainly widely held assumptions about inflation strongly work against adopting life cycle costing approaches.

3. Cited in *The Affordable Housing Handbook*, New Jersey Department of Community Affairs and Tri-State Regional Planning Commission (1981), p. 34.

4. *The Costs of Sprawl*, Real Estate Research Corporation, prepared for U.S. Council on Environmental Quality, Department of Housing & Urban Development and Environmental Protection Administration, (Chicago, 1974). The specific density assumptions used to define each of the five housing types were as follows (p. 6):

	Gross Density (per acre)	Net Density (per acre)
Conventional	2.0	3.0
Cluster Subdivision	2.5	5.0
Townhouse	3.3	10.0
Garden Apartment	5.0	15.0
Highrise Apartment	10.0	30.0

None of these are particularly high densities for these housing types.

5. Although the author is not aware of any court decisions in which this conclusion has been explicitly reached, it is recognized by commentators; see Williams, *American Land Planning Law*, Vol. 5, p. 289.

6. See, e.g., *Affordable Housing, supra.*; U.S. Department of Housing & Urban Development, *Affordable Housing: How Local Regulatory Improvements Can Help* (Washington, D.C. 1982); Central Naugatuck Valley Regional Planning Agency, *Least Cost Housing: Minimizing the Fiscal Impact of Zoning and Subdivision Regulations* (Waterbury, CT, 1978); California, Office of Appropriate Technology, *The Affordable Housing Book* (Sacramento, 1982).

7. See *Divan Builders, Inc. v. Planning Board of the Township of Wayne*, 66 NJ 582 (1975). New Jersey, along with Illinois, can be characterized as among the more restrictive states in terms of their case law governing exactions.

8. The formula used by the city of Newport Beach, California, to calculate the fee to be paid by a developer in lieu of parkland dedication can yield a cost of nearly $6,000 per dwelling unit for that item alone.

9. See *Associated Home Builders of Greater East Bay v. City of Walnut Creek*, 4 Cal 3rd 633, 484 P2d 606 (1971). This case is generally considered the leading case for the expansive view of the scope of permissible exactions.

10. The case law dealing with exactions and that dealing with exclusionary zoning have rarely been meshed in any decision; a partial exception is *Oakwood at Madison v. Madison Township*; see 72 NJ at 520-523.

11. U.S. Department of Commerce, Bureau of the Census, *Statistical Abstract of the United States 1982-1983*, Table 1341, p. 748. Average floor area of a new house in 1950 estimated at 900 sf; see California Office of Appropriate Technology, *The Affordable Housing Book*, p. 71.

12. See Williams, *American Land Planning Law*, Vol. 2, pp. 623-664. In 1979, the New Jersey Supreme Court held, in *Home Builders League of South Jersey et al. v. Township of Berlin et al.*, 81 NJ 127, 405 A2d 381, that such requirements were illegal as exclusionary zoning, except when directly linked to health standards and occupancy standards applicable to the unit in question.

13. Professional Builder, *Affordable Housing Ideas*, (Denver, 1982).

14. These floor plans were selected from an extensive catalog of plans in Princeton University, Research Center for Urban and Environmental Planning, *Planning & Design Workbook for Community Participation* (1969). These are "model" plans, and do not correspond literally to built plans.

15. The project described in the text is Niguel Beach Terrace, in Laguna Niguel, California. A similar range of floor areas is found in another inclusionary project in Orange County — Aliso Creek Villas in El Toro, in which the range was from 711 to 1197 square feet.

16. Historic Towne of Smithville (near Atlantic City), New Jersey. Initial sales prices were $38,990 for the one-bedroom units and $48,900 for the two-bedroom units.

17. "Better Living in Smaller Space," *Housing*, 1980, designs by Gene Dreyfus.

18. An excellent description of the *modus operandi* of one of the better known of the efficient volume builders, Fox & Jacobs, of Dallas, Texas, will be found in Martin Mayer, *The Builders* (New York: W.W. Norton & Co., 1978), pp. 229-242. This book is an excellent introduction to the industry generally.

19. *Professional Builder*, October 1981. This survey found other interesting information, including the fact that 75 percent of large volume builders (over 150 units per year) now use computers for construction-related purposes, compared to only one-sixth of smaller builders.

20. One exception is the Cleveland, Ohio, firm of Forest City Dillon, which has had considerable success with a highrise system based on manufacturing slabs, which are assembled on-site (sometimes known as the "house of cards" technique). This firm was able, however, to develop a strong position in the limited highrise market, particularly in the area of federally-financed senior citizen housing. While their product is highly competitive with conventional highrise construction, it is far more expensive than efficient on-site stick construction.

21. Schwartz, Johnston & Burtraw, *Local Government Initiatives*, pp. 34-36.

22. Since the money is not drawn down in advance, or if it is, a substantial amount is reinvested, the rule of thumb dictates that the actual net cost to the developer is roughly one-half of the total cost; i.e., the net cost to borrow X dollars at 18 percent for one year for construction is approximately 9 percent of X.

23. The level of profit which a developer considers "acceptable" varies widely from developer to developer and from year to year, depending on a multitude of factors. As a result, it is more or less impossible to establish a specific number as a "fair" or "reasonable" profit on a development. Depending on the circumstances, it may range from 8 percent to 20 percent or more. It must be remembered that the profit calculated before construction begins is hardly assured profit; it is, in essence, a backup risk and contingency factor which, given the nature of the development industry, is often substantially eroded by the time the books are closed on a project.

24. This does not mean, however, that there are not hundreds of gimmicks, most of which upon close examination, turn out to be variations on a small number of generally unconscionable, basic patterns.

25. As of this writing, federal law provided that effective December 31, 1983, there would no longer be any exemption from federal taxation on the interest earned from bonds issued to finance *owner-occupied* housing (the exemption would continue to apply to rental housing). Bills to repeal this "sunset" date were pending in Congress, and action was widely expected during 1984.

26. Most probably inadvertently, the legislation mandating this requirement did not provide for any variation in the income ceiling by *family size*. As a result, a bizarre pattern has come into being. In calculating allowable rents for a project net of utilities, a utility allowance is subtracted from the ceiling rate, which is 30 percent of the ceiling income. Since the ceiling income and ceiling rent are the same for all household and unit sizes under this standard, but since the utility allowance increases with larger units, the maximum *net* rent that can be charged for these units decreases with unit size; in other words, the allowable rent for a 3-bedroom unit is less than for 2-bedroom units, which is less than for a 1-bedroom unit.

27. There have been various proposals during the past few years to substitute a program of federal interest rate subsidies in some manner for the tax-exemption on housing revenue bonds. Although this may be attractive from the standpoint of pure fiscal efficiency, no state or local agency is eager to turn control of this area — one of the last remaining areas in which local government has some considerable policymaking flexibility — to the federal government.

28. For a variety of technical reasons, bond issues for rental housing are generally done on a project-specific basis, while bond issues for owner-occupied mortgages are generally pools of funds, to be used within broadly defined geographical areas.

29. *Professional Builder*, p. 51. From 1976 to 1981 the average construction time of the builders surveyed declined from 84 to 79 days.

30. See, e.g., the case studies from Frieden, *The Environmental Protection Hustle*; also, *Report of the President's Commission on Housing* (Washington, D.C., 1982) p. 208; "Housing America: Land Use is the Challenge of the '80s," *Professional Builder*, pp. 190-205.

31. California Planning and Zoning Law, Section 65913.3 (amended by Stats. 1981, ch. 846).

32. Downs, *Opening Up the Suburbs*, p. 47.

33. *Report of the President's Commission on Housing*, p. 11.

34. "The First Time Market," *Affordable Housing Ideas*, p. 137.

35. Chicago Title Insurance Company, cited in *Statistical Abstract of the United States 1982-1983*, p. 762.

36. Data from the U.S. Department of Housing & Urban Development, cited in Muth, "Condominium Conversions and the 'Housing Crisis'," in Johnson, *Resolving the Housing Crisis*, p. 324. The data, which apply to FHA-financed houses (which are reasonably widely distributed nationally), show a range of variation between 1.66 and 1.85 percent between 1970 and 1978.

4

The Economics of Inclusionary Housing Programs II: The Distribution of Market Effects

The distribution of market effects arising from the imposition of an inclusionary housing program has been the subject of considerable attention, perhaps more than has been devoted to the underlying economic feasibility issues surveyed in the preceding chapter. Much of this attention has been focused on what can be characterized as the "fairness" issue, an issue of as much political as economic interest. This is the question of who pays the cost and who benefits from the achievement of inclusionary housing goals.[1]

It is a self-evident proposition that inclusionary housing is by design an effort at redistribution by providing benefits in the form of affordable housing to families for whom that housing would not be available in the absence of such programs. Although there are those who would argue that it is not the most efficient or rational means of meeting housing needs — an issue that was discussed in some detail in chapter two — few would challenge the basic premise that all households should have decent places in which to live, at prices which they can afford to pay. The issue, rather, is who is to pay and in what manner for the benefits being redistributed.

That there will be costs to be paid in the great majority of cases is not seriously in doubt. Evaluation of the major California programs has established that low- and moderate-income housing units built under inclusionary housing programs are consistently sold below their market value.[2] While that does not in itself mean that a loss, in the literal sense, is being taken by the developers, it does dictate, at a minimum, that profits are being foregone which would otherwise be available. The loss of profits is not a trivial consideration. Not only are profits essential to the continued viability of any enterprise in a capitalist economy, but they are particularly important in a highly volatile industry such as housing, where substantial amounts of money must be placed at risk anew for each undertaking, and where the possibility of loss on a given project, for reasons beyond the developer's control, is always present. The highly leveraged nature of the development industry may result in some developers becoming extremely wealthy, but it leads to many others losing everything when any of a host of reasons results in the failure of a development project.

In other cases, particularly where a community is applying the standard established by the New Jersey Supreme Court in *Mount Laurel II*, it may literally not be possible to sell or rent some units in a manner that will enable the developer to incorporate all of the true costs of development in the selling price. This is particularly likely to be the case if the developer is required to provide for the full range of off-site improvements and exactions that may be required of a typical development in many suburban jurisdictions.

Under any of these circumstances, the issue of who pays is germane. It is a complex issue, not amenable to simplistic formulations; e.g., that a developer pass the cost on to buyers of market-rate units or that he absorb the cost from his profits, excess or otherwise. Before any effort can be made to determine whether the allocation of costs is reasonable or "fair," a systematic effort must be made to determine, as best one can, what the actual allocation of costs is. That, in turn, must be done in a realistic framework, taking into account the degree to which the development process deviates from classical economic principles and premises, rather than on the basis of abstract economic models. Furthermore, the market interactions resulting from the provision of more modest housing units in a community or within a development project must be taken into consideration. Although that subject raises questions about which it is possible only to speculate, in the absence of an adequate body of substantive data, informed speculation may still be useful in establishing the context in which programs currently in place can be evaluated, and future programs formulated.

Finally, whatever the distribution of costs, it is important to examine the distribution of benefits as well, and the reasonableness with which those benefits appear to be allocated. This is, in essence, a question of social policy rather than pure economics; specifically, are the benefits of such programs, as defined by both the number and the characteristics of the beneficiaries, commensurate with the costs imposed on those paying for the implementation of inclusionary housing programs?

Who Pays for Inclusionary Housing Programs?

The simplest case in which to examine the question of who pays the costs of an inclusionary housing program is one in which no *public* costs, such as those which may be associated with off-site improvements or tax-exempt bond financ-ing, are engaged in the program. In such a case, the costs of an inclusionary housing program can be borne in three ways. First, the costs can be absorbed by the developer from the profits that he would otherwise presumably make. Sec-ond, the costs can be passed forward to the buyers of the market-rate units in the development. Third, they can be passed backward, in that the developer of a project subject to an inclusionary housing program will not be willing to spend as much for land, all other factors being equal. *In the long run*, under most circum-stances, the last should predominate; in other words, most of the costs will be passed backward to the owners of land, as Ellickson and Hagman appropriately point out. There are enough exceptions, however, to justify some discussion.

In the long run, any program which imposes significant costs on a developer, which he must absorb and cannot pass either forward or backward, is likely to be unstable. The ability of a developer to make reasonable profits, more or less con-sistently, is a *sine qua non* of that developer's willingness to remain a developer. If the market generally makes it impossible to make a reasonable profit, the de-veloper will not build. If circumstances particular to a specific community or area make it impossible, he will build elsewhere. This is not to suggest that there will not be occasions when a developer will reduce his profit in order to satisfy an in-clusionary requirement, but it does suggest that no policy that expects any devel-oper to do so consistently and substantially can be considered a realistic policy. It should be acknowledged, however, that while that statement is generally correct, there are certain eccentric housing markets, as will be discussed below, in which it may not be entirely true.

The ability of a developer to pass costs forward to the prospective buyers of market-rate housing in his development is also constrained. The assumption made in some examples of the literature that a developer will seek consistently to maximize the price he charges for the units he builds is not necessarily accurate.[3] The manner in which a developer prices his product is a compound of a variety of factors, including his production costs, the type of housing product that he typi-cally builds, the size of the development, the length of time he is willing to re-main involved with that development, and finally, the price that the market will allow at a given rate of market absorption. Market analysis is far from an exact science, and the more aggressively a developer prices a particular housing prod-uct, the greater the risk he incurs of either not being able to sell at all or signifi-cantly slowing down the rate of sale of the units. Slow sales can be a major problem for a developer, since the cost of carrying inventory can easily consume all or most of what would otherwise be the developer's profit.

The point is well made by Ellickson that the ability of a developer to pass on the costs associated with an inclusionary housing program, or for that matter, any costs over the customary costs of development, vary significantly depending on the nature of the community and its place in the regional housing market.[4] If the community, in Ellickson's terminology, has no unique attributes, and has no features which would prompt a buyer to spend more money on a house in that community than on an identical house elsewhere, no builder active in that community can pass on "non-standard" costs to homebuyers. If, however, the community is perceived by some substantial part of the marketplace as unique, so that buyers will pay a premium price to live in that community, a builder can pass forward costs up to the level of the premium generated by the community's unique position in the marketplace.

It should be stressed that this model applies to a variety of cost factors over and above inclusionary housing programs. It would be incorrect to suggest, as some of the critics of inclusionary housing programs would appear to do, that costs generated thereby have a different effect than other "non-standard" costs. The same logic that may make it impossible for a developer to pass foward the costs of an inclusionary zoning program in a non-unique community, makes it impossible for that developer to pass forward any costs over and above those typical of development in that community. It is largely for that reason that sites that are either unusually expensive, in need of extensive site preparation, or require extensive off-site improvements for development are unlikely to be developed in non-unique communities and significantly more likely to be developed in unique communities, where the premium prices that can be obtained allow a developer to pass forward the cost of building on expensive land or to spend substantial sums for site and off-site improvements.[5]

Since the pricing of housing in unique, or premium, communities is such as to accommodate a wide range of costs associated with site acquisition and improvement, it is not unlikely that some builders in these environments can pass the costs of inclusionary housing forward, particularly if their land acquisition or improvement costs are below the maximum level tolerated by the market. It is notable that a large number of inclusionary programs have been implemented in such unique communities, a category which would certainly include Orange County or Palo Alto in California, or Bedminster and Cherry Hill in New Jersey.

Still, while the economics of development in a premium community may offer a developer greater flexibility in pricing his product, the flexibility is far from unlimited, particularly if, as in the case of Orange County, there is a relatively competitive building industry active in the area, albeit one competing at the premium price levels made possible by the character of the area. While the strength of the market demand at premium prices supports substantial development activity, it does not support infinite premium pricing, as a number of developers in that area discovered in the early 1980s.

While absorbing or passing the costs forward are not tenable long-term resolutions of the question, they do occur — particularly in situations where a developer becomes subject to an inclusionary housing program requirement after the land for the proposed development has already been acquired, or after substantial investments have already been made. The former is far from unusual, since considerable stockpiling of land does take place. Under such circumstances, there s no possibility of passing costs backward to a landowner, since the landowner and the developer are one and the same. Leaving aside what can be considered transitional cases, however, the tendency from that point onward will be to pass the cost or the reduction in profit potential backward to the landowner in the form of a lower price for his or her land. In essence, the effect of an inclusionary housing program on land value in a given zone, all other standards being held constant, is identical to that of a downzoning of the same land. As the prospective income stream from the property is reduced, the value of the land is proportionately diminished. Indeed, given the legal interpretation previously offered as to the nature of inclusionary housing programs — i.e., that they are intrinsic to the use of the land — the outcome logically should be precisely that.

Land markets, however, often behave in ways unrelated to rational economic behavior, and their irrationality can act as a potential drag on the successful implementation of an inclusionary housing program. As has been noted earlier, landowners develop expectations of the value of their land which tend to be highly sensitive to upward movement of the land market and highly *in*sensitive to downward movement. In what has been characterized as a "price ratchet," land prices tend to remain fixed at the upward end of a price cycle for an extended period after changes in objective reality have come to dictate lower prices.

How significant the effect of the price ratchet will be depends entirely on the relationship between supply and demand within a given local market. Two diametrically opposed cases can be presented. In the first case, the supply of land within a particular premium community in which development demand is strong is extremely limited or concentrated in a few hands. In this case, if the landowners hesitate to reduce their prices down to the new level dictated by the market, developers may have to re-evaluate their ability to continue to build under the inclusionary housing program at higher land prices than they consider to be reasonable. A particularly efficient developer may, for example, determine that he can achieve economies to compensate for the higher land price, or for his inability to pass his costs backward to the landowner. Once, of course, a major land transaction takes place *post*-inclusionary housing program at *pre*-program land values, the ratchet will be fixed. Few, if any, subsequent land transactions will reflect the reduced land value theoretically dictated by the market.[6]

Alternatively, if the supply of land is substantially in excess of the demand, particularly if developers have land stockpiled so that they continue to build for some length of time without acquiring additional land, there is a realistic probability that over time the price of land in that community will indeed decline to the level set by the change in profit potential resulting from the establishment of the inclusionary housing program. In most premium communities, however, it is likely that circumstances are closer to the former rather than the latter case. Land available for development appears in short supply, whether by virtue of the absence of vacant parcels, development constraints such as growth controls or lack of infrastructure, or other factors.[7]

The above discussion has considered only the simplified case in which no public costs are involved and all cost relationships are between the developer and his market "partners" — the landowners and homebuyers. In a well-designed inclusionary housing program, however, there may be a substantial measure of public involvement, including fast-track or accelerated processing, waiver of fees or off-site improvement requirements, and provision of assistance through tax-exempt bond financing or use of Community Development Block Grant funds. When such involvement is part of the development process, some measure of cost has been diverted onto actors other than the basic landowner/developer/homebuyer trinity.

To the degree that a municipality offers concessions with regard to customary municipal requirements or procedures, those concessions redirect costs away from the developer. The costs will be passed either to other developers not engaged in providing low- or moderate-income housing, or to the community as a whole through the local tax base. If a fee customarily required in lieu of park dedication is waived, the costs of providing the open space that would otherwise have been provided with those funds is borne either by the citizens of the municipality, or by other developers, or by a combination of the two. Alternatively, that particular open space is not provided, which may represent a cost to some or all of the citizens of the community in the form of reduced level of public goods. The same supposition applies to any other public improvement which might ordinarily be demanded of a developer. Expedited processing of an application, if it results in delays to other applications pending before the municipality, also shifts some costs from the developer of low- and moderate-income housing to his peers seeking to develop other types of projects in the community.

Use of funds raised through sale of tax-exempt revenue bonds, or obtained under the Community Development Block Grant program, spread the cost beyond the local purview and onto the federal treasury and, by extension, onto all taxpayers. This is arguably as it should be; if the provision of housing to meet the needs of low- and moderate-income households is a broad societal responsibility, then it should be met by a levy against the society as a whole. Since that is not going to take place, it need not be pursued further; still, there is little dispute that to the degree that such funds are available, it is reasonable to utilize them to support inclusionary housing programs and to distribute the costs associated with those programs more widely.

The use of public resources in the execution of inclusionary housing programs is not limited to substituting for costs that would otherwise be borne by private entities. Much of the use of public resources is directed at *supplementing* private resources; i.e., making units affordable to households of substantially lower income than would be the case if only private resources are engaged.[8] Indeed, California statutes explicitly require that

> Where there is a direct financial contribution to a housing development . . . through participation in costs of infrastructure, writedown of land costs, or subsidizing the cost of construction, the city, county, or city and county *shall assure continued availability for low- and moderate-income units for 30 years*.[9] [Author's emphasis]

Under these same statutes, municipalities are obligated to provide "incentives" to developers providing 25 percent of the units in their developments as low- and moderate-income housing. The above provision, however, applies only where the incentive incorporates a direct financial contribution, which may come from the municipality, or from state or federal funding sources to which the municipality has access.

The question of cost assumption is further muddied in a case such as that of Orange County, where a program of transfer credits has been established, as discussed briefly in chapter three, and in more detail in chapter seven. If developers who do not want to build low- and moderate-income housing are willing to buy credits from overachieving developers and pay substantially more for those credits than the apparent true cost to the overachieving developers — which appears to be the case — then a significant shift in the incidence of these costs has taken place. A substantial part of the cost of carrying out the Orange County inclusionary housing program, therefore, is being assumed by the developers who purchase the transfer credits.

The above discussion is meant to serve two purposes. One is as a prelude to the discussion of the "fairness" of the distribution of costs of an inclusionary housing program. A second is to serve as a framework for the evaluation of ordinances, programs, or specific projects. Whatever one's position on the underlying philosophical premises, the ability to evaluate such programs and projects must be grounded in the more fundamental ability to trace the costs and the benefits of the program through the various paths outlined above.

In that context, it should be emphasized that while one can undoubtedly reach a conclusion of some sort, based on some combination of facts and ideological premises with regard to the fairness of *any* particular way of distributing costs, it is a much harder matter to arrive at a conclusion with regard to a program in its entirety, particularly a complex multilayered one such as that administered by Orange County. In such a program, the networks of cost incidence that come into being are highly complex; to arrive at a single-minded ideological conclusion would appear, at the very least, to be intellectually suspect.

Fairness and the Distribution of Cost of an Inclusionary Housing Program

As has been described, leaving aside the complexities associated with the wide diffusion of costs among private and public sector actors, the simple model of inclusionary housing cost incidence distributes those costs in some manner within the landowner/developer/homebuyer trinity. The fairness of this outcome has been challenged, on the grounds that the costs associated with carrying out a redistributional social policy should be borne by the society as a whole. This is, of course, a reasonable argument in the abstract. It is, however, no more than a statement of an ideal, which bears at best a tangential and occasional relationship to the reality of American social and economic policy. Furthermore, the course of such policy in the 1980s strongly suggests that society is moving away from that ideal and dismantling many of the efforts for a national assumption of the costs of social policies that were initiated during the 1960s and 1970s. To the extent that redistributional social policies are to be carried out during the coming years, it can reasonably be assumed that the cost of such policies will be unevenly distributed. Tests of fairness, therefore, will have to be other than simply a determination of whether costs are or are not equally distributed throughout the entire society.

Given the likelihood of an uneven distribution of burdens, a central issue is whether those on whom the burden falls are reasonably capable of bearing it. A second question is whether placing the burden there violates any important norms or values of the society. In both cases, an objective assessment would suggest that the anticipated distribution of costs associated with inclusionary housing programs is not, in itself, either unfair or unreasonable. This does not mean, of course, that the workings of particular programs under particular circumstances cannot be unfair or unreasonable — a rather more technical question which is dealt with in following chapters.

As has been pointed out, the homebuyer will either pay slightly more for a given unit, after the costs of an inclusionary housing program have been added, in a community with unique attributes, or buy a similar unit for less in a community in which there is no inclusionary housing program. The likelihood that any affluent households will be priced out of the market as a result of inclusionary housing programs is too small to be seriously entertained; the worst outcome that can be envisaged is that some households will be forced to substitute somewhat less desirable units, in terms of either size, features, or location, than they might have preferred. This substitution, to varying degrees, is intrinsic to every normal market and occurs whenever any change of circumstances affects the affordability of housing in the market, whether it be changes in mortgage interest rates, construction costs, or property taxes.

The practical consequences of assuming cost burdens are potentially far more serious for a developer. While an affluent household that finds a unit in a particular community too expensive can easily select another community in which to live, the developer lacks the same flexibility. If a developer builds housing which ends up costing more than the market in that community can bear, he has little recourse. The majority of developers have extremely limited geographic mobility. They are effectively limited to a small geographic area by virtue of their land investments, familiarity with the political and economic dynamics of the area, and a network of relationships with subcontractors, financial institutions, and workers. A cost burden, therefore, that places a developer at a serious disadvantage to his competitors can be fatal to the affected developer.

This is not so much a philosophical as a practical concern. It would be preposterous to argue that a municipality is in any way obligated to ensure that a market exists for a developer's product on any particular parcel. The municipality need only go as far as to prevent a claim of a taking, and as has been discussed, that is not far at all. The practical concern is that if the developer cannot make enough profit to continue developing and building, the inclusionary program could become a nullity. Worse, it could become a cover for exclusion. Indeed, it does not take great insight to perceive that a municipality bound on exclusion, in a legal climate such as that of New Jersey, could hardly do better than to adopt an *inclusionary* ordinance, of such stringency in terms of the number of low- and moderate-income housing units required and the rigor of the affordability standards imposed, that no builder would find it possible to meet its conditions. Admittedly, such an ordinance could be challenged in court, but such a challenge would be far more difficult, and require far more sophisticated economic evidence, than a conventional exclusionary zoning lawsuit.

The third member of the trinity, the landowner, in many ways has the least claim to any particular level of economic benefit associated with the use to which his land can be put by virtue of a particular body of government regulations. It has long since been recognized that within broad locational parameters it is public regulation that creates value for land, coupled with public improvements, rather than any virtue intrinsic to the land or its owner. A substantial body of literature has developed on the subject of capturing the incremental value created by public improvements — a notion which has been translated into law in a number of countries, most notably Great Britain.[10] As was noted earlier, the effect of the imposition of an inclusionary zoning condition on a parcel of land can be considered analogous to downzoning of that parcel; the value is reduced, but is not reduced from some intrinsic value that the land supposedly had, but from a value that was created by the public zoning action in the first place. Furthermore, downzoning is commonplace for other reasons, and often to a far more drastic degree; as Hagman ironically comments, "if downzoning to provide a place where frogs can croak and birds can chirp is in the public interest, it should be equally possible to downzone a place so that low- and moderate-income persons can there sing."[11]

It is possible to anticipate the effects of imposing costs associated with inclusionary housing programs, despite their newness, with considerable reliability, since from an economic standpoint (with certain very limited exceptions, discussed below) they are not different than other costs imposed by public bodies on the development of land, which in turn must be absorbed within the landowner/developer/homebuyer trinity.

Reference is made to the imposition of costs for on-site and off-site improvements, known generically as exactions. Exactions, including both those mandated by ordinance and those negotiated informally with developers as a part of the approval process, affect the cost of development substantially more in many cases than any rationally designed inclusionary housing program. Indeed, there is a certain irony in many builders' protests over the enactment of inclusionary housing programs, inasmuch as substantially greater costs, arguably serving the public interest less, have long since been recognized as a part of the cost of doing business by the industry.

Although there has been little systematic study,[12] it appears clear that the economic effect of development exactions is essentially the same as that predicted for inclusionary housing programs. It is a self-evident proposition that the availability of infrastructure to a parcel of land — in particular, roads, sewers, and water supply — increases its value. This is largely by virtue of the fact that a developer or landowner does not have to bear the costs of providing these facilities, which costs result in the land value of parcels lacking infrastructure being substantially reduced. The extent to which land values are reduced is a function of the elasticity of demand in the market. The more readily the developer can pass on the costs of providing infrastructure or other off-site improvements and costs, such as fees in lieu of park dedication to the buyers of his units, the less the land value will suffer by the absence of infrastructure. As noted earlier, the market in unique or premium communities appears to adjust readily not only to higher land costs, but to a higher level of exaction and improvement cost. As a result, such communities can impose conditions, such as land dedication and payment of substantial fees, which would effectively stifle development activity if imposed in other communities less attractive to the marketplace. The fee in lieu of park dedication in Newport Beach, California, has been mentioned; another example is a fee charged developers in Princeton, New Jersey, which is used to rehabilitate the sewer system in the older part of the community at $800 per bedroom, or $3200 for a typical four-bedroom house.[13] Through negotiations, other communities have obtained bicycle paths, pedestrian bridges over highways, extensive off-site road improvements, fire stations, school sites and school buildings, and sites for general-purpose municipal buildings.

The close relationship between developers' willingness to pay the costs exacted and the elasticity of market demand in the community is likely to have a significant bearing on the feasibility of inclusionary housing programs. The two may not be analogous from a legal standpoint, but do bear an economic relationship.[14] While it does not appear that there are compelling "fairness" arguments raised by inclusionary housing programs, the analogy with exactions, however, suggests that tests of reasonableness that must be met if inclusionary housing programs are to be successful are closely bound up with marketplace interactions. It is this area which must be explored next.

Inclusionary Housing Programs and Market Forces

Pursuing the analogy between inclusionary housing programs and exactions, it logically follows that the costs of an inclusionary housing program will be more readily absorbed by the market in unique or premium communities than in communities with less compelling market attractions. The premium price that buyers will pay to live in the Princetons or Palo Altos of the world enables a developer to incorporate a variety of costs into the purchase price of his units which would not be possible elsewhere. It is most probably the case in such communities that the costs of a reasonable inclusionary housing program can be absorbed without any decline in the price of land paid by developers. This is potentially important, since it is precisely such communities in which the price of land is most likely to remain high, whatever inclusionary program is adopted.

There is a sort of poetic justice inherent in this conclusion. Since housing in premium communities is the most expensive housing, the need is greatest there for an inclusionary program if anyone other than the wealthy are to be able to live there. Furthermore, since these are the most affluent communities, the redistributional effect of an inclusionary housing program is likely to be greater than in a community where the income gap is less pronounced.

That notwithstanding, this conclusion raises serious problems. First, premium communities are, by definition, a relatively small part of any geographic area or housing market. An inclusionary housing program, therefore, which found itself limited to premium communities would affect only a small part of the region's housing production and would be destined to have no more than a modest impact on the region's housing needs. Second, the question arises whether the imposition of an inclusionary housing program, with a resulting increase in the number and visibility of low- and moderate-income households in the community if sufficiently widespread,[15] could potentially have a negative impact on the premium character of the community, or at a more modest scale, the premium character of specific developments in which low- and moderate-income housing were incorporated.

The first issue is philosophically straightforward, although possibly technically complex. If inclusionary housing programs are to be a significant means of meeting low- and moderate-income housing needs, they must be economically sound propositions in a much wider variety of communities than just the small number of elite suburbs. Limiting the reach of inclusionary programs to premium communities would be preposterous both as law and as housing policy. The economic factors involved, however, dictate that great care be taken with the design of each program. Programs must be designed in such a way that the level of the inclusionary objectives — i.e., the number and type of low- and moderate-income housing units sought — and the level of incentives offered yield a reasonable outcome for a capable developer. The extent of the low- and moderate-income housing requirement can and should reasonably vary with the marketplace character of the community imposing the requirement. Achieving such an outcome is not unrealistic, given the level of affordability that can be achieved where land and improvement costs can be kept down, and with reasonable cooperative effort between developers and local governments.

The second issue, although wildly speculative, is worth some discussion. It is clear that at least part of the motivation of those seeking to live in elite communities is the opportunity to live among other well-to-do people of putatively similar socioeconomic status or class. Generally speaking, in the United States private housing choices have tended to maintain socioeconomic segregation, rather than combat it; Ellickson writes, "the trend is a clue that upper-income groups disvalue the proximity of lower-income groups more than lower-income groups value the proximity of upper-income groups."[16] This may not be strictly true, because the ability of the upper-income groups to enforce their preferences is so much greater than that of the lower-income groups; it has, nonetheless, enough truth to it to be given careful consideration. Areas such as the West Side of Manhattan or Venice in Los Angeles, in which a widely heterogenous economic mixture appears to exist with some measure of stability, are the exception, rather than the rule. Furthermore, even in such areas, there appears to be a gradual diminution of whatever heterogeneity may exist at one time; in any area which becomes highly attractive to a wealthy population, the more affluent in-migrants will be able to outbid any less affluent households seeking to move into the same community. Over time, more and more of the units occupied initially by lower-income households turn over and are occupied by well-to-do households. Elite communities tend over time to increase their elite status relative to the regional mean as a result of an ongoing process in which each change reinforces the prevailing tendency.

Although in theory any in-migration of lower-income households or any explicit provision for such households through new construction, however modest, could dilute the elite tendency described above and thereby reduce the degree to which that community was more attractive than others in its region, there is some empirical evidence that indicates that that is not so. One case in point is Princeton Township, New Jersey, an affluent municipality by any standard, in which two substantial low-income housing projects were constructed during the 1970s, representing slightly over 7 percent of the total housing stock in the community by 1980.[17] There is no evidence that the construction of these projects had any effect whatsoever on the market perception of Princeton as a residential community for affluent households. Similarly, the elite status of many communities can survive the continued existence of slum areas or "pockets of poverty," as long as, one assumes, such areas are geographically limited and relatively clearly defined.

While it is quite possible that there is a "tipping point" in such matters, there is no particular evidence to indicate that the market position of an elite community taken as a whole is likely to be affected by the establishment of an inclusionary housing program. The impact of such a program on the market position of a specific *development* within that community is potentially more significant. Ellickson comments, "homebuilders seem to have learned from experience that their economic survival requires them to target each of their projects at a rather narrow stratum of the housing market."[18] As realtors know, a given house is likely to sell for more if surrounded by houses of similar or greater value, than if surrounded by lower-priced houses. The presence of less expensive homes within a subdivision, as a result of an inclusionary housing program or for any other reason, could reduce the price which a developer could get for the more expensive product in the development. Empirical evidence, however, that would make it possible to quantify this effect does not appear to be available.

A number of empirical rules of thumb, based on developer practices as well as intuitive judgments, exist. It would appear that first, the tolerance of substantial economic or price disparities is less in single-family than in multifamily developments; and second, that the larger the development, the wider the range of prices as well as housing types and sizes. Essentially, both of these conclusions flow from the relative ease or difficulty of using design and planning techniques to muffle the differences, as it were, at least as they are perceived by residents of the development.

Design treatments can result in considerable visual homogeneity in a multifamily development containing dwelling units of significantly different size and price; the same techniques are less adaptable to a conventional single-family development. The size of a single-family detached house dictates to a large extent its external appearance. A wide variety of interior configurations, however, can be accommodated in multifamily structures of essentially similar appearance. Similarly, within a large-scale development, such as a planned unit development, clusters of relatively homogeneous units can be separated from other clusters at different price levels by a variety of visual buffers, including woods, parklands, berms, roads, and nonresidential commercial or office development. In this manner, within the totality of a large development, a diverse socioeconomic mixture of populations can be successfully accommodated.[19]

The above pattern has, indeed, been more the rule than the exception in developments containing one thousand or more units. This is particularly the case in other than premium communities, since market considerations dictate that a developer appeal to as broad and diversified a market as possible. A development such as Twin Rivers in central New Jersey, or Smithville, in the Atlantic City area, contains both single-family and multifamily sections, as well as units for both sale and rental occupancy. In fact, in developments of this nature, the economic mix is arguably as diverse as that generated by many inclusionary programs. On occasion, subsidized housing has been integrated into such developments, as in Columbia, Maryland, or Echelon, New Jersey. In the latter case — a development by Rouse Corporation in a suburb of Philadelphia — the subsidized housing is limited, however, to housing for senior citizen occupancy. Still, many of the occupants of the unsubsidized rental units in that development would most probably fall into the moderate, if not low-income range as defined in *Mount Laurel II*.

In such developments, and particularly in those where a formal inclusionary housing program is a part of the development scheme, it is the intuitive market judgment of developers that if more affluent households are to be persuaded to live in the development, a *non*-low- and moderate-income character must be established initially for the development. In discussions with a number of developers, it was clear that no developer was willing to begin construction of low- and moderate-income units required by an inclusionary housing program until he had first constructed enough more expensive units to ''establish the character'' of the development.[20] This typically entails constructing twenty to twenty-five percent of the more expensive units prior to construction of the first low- or moderate-income unit.

This process is analogous to that of establishing a pattern of what Downs terms ''middle-class dominance'' for a neighborhood coming into being. As Downs points out, ''middle and upper income households can attain their basic residential objectives through *dominance* of their neighborhoods and do not require *total exclusion* of low and moderate income households.'' [Author's emphasis].[21] Similarly, the presence in developments of less expensive units occupied by low- and moderate-income households does not necessarily deter more affluent buyers, as long as the character of the development is clearly that of a middle- or upper-income community. The question remains, however, whether those affluent households will pay the same price to live in a development in which they know low- and moderate-income households are also present if alternative developments, similar in all but that regard, are available. The answer is that no one really knows, at least at this point. The uncertainty, however, is at least significant enough that many developers perceive inclusionary housing programs as significantly adding to their market risk.

A final consideration worth noting is the spread, as it were, of the economic mix resulting from an inclusionary housing program. Although statistical evidence is lacking, intuitive considerations suggest that the narrower the income differences within a development, the more easily marketable and acceptable to households at both the top and bottom of the range the project will be. The evidence is present to suggest that substantially more variation in income within developments, even relatively small-scale developments, may be more tolerable than is sometimes believed. An extensive study of mixed-income rental developments in Massachusetts concluded that,

> Income mix "works" or does not "work" according to whether the mix occurs in a well-designed, well-constructed and well-managed development. These latter factors are the crucial determinants of satisfaction. Income mix and racial mix are, in themselves, of no particular relevance.[22]

As has been noted, developments in which rental apartments and sales units are combined, by virtue of the different markets served by the two tenure types, often accommodate a relatively wide income mix.

The fact remains that none of these demonstrably successful economic mixtures has included a particularly wide income range, by national standards; the projects in the Massachusetts study were all relatively "affordable" rental projects, in which it is likely that the highest income category was not substantially above the regional median.[23] Still, these conclusions are potentially significant. The Massachusetts study found that if the more traditional determinants of resident satisfaction were amply present, income mix receded into the background. It is not inconceivable that, under many circumstances, the degree to which economic integration as well as racial integration is a problem will be in direct proportion to the extent that it is brought forward and stressed as a problem by those responsible for carrying it out.

These uncertainties, coupled with the awareness discussed in chapter two that the smaller the scale or the finer the grain of economic integration, the more problematic it is likely to be, have prompted consideration of different options within the overall framework of inclusionary housing programs. These options include the ability to purchase credits from other developments, as in Orange County, California; the ability to construct the required low- and moderate-income units on a site other than that which is the subject of the development proposal; or the ability to make a payment to the municipality in lieu of providing low- and moderate-income housing. Off-site provision of low- and moderate-income units has been permitted by the New Jersey Department of Environmental Protection, which imposes inclusionary requirements on certain developments under regulations adopted pursuant to the Coastal Area Facilities Review Act.[24] Both off-site development and the payment of fees in lieu of housing units have been approved under the Newton, Massachusetts, inclusionary housing program.[25]

While allowing a developer to meet low- and moderate-income housing requirements on a site other than his proposed development site may strike some as inconsistent with the principles of inclusionary housing programs, as may allowing a developer to "buy out" of an inclusionary requirement, that is not necessarily the case if the alternative sites are appropriately situated and any funds thus obtained used appropriately and responsibly. The purpose of inclusionary housing programs is not to impose burdens on developers, but to increase low- and moderate-income housing opportunities within a broad context of social and economic integration.

The market imperatives discussed above suggest that significant constraints exist on the potential benefits and beneficiaries of inclusionary housing programs. Since such programs depend on the activities of the private sector, they are constrained by economic considerations affecting developers and landowners and the market choices made by prospective homebuyers and tenants. It is for that reason that so much emphasis has been placed in the preceding pages on the notion of reasonableness. Above all else, programs must be reasonable, in the sense of setting realistic achievable goals and providing the means of achieving those goals, if they are to succeed.

One area in which the test of reasonableness imposes constraints is that of the downward reach of the economic mix, both of the percentage of low- and moderate-income units that can reasonably be required, and of the definition of low and moderate income that can be applied. The latter is of particular significance. The efficient development exercise presented in chapter three suggests that development under near-optimal conditions, but with no subsidy as such, can approach affordability for households earning 80 percent of the regional median income, adjusted by household size. This conclusion is supported by the experience of the Orange County, California, program in which a number of developers have produced substantially more "affordable" units than required by the county inclusionary programs, including three projects in which over 90 percent of the units were "affordable" units by the county definition.[26]

Accepting this as a general proposition, it would logically follow that inclusionary requirements in which income standards of 100 to 120 percent of median are set can be achieved in many cases where conditions are substantially less than optimal; e.g., more expensive land or site improvement costs, or more expensive construction costs typical of smaller builders. Conversely, it is unlikely that a unit affordable to a household earning 50 percent of the median or less can be provided except through some form of subsidy, either publicly provided or imposed internally on the other units in the development. While, as has been argued above, there is nothing philosophically repugnant about imposing such costs on the other units, market considerations constrain a rational builder's ability and willingness to do so. The extent to which a developer can do so will vary substantially from community to community, and from site to site. Furthermore, that extent will be affected significantly by factors unrelated to the development process, such as the property tax rate in the community or the best available mortgage interest rate.

The extent of the cost difference to a developer of making a unit affordable to a

EXHIBIT 1
Developer Profit/(Loss) Associated with Producing Housing Units
Affordable to Households at 80 Percent and 50 Percent
of Newark, New Jersey, SMSA Median Income

Number of Bedrooms	House-hold Size	Income Ceiling	Unit Sales Price	Afford-ability Ceiling*	Developer Profit or (Loss)
Moderate Income (80 percent of median adjusted for family size)					
1	2	$20,150	$35,000	$37,613	+ 2,613
2	3	22,700	42,500	42,373	(− 127)
3	4	25,200	51,500	47,040	(− 4,460)
Low Income (50 percent of median adjusted for family size)					
1	2	$13,100	$35,000	$24,453	(− 10,547)
2	3	14,700	42,500	27,440	(− 15,060)
3	4	16,350	51,500	30,520	(− 20,980)

Note: *Affordability ceiling represents the most expensive unit that a household earning the maximum for the appropriate income/household size can afford, based on the assumptions given in Exhibit 7, Chapter 3.

Source: Income data from U.S. Department of Housing & Urban Development, Newark Area Office (1983); unit sales price from efficient development exercise, page 3-39

household at 80 percent of median compared to making the same unit affordable to a household at 50 percent of median is considerable. Applying the numbers used in the efficient development exercise to the low- and moderate-income levels of the Newark, New Jersey SMSA, one obtains the effects shown in Exhibit 1.

These figures should not be taken as absolute numbers since there are a variety of options available to developers to reduce carrying costs. Buydowns and use of tax-exempt bond financing, either or both of which increase affordability, bring the "affordability ceiling" closer to the actual cost of the unit and reduce the loss associated with producing the unit. The message of the exhibit is nonetheless straightforward. A section of a development targeted to households earning 80 percent of median can be incorporated into a larger development with little or no effect on the economics of the development as a whole. The losses potentially associated with producing housing targeted to households earning 50 percent of the median income, however, could create serious difficulties within a development, unless (a) the number of such units in the development was very limited; (b) the development or the community in which it was located had enough unique attributes to make buyers pay a premium price for the market-rate units; (c) the developer was in a position to take advantage of atypical savings or economies, such as exceptionally low land costs; or (d) outside assistance, typically in the form of public-sector support, was available. It is likely, furthermore, that the inclusion of a substantial percentage of low-income units at that price level could have a negative effect on the marketability of the more expensive units, by virtue of its effect on the perceptions of developers and potential homebuyers.

The above is not an argument against inclusion of units affordable to households earning 50 percent of area median income or less, since a substantial number of developments will fall into one or another of the above categories. Prior to 1983 and the New Jersey *Mount Laurel II* decision, no inclusionary program had made provision for such households, except where federal subsidies were available; since that decision, numerous municipalities and developers in New Jersey have begun to address themselves to that population. Preliminary evidence suggests that developments with as much as ten percent of the units affordable to households earning under 50 percent of the area median and with additional units affordable to households earning between 50 and 80 percent of the median are often economically feasible. This is discussed further in chapter eight.

The foregoing example points out how important careful program design is to the success of an inclusionary program. An apparently simple matter like the definition of low and moderate income can have a significant bearing on the outcome of the program, as will such additional considerations as the percentage of units required, their phasing relative to the more expensive units in the development, and the extent and nature of the incentives that the municipality is in a position to offer a developer participating in an inclusionary housing program. It will be the purpose of the next chapter to explore those matters in detail and to provide a more detailed picture of the policies that must be adopted and the actions that must be taken by both local government and developers to make inclusionary housing programs a success.

NOTES

1. The author would like to express his debt in framing and resolving the issues discussed in this chapter to the following works: Robert Ellickson, "The Irony of 'Inclusionary' Zoning," in M. Bruce Johnson, ed., *Resolving the Housing Crisis* (San Francisco: Pacific Institute for Public Policy Research, 1982); Schwartz, Johnston & Burtraw, *Local Governmental Initiatives for Affordable Housing* (1981); and Donald G. Hagman, "Taking Care of One's Own: Bootstrapping Low and Moderate Income Housing by Local Government," *Urban Law & Policy*, Vol. 5, No. 2 (June 1982). Each of these essays brings considerable insight and experience to bear on the political and economic issues which are the subject of this chapter.

2. Schwartz, Johnston & Burtraw, *Local Government Initiatives*, p. 34; Ellickson, "Irony of 'Inclusionary' Zoning," pp. 140-141.

3. See, e.g., Hagman, "Bootstrapping Low and Moderate Income Housing," p. 19; also conversation with Sylvia Seman, Palo Alto Housing Corporation. Admittedly, the cities of Santa Monica (Hagman's example) and Palo Alto are unusual in that they are both premium communities with unusually severe constraints on development activity.

4. Ellickson, "Irony of 'Inclusionary' Zoning," pp. 151-155.

5. The reverse side of this dynamic is that a developer in such a community who manages to obtain

lower land costs (through, for example, his obtaining rezoning of a parcel at substantially higher density than that on which his purchase price was based) or lower off-site improvement costs, can price his product *as if* his costs were at the marketplace level and, thereby, make a substantial windfall profit.

6. A factor other than supply and demand that can, under certain conditions, have a significant effect on the price ratchet is the price basis of the landowners, i.e., the price at which they acquired the land themselves and their costs of carrying the land since its acquisition. When land has been bid up, through a speculative process, and substantial numbers of speculative transactions take place at or near the peak price, those buyers will be particularly reluctant to sell at a lower price, even if objective conditions dictate that their property has declined significantly in value. In many cases they may prefer to hold on to their land in the hope that property values will rise again, rather than take a loss. This was very much apparent in the real estate market in Atlantic City, New Jersey, during the late 1970s and early 1980s.

7. A possible case in point is Orange County, where, although there is great acreage of vacant developable land, it is held by a very small number of owners, notably the Irvine Company, who release land for development only gradually in order, one assumes, to maintain the price. See Schwartz, Johnston & Burtraw, *Local Government Initiatives*, p. 61 (n.61).

8. An example of the difference could be in the use of mortgages based on tax-exempt bonds. If a developer was required, initially, to make his units affordable to the target population on the basis of conventional interest rates, and the tax-exempt bonds were used to further reduce costs, that would be a supplement to private resources. If the developer were allowed to cost the project using the assumption *ab initio* that tax-exempt bonds would be available, it would be a substitution.

9. California Planning and Zoning Law, Sec. 65916 (adopted Stats. 1979, Ch. 1207).

10. See, e.g., Donald Hagman & Dean J. Misczynski, eds. *Windfalls for Wipeouts: Land Value Capture and Compensation* (Chicago: American Soc. of Planning Officials, 1973).

11. Hagman, "Bootstrapping," p. 21. This essay contains an excellent discussion of the arguments regarding the fairness of inclusionary housing programs to landowners.

12. It is notable and unfortunate that Johnson, ed., *Resolving The Housing Crisis*, which is cast as a broadly framed plea for the deregulation of the housing industry, does not address the issue of exactions in any meaningful way, devoting instead considerable space to such atypical cases as the California Coastal Commission.

13. This particular exaction is almost certainly illegal under New Jersey law; see discussion in chapter seven, esp. footnote 6. The interesting aspect is that legality and cost burden notwithstanding, developers to date have paid the fee, rather than challenge it.

14. In view of the lack of legal comparability, the economic analogy should not be overdrawn. An alternative comparison might involve large lot zoning; developers can often build on lots of one, two, or three acres in premium communities, where such large lot zoning in other suburban communities could be considered tantamount to a taking.

15. The tendency in such communities is for a steady decline to occur in the number of low- and moderate-income households. Since this decline is a largely invisible one, any change in the pattern is likely to be perceived as an increase, although it would probably not register as such statistically.

16. Ellickson, "Irony of 'Inclusionary' Zoning," p. 161.

17. The two projects, one constructed under Section 236 and the other under the Public Housing Program, contained 384 units (out of a total of 5065 in the municipality). These units represented nearly 50 percent of all units built in the municipality between 1970 and 1980. Roughly one-third of the units in the two projects were for senior citizen occupancy. It is interesting to note that the earlier, much larger, project was constructed in an isolated location, largely invisible from any other part of the community, and was built with little community opposition. The second project was built in a highly visible location, in an area characterized by moderately expensive single family houses, and engendered considerable community opposition, which was successfully overcome by a local political leadership committed to the project.

18. Ellickson "Irony of 'Inclusionary' Zoning," p. 162.

19. See the discussion of "price range" in Urban Land Institute, *Residential Development Handbook* (Washington, D.C., 1978), p. 137. This source suggests that such mixing of price ranges becomes feasible in developments of more than 400 units.

20. Discussions with John Kerwin, President, The Hills Development Company; and with J.S. Bilheimer, President, Centex Homes of Washington, D.C.

21. Downs, *Opening Up the Suburbs*, p. 95.

22. William Ryan, et al. *All In Together: An Evaluation of Mixed-Income Multi-Family Housing* (Boston: Massachusetts Housing Finance Agency, 1974).

23. The study report does not provide income data as such; the fact that the sample of successful projects were, by and large, low-rise suburban rental developments (garden apartments) would suggest a more modest income distribution than would be the case in the suburban population as a whole.

24. N.J. Administrative Code Section 7:7E-7.2. This regulation allows developers to build "affordable units off-site if affordable units on-site are infeasible." Practical determinations are made by the agency staff, taking into consideration factors such as the physical characteristics of the proposed development, land and site improvement costs, and the scale of the development. As of the end of 1983, no off-site proposal had been submitted to the Department.

25. Joel Werth, "Inclusionary Zoning Regulations: An Update," *PAS Memo* 80-3 (Chicago: American Society of Planning Officials, 1980).

26. Schwartz, Johnston & Burtraw, *Local Government Incentives*, p. 36.

5

Making Inclusionary
Housing Programs Work

The preceding chapters have identified any number of potential pitfalls which can hinder the effective carrying out of an inclusionary housing program, but have also suggested that means are available to navigate most of the obstacles that stand between theory and practice. The obligation to provide those means falls largely on the municipality or county designing and implementing the program; while it is necessary, of course, for developers to approach such programs reasonably and constructively, they can act only within the context of the program devised by local government.

From a philosophical standpoint and, at least in New Jersey, a legal standpoint as well, the obligation to make inclusionary housing programs work is shared by the municipality and the developer. The *Mount Laurel II* doctrine holds that the municipality must provide the opportunity for the development of low- and moderate-income housing, but that opportunity can be provided by imposing a duty upon developers in the community to provide those units within their developments. Thus, from the developer's standpoint, the construction of low- and moderate-income housing becomes as much an intrinsic part of the manner in which he does business as the accommodation of indigent patients was held to be an intrinsic part of the nursing business in *New Jersey Association of Health Care Facilities v. Finley.*[1]

Still, it is the municipality which at least in theory has the initiative. Where planning and zoning powers are properly being exercised, the municipality establishes the ground rules which must be adhered to by a developer seeking to build.[2] This is particularly the case with regard to inclusionary housing programs, whether or not it is true of the general course of municipal land use regulation. The typical developer is not likely to include low- and moderate-income housing in an otherwise more expensive development except in response to an explicit regulatory mandate. Framing that mandate, therefore, in all of its dimensions so that the program will indeed trigger the development of low- and moderate-income housing, becomes the most important consideration in the design of an inclusionary housing program. At the core of that mandate lies the zoning or land use ordinance setting forth the terms and conditions under which a builder in the community must develop.

The Contents of the Inclusionary Zoning Ordinance

The threshold standards that an inclusionary zoning ordinance must meet can be stated succinctly: *The ordinance must establish a reasonable and non-excessive goal for the development of low- and moderate-income housing, and must establish other land use standards which do not interfere with the achievement of that goal.* A large number of inclusionary zoning ordinances fall short, however, of the above standard, although more often with regard to the latter requirement than the former.

In any specific development scenario there is a point up to which low- and moderate-income housing requirements are feasible and not unreasonably burdensome, but beyond which they become burdensome. Although from a practical standpoint it is rarely possible to identify that point with precision (contrary to some developers' claims), the economic tools described in previous chapters can often provide a good approximation. Inclusionary zoning ordinances can be burdensome in two separate ways: by requiring an excessive percentage of low- and moderate-income units, or by defining low- and moderate-income housing too narrowly or restrictively. An inclusionary ordinance in Bridgewater Township, New Jersey, for example, required that 40 percent of the units in the multifamily zone be low- and moderate-income housing, of which 15 percent must be low-income and 25 percent moderate-income housing. This ordinance has been in effect since 1977, in a municipality well situated for development, and has yet to stimulate construction of a single housing unit in the zone governed by this provision.[3]

Such an ordinance creates burdens for a developer in a number of ways. Not only does it drastically reduce the number of units on which he can reasonably anticipate to make a substantial profit, but, assuming (as is nearly always the case) that construction of low- and moderate-income housing requires the reallocation of certain land and improvement costs from the low- and moderate-income housing to the balance of the development, it drastically reduces the ratio of units to which costs are to be allocated, to units from which they are to be removed. In an ordinance in which 20 percent of the units must be lower-income housing, the ratio is 4 to 1 (80 percent to 20 percent). As a result, a cost reduction of $5000 on the lower-income units has a cost-increasing effect of $1250 on the other units, an increase which in many cases is easily absorbed. The same cost reduction on the lower-income units in a development with a 40 percent requirement, in which the ratio is 1.5 to 1, has a cost-increasing effect of $3333 on each more expensive unit, nearly three times the effect and a substantial burden. Furthermore, although it is a matter involving considerable subjective judgment, it is widely believed by developers and real estate professionals that while a 20 percent lower-income share can be absorbed in a larger development without significantly impairing marketability, the same would not be true of a 40 percent share. While this may or may not be true, the fact that it is widely believed to be true is enough to discourage a developer from assuming such a risk.

Even if the total lower-income housing requirement were not excessive, it is likely that at least under some circumstances, an ordinance that required that 15 percent of the units be low-income housing as defined in *Mount Laurel II* could impose an excessive burden on the developer. The level of subsidy that may be required in order to produce units affordable to households earning 50 percent or less of the area median income may well be such that it is impossible to absorb the subsidy in the remaining units without either rendering them unmarketable, or forcing the developer's return below minimally acceptable levels.

An ordinance can as easily err on the other side, establish a minimal lower income target, and risk becoming trivial. The Cherry Hill ordinance, which was sustained in the previously cited *Uxbridge* case, required only that 5 percent of the units in a single multifamily zone be "low or middle income housing units."[4] Such an ordinance arguably creates far fewer lower-income units than it could, while requiring an effort on the part of the developer and the municipality not significantly less than that required to achieve a more substantial goal.

If the above burdens are quantitative in nature, qualitative burdens appear in ordinances as well. An ordinance that required that the low- and moderate-income units in a development be identical to the more expensive units would preclude a developer from using a crucially important tool to make low- and moderate-income housing work economically — his ability to reduce the floor area of the unit and modify other internal features. The Inclusionary Housing Policy of San Diego County provides that "all units made available under this program shall be designed to be in keeping with the *interior and exterior* design of the other units in the project."[5] Although it can be argued that the language is ambiguous, a strict interpretation could easily discourage developers from building under such a policy.

A more thoughtful approach to the issue which the San Diego County policy presumably sought to address — that of compatibility within a development between the lower-income and other units — is found in the inclusionary ordinance of the City of Santa Cruz, California:

> Inclusionary units should be reasonably disbursed [sic] throughout the development, should contain on the average the same number of bedrooms as the market rate units in the development, and should be compatible with the design and use of remaining units in terms of appearance, materials, and finish quality. The applicant shall have the option of reducing the interior amenity levels and square footage of inclusionary units, provided all units conform to the requirements of the City Building and Housing Codes.[6]

Even here, however, difficulties can arise; a developer may see the level of dispersal sought by the city as potentially harmful to the marketability of the more expensive units. Some studies have indicated that developers feel that the ability to cluster the lower-income units is important to the success of an inclusionary program.[7] In view of this widely held belief, it is arguably incumbent on a municipality, before adopting such an ordinance provision, to be thoroughly convinced that the benefits of the finer grain of integration that would result from a literal application of the ordinance clearly outweigh the risks thereby imposed, and the potential loss of builder interest in developing in the community. It should also be noted that there is no readily apparent rationale for the requirement that the inclusionary units have the same number of bedrooms as the other units; needs may vary, and some flexibility should be allowed the developer to tailor his low- and moderate-income units. It is more than likely, in any event, that the bedroom mix chosen by a developer for his market rate units is a function of his perception of market demand at a particular price range, and has little or nothing to do with the demographic distribution of housing needs. Building a lower-income cluster with the same number of bedrooms as a luxury development could turn out to be financially unpalatable to the developer, while not necessarily furthering the social objectives of the program.[8]

More common than burdensome low- and moderate-income housing requirements, however, are burdensome or unreasonable land use standards which have no explicit bearing on the inclusionary program, but effectively undermine it through the imposition of general constraints on development. An example of this is found in the Planned Development District ordinance adopted in the early 1970s by East Windsor Township, New Jersey, a rapidly growing suburban community in the central part of the state. This ordinance required as a condition of development that 5 to 10 percent of the units be provided for low-income households at public housing income levels, and an additional 10 to 15 percent for households eligible for the now moribund federal Section 235 program. These are not, on their face, unreasonable requirements. The balance of the planned development district requirements, however, was problematical:

- a minimum 400-acre parcel was required to qualify for the district designation;
- no less than 30 percent of the gross tract area must be developed for office or industrial uses;
- 50 percent of the remaining acreage was to be dedicated for open space;
- the remaining acreage (35 percent of the total) which could be developed for residential uses was subject to an extensive series of requirements and conditions.

In the final analysis, the maximum gross density that could be attained in a planned development under the ordinance, construing ambiguous language in the most liberal manner, was under 2 units per acre. That would only be possible, however, if 400 acres could be assembled within a district, which in its entirety contains little more than 400 acres in multiple and fragmented ownership.[9]

This is an extreme case, and it is not difficult to conclude that the municipality enacting this ordinance had no serious intention of encouraging, or even allowing, substantial development of any kind to take place through the planned development approach. A more unusual example is found in Cranbury Township, a close neighbor of the above municipality. In 1983, governed by the desire to preserve a large agricultural area in the municipality, the township adopted an unusual ordinance. A high-density planned development district was created, in which the following provisions applied:

- The maximum development density at which one could build *as of right* was one unit for every two acres;
- One could increase the permitted density up to a maximum of four units per acre through the purchase of development rights from agricultural lands in the farming district;
- One could, having done so, further increase the density to five units per acre, by constructing 15 percent of the total number of units as low- and moderate-income housing consistent with *Mount Laurel II* standards.[10]

Leaving aside the doubtful success of a voluntary program grounded in such a modest density bonus, the central problem lies in requiring the purchase of development rights as a precondition to achieving a density at which low- and moderate-income housing become potentially feasible. The specific provisions of the ordinance are onerous; for each additional unit (not unit per acre, but individual unit) that may be added to the "high-density" tract, the development rights to roughly 2½ acres must be purchased.[11] Given the location and character of the community, one can speculate that the cost per incremental unit could exceed $25,000.[12]

The specific character of the Cranbury ordinance provisions clearly render it a

EXHIBIT 1
Recommended Maximum Density Standards
for Multifamily Housing

Unit Type	Representative Sources*			
	CB	HUD	DCA	AM
Townhouse	14	13	10-20	10
Garden				
Apartment (2 ST)	18	19	15-25	20
Mid-rise				
Apartment	45	70	25-50	45

*Sources: (CB) Urban Land Institute, *Community Builders Handbook*.
(HUD) HUD, *Manual of Acceptable Practices*. This Manual does not specify densities, as such, but provides a scale by which density can be calculated based on unit size, open space allocation, etc. The above densities were computed by applying typical open space and unit size figures to the HUD formula.
(DCA) NJ Department of Community Affairs, *Affordable Housing Handbook* (preliminary draft).
(AM) Alan Mallach Associates, *Least Cost Housing*, prepared for New Jersey Department of The Public Advocate.

nullity as far as the capability to "provide a realistic opportunity" for low- and moderate-income housing. Even if the specific provisions were less burdensome, the cost of development rights less, and the final density ceiling higher, the underlying conclusion is still the same. Any ordinance which seeks to serve two inconsistent, perhaps conflicting, purposes will diminish the feasibility of achieving one, if it is made conditional on the other. The same is true of an ordinance which requires major and expensive off-site improvements as a condition of development. This is not to suggest that a municipality cannot, or should not, seek to achieve other planning and development objectives. If, however, the thrust of the ordinance is to treat the provision of low- and moderate-income housing as simply another exaction, set on top of other exactions bearing a higher priority, that ordinance will fail as a *bona fide* inclusionary ordinance.

A major consideration in framing an inclusionary zoning ordinance, going beyond simply refraining from placing unreasonable impositions or burdens on the developer, is that of *establishing standards which allow a builder to build as efficiently as possible*. Two essential elements in this regard, often treated poorly or inappropriately in such ordinances, are (1) providing density standards that allow for efficient development; and (2) providing flexibility in terms of the physical configuration of the buildings in the development.

Density: Efficient development is dependent on the reasonably high gross density, in terms of the total number of units that can be built on a site and, even more, on a high *net* density, which is a reflection of the degree to which units can be effectively clustered within the site. A gross density of four units per acre, as in the Cranbury ordinance, with the particularly high land costs associated with achieving that density, clearly works against the objective of achieving high efficiency of development. Within the same ordinance, net density standards of 8 units/acre for townhouses, and 10 units/acre for garden apartments are set forth.[13] These are substantially lower than standards widely held by practitioners; indeed, there is something very close to a consensus on acceptable net density standards in the literature (see Exhibit 1), a consensus that notably fails to be reflected in many zoning ordinances. The values in the exhibit, however, are definitely on the conservative side, inasmuch as they are all proposed as generalized standards that can be widely adopted without regard to specific developments or specific sites. There is ample evidence that sensitive design and site planning can generate attractive and livable low-rise housing at densities of 30 to 50 units per acre, as has been achieved frequently in California settings, where traditional prejudices against high-density development appear substantially less than in the northeastern United States.[14]

A rational ordinance should not set forth both gross and net density standards, but rather one or the other. In a planned development, for example, if reasonable net density standards are set forth for each unit type (townhouses, garden apartments, etc.), in conjunction with reasonable standards for open space, collector roads, and the like, a total number of units and, therefore, a gross density will logically emerge. Where both are set forth in the ordinance, barring unusual luck, inconsistencies and therefore unnecessary constraints will invariably emerge.

Design Flexibility: Ordinances are rife with provisions limiting the design flexibility of the developer and his professional staff. An ordinance will require a particular mix of units (a set percentage of single family units, a percentage of townhouses, etc), and impose extensive design standards on each unit type. The Cranbury ordinance, for example, requires that multifamily buildings contain no more than six dwelling units per structure.[15] All such provisions reduce the ability of a developer to build efficiently; in the above instance, as has been noted earlier, arguably the most efficient multifamily building type is a building in which eight units are on each floor, with a total of sixteen (2-story) or twenty-four (3-story) units in the structure.

It is not suggested that these requirements have been adopted by these municipalities for the purpose of thwarting an inclusionary housing program; on the contrary, they are typical of zoning ordinances throughout suburban America. What is significant is that they reflect the attitude, inimical to successful production of low- and moderate-income housing, that an inclusionary zoning provision can simply be superimposed on top of an ordinance that is substantively exclusionary, and that by so doing, the underlying ordinance is thereby cleansed. Such an attitude will not make an inclusionary housing program work.

EXHIBIT 2
Effect of Highland Park, Illinois,
Density Bonus Ordinance

Ordinance Provisions		Effect of Ordinance*		
Percent Density Increase	Percent Lower Income Units	Total Units	Lower Income Units	Market Units
None	None	100	0	100
1%	2%	101	2	99
2	4	102	4	98
3	6	103	6	97
4	8	104	8	96
5	10	105	11	94
6	12	106	13	93
7	14	107	15	92
8	16	108	17	91
9	18	109	20	89
10	20	110	22	88

*Note: The hypothetical example given has been based on a density by right of 10 units/acre. The effect of the ordinance, of course, is the same at any base density.
Source: Analysis by author based on relevant provisions of Highland Park, Illinois, zoning ordinance.

Incentives

A municipality or county can, over and above providing a "clean" zoning ordinance under which to build, offer a developer a variety of incentives to make the development of low- and moderate-income housing more attractive. Within this area, it is important to distinguish between zoning incentives, which are a part of the land use regulatory scheme, and other incentives, such as financial assistance or processing assistance.

Zoning Incentives

The preceding discussion has implicitly assumed that the ordinance under consideration would require the provision of low- and moderate-income housing as a condition of development, so that the concept of a zoning incentive, or density bonus, was fundamentally irrelevant, for a variety of reasons discussed in some detail earlier in this book. The concept of the density bonus is, however, central to the notion of the voluntary inclusionary program; indeed, the entire logic of the voluntary inclusionary program is that the opportunity to build at greater density is an incentive sufficient to prompt a developer to incorporate low- and moderate-income housing in his development.

The range of density bonus incentives found in voluntary inclusionary ordinances is wide. At least one ordinance, that of Highland Park, Illinois, provides such a limited density increase relative to the required low- and moderate-income housing units that the builder ends up building *fewer* market rate units under the density bonus than he is permitted to build by right.[16] The workings of this ordinance are shown in Exhibit 2.

This is an extreme case, and it would be surprising if it were found to be successful in the absence of federal subsidies. While it has generated some low- and moderate-income housing, they have been exclusively units subsidized under the Section 8 program. This suggests an interesting, but not unreasonable, conclusion; namely, that under many market conditions it may well have been *more* profitable for developers to build Section 8 housing than conventional or market units.[17]

Exhibit 3 presents the effect of three more representative density bonus ordinances in which the number of conventional units increases as a result of the bonus. The range of increase varies from two-thirds of a conventional unit for each lower-income unit (Piscataway Township, New Jersey) to two conventional units for each lower-income unit (Lewisboro, New York). The author is not familiar with any density bonus ordinance which provides a more generous incentive in this regard than that of Lewisboro. This is one of the very few voluntary density bonus ordinances that has resulted in any lower-income housing being provided without federal subsidies.[18]

Two developers have utilized the provisions of the East Brunswick ordinance to produce lower-income housing, utilizing the Federal Section 235 and 236 programs respectively. Recently, the township has awarded a density bonus to a developer who is providing units affordable to households earning up to 105 percent of the area median income, without federal subsidy. The difference between the price of that housing and other housing being built in the general vicinity appears to be nominal, and even the township officials have acknowledged that this project was not providing low- or moderate-income housing in the *Mount Laurel II* sense.[19]

Both in East Brunswick and Piscataway, as well as elsewhere, the majority of developers do not seek to take advantage of these density bonus provisions. In East Brunswick, even during the period in which federal subsidies were available, it would appear that as many multifamily projects were developed without the density bonus as with its provisions. The available evidence strongly suggests that these provisions are not an efficient means of providing low- and moderate-income housing. They may be effective where federal programs make the provision of lower-income housing profitable in and of itself; even there, however, many developers are likely to be reluctant to involve themselves with such

EXHIBIT 3
Effect of Three Density Bonus Ordinances
on Hypothetical 50-Acre Site

	Total Units	Lower-Income Units	Market Units	Percent Increase In Market Units
Piscataway Township, New Jersey				
By Right	300	0	300	
Maximum	400	60 (15%)	340	13.3
East Brunswick Township, New Jersey				
By Right	250	0	250	
Maximum	400	75 (18.75%)	325	30.0
Town of Lewisboro, New York				
By Right	100	0	100	
Maximum	140	13 (9.3%)	127	27.0

Source: Analysis by author based on relevant provisions of three zoning ordinances.

efforts, and will therefore choose not to take advantage of the density bonus. Without federal subsidies, the only units built under these programs for which developers have been given density bonuses — as in Lewisboro or East Brunswick — are low- and moderate-income housing only by a definition substantially broader than that of *Mount Laurel II*.

There are other approaches which a municipality may want to entertain. A number of California municipalities have enacted, as a part of a growth control program, what can perhaps be characterized as a coercive voluntary program. In order to receive priority under the program, without which approval to build is not likely to be granted, a developer has to accumulate a certain number of points, of which a substantial number are available only for production of lower-income units. Under the program enacted in Davis, California, it has become effectively impossible to obtain building permits without providing a substantial number of low- and moderate-income housing units.[20] A similar program, but one giving much less weight to low- and moderate-income housing production, has also been enacted in Petaluma, California.[21]

A different approach, under consideration in some New Jersey communities as a response to the *Mount Laurel II* decision, is the inclusionary overlay zone, or conditional use. In a version of that approach being developed by a planning team including the author, the overlay zone or conditional use would apply to roughly two-thirds of a municipality. Within that area a developer could build under the existing zoning by right, which would be limited with rare exceptions, to development of single-family houses on relatively large lots. The developer could, alternatively, seek to build under the conditional use, which would provide for an increase in density in the area of 600 percent; e.g., from one unit per two acres to three units per acre. In order to qualify for that increase in density, the developer would have to either:

1. Incorporate roughly 20 percent of low- and moderate-income units in his development;
2. Combine the proposed site with a second site, and incorporate roughly 20 percent of the total units proposed as low- and moderate-income housing, on either site; i.e., place all of the lower-income units on one site, and the market units on the other; or
3. Make a substantial cash contribution to a designated local housing agency or trust, to be used exclusively for the production of low- and moderate-income housing.

An economic analysis is being conducted to establish the relative costs of the options, in order to calibrate the alternatives so that alternative (1) will be less costly than alternative (2), which will be less costly than alternative (3). This reflects the policy decision that it is preferable to have developers build the units rather than contribute cash, and preferable to have them build the units on the same site as the market units rather than on a separate site. It is anticipated that developers will make cash contributions in most cases, notwithstanding the economic analysis, in view of the perceived market risks associated with producing the lower-income units.[22]

It is uncertain whether such a program will provide a significantly greater incentive than the more familiar forms of density bonus programs. It seems clear that a necessary condition for the success of such an overlay approach is that the underlying permitted use be *significantly* less appealing from a development perspective than the overlay, even with the low- and moderate-income housing. If the difference is not dramatic, the program is not likely to succeed.

One technical advantage of the overlay zone over the conventional density bonus is that it is less likely to trigger speculative increases in the price of land than is an ordinance which clearly limits the workings of the density bonus to a small number of sites. If the overlay is cast widely enough across a municipality, the probability of intensive development of any single site is small enough so that the increase in land value may be modest. If this is so, then it may provide a stronger incentive to developers to take advantage of the overlay, because the developer will be able to benefit from the greater part of the incremental land value resulting from the higher density. On the other hand, municipalities may be reluctant to relinquish the level of control over the location and timing of intensive development which they would have to forego to provide an overlay zone large enough to have a serious probability of success.

The provisions of the overlay zone discussed above include one feature of broader significance: specifically, the idea of offering developers alternative routes to the satisfaction of the inclusionary objective. As will be discussed below, developers vary widely in terms of their technical capability to produce lower-income housing, their perception of its feasibility and compatibility with their conventional product, and their fundamental willingness to embark on inclusionary housing developments at all. A municipality framing an inclusionary program should examine carefully whether its objectives can be achieved, in some cases, through alternatives to "straight" inclusionary development; i.e., alternatives to incorporating low- and moderate-income housing within each major development in the community. The principal alternatives that have been identified are:

1. *Off-site Development*: Permitting the developer to construct the lower-income units on a site separate from that on which he proposes to construct his market-rate units;
2. *Payment in Lieu of Development*: Permitting the developer to make a payment to an appropriate public or nonprofit entity, which will use the proceeds to further lower-income housing in some manner, in lieu of constructing any lower-income units;
3. *Transfer Credits*: Permitting the developer to purchase credits from other developers who have produced an excess of lower-income units. As in Orange County, California, where this has been implemented, the existence of transfer credits, and the substantial price that developers are willing to pay for them provide a meaningful incentive for certain developers to produce more lower-income units than strictly required under the county's inclusionary program; and
4. *Donation of Land*: Permitting the developer to donate a parcel of land within his development to a public or non-profit agency, on which the agency will have the required lower-income units constructed.

Each of these alternatives may be worthy of consideration in some communities under some circumstances, and irrelevant or inimical to the success of an inclusionary program in others. These considerations are discussed in some detail, particularly with regard to the alternative of payments in lieu of construction, in chapter seven. The point that should be stressed, however, is that such alternatives should, at a minimum, be *considered* in the framing of any inclusionary zoning ordinance.

Other Inducements and Financial Benefits

Municipalities have the power to offer a variety of other potential inducements to developers in order to generate the production of low- and moderate-income housing. In other cases, municipalities may be able to obtain such benefits for developers from third parties, notably the state and federal government. Such inducements serve the purpose of reducing the cost, either initially or over time, to low- and moderate-income residents of housing produced through inclusionary housing programs beyond that which a developer can reasonably achieve through internal subsidies. Such inducements, such as tax abatement, use of tax-exempt bonds, and the like are arguably more important to offer in the context of a mandatory than a voluntary inclusionary program. In the latter, in the final analysis, the developer can choose not to take advantage of the inclusionary option; but in the mandatory program, the developer has no choice other than to leave the community or cease being a developer at all. This clearly places a greater obligation on the part of the community to seek out and provide assistance from whatever sources may be available, to the greatest degree possible.

Many of the available non-zoning incentives have been mentioned, and a few discussed in some detail, earlier in this book. This section will provide a short checklist, as it were, of the more effective and more readily available incentives.

(1) *Tax-Exempt Bond Mortgages*: The first state to utilize the device of selling tax-exempt revenue bonds and using the proceeds to make mortgages to finance low- and moderate-income housing was New York State, which created the New York Housing Finance Agency under what became known as the "Mitchell-Lama Program" in 1959. Most major industrial states adopted similar statutes in the late 1960s, and by the end of the 1970s nearly every state in the United States had an agency, authority, or other body created for the purpose of issuing tax-exempt bonds for home mortgages, rental project financing, or both. In many states, particularly those in the West and Southwest, state law permitted counties and municipalities to issue their own tax-exempt bonds for this purpose, either directly or through an instrumentality such as a housing or development authority. While various restrictions have been placed on the use of such bonds, in large part as a result of their proliferation, and most notably by the Mortgage Bond Tax Subsidy Act enacted by Congress in December 1980, they still continue to represent a substantial part of the tax-exempt issue calendar and a major resource in creating affordable housing.

The lower interest rate of tax-exempt bonds, typically 3 percent to 4 percent below the conventional mortgage interest rates at any given time, provides a substantial boost to the affordability of a unit at a given cost. The level of subsidy that is likely to be required, without tax-exempt bond financing, to produce housing that is realistically affordable to low-income households as defined in *Mount Laurel II* is greater than that which most developers may realistically be able to provide. In such circumstances, it may be reasonable to require certain levels of low-income housing production only if tax-exempt bond financing is available.

The specific circumstances under which it may be available will vary from state to state. Where state law provides that a municipality or county can issue such tax-exempt bonds directly, such a commitment should be seriously considered by any community imposing an inclusionary housing obligation on a developer. In other cases, the county or municipality may be able in some manner to facilitate a bond issue by a state or county agency, or make it possible for a developer to obtain funds from such sources, which would be difficult or impossible without the intervention of local government. In New Jersey, a statute provides a means by which a municipality (which cannot issue tax-exempt bonds for housing under state law) can guarantee rental housing revenue bonds issued by a county authority.[23] In a number of states, a developer may not obtain such financing from the state agency issuing housing revenue bonds unless the municipality has adopted a resolution authorizing such financing, although the municipality involved need not otherwise take an active role in the matter.[24] Although there are some cases in which no municipal action is required, in most circumstances the municipality or county can through its actions substantially increase the availability of tax-exempt bond financing to developers producing low- and moderate-income housing.

(2) *Community Development Block Grant (CDBG) Funds*: All municipalities and counties in the United States are potential recipients of funds under the Community Development Block Grant program, a federal program available to support a wide variety of local activities, particularly those in support of improving the housing conditions of low- and moderate-income households. Some municipalities and counties, including all large urban centers, are considered "entitlement" communities, and receive such funds on a noncompetitive basis; other communities are eligible to compete for a pool of funds set aside for non-entitlement communities, known as the Small Cities program. In many states, as a result of recent program changes, the Small Cities program is administered by the state rather than the federal government.

While CDBG funds cannot be used directly to finance construction, they can be used in a variety of ways which directly facilitate the construction of low- and moderate-income housing or make the end product more affordable to lower-income households. Among the more widespread uses of such funds are landbanking or the acquisition of land for low- and moderate-income housing with CDBG funds;[25] use of CDBG funds to provide infrastructure for low- and moderate-income housing sites, particularly for the funding of necessary off-site improvements;[26] and interest-rate reduction, by incorporating grant money into financing packages either as a grant or as a low-interest loan.[27]

The law provides for a diversity of techniques by which CDBG funds can be used to reduce costs associated with the provision of lower-income housing, so that a municipality, in conjunction with one or more developers, can readily design a program that utilizes available funds in the most efficient manner in each particular case. Furthermore, this program represents a significant source of funds, with annual appropriations in recent years being in the area of $5 billion. As a result, there is no question that by targeting CDBG funds to defray costs associated with providing low- and moderate-income units in larger developments, more units more affordable by lower-income households can be obtained.

There has been to this point only limited application of CDBG funds to inclusionary housing programs; indeed, there has been only limited application of CDBG funds to support construction of lower-income housing in suburban areas generally. Much of this has been a function of local governments faced with the controversial nature of lower-income housing development in the suburbs following a path of least resistance. Given the great variety of legal purposes to which these funds can be put, the number of competing interests in a community seeking a share of the funds, and the relative lack of oversight by the federal government to ensure that the funds are indeed used to benefit lower-income households, it is not surprising that CDBG funds are used in other areas. Most housing funds, it would appear, have been used for rehabilitation and home improvement programs, while other funds have been used for infrastructure improvements and recreation and community facilities in existing neighborhoods, which may or may not have been areas of lower-income population concentrations. Other funds have been used for economic development activities, such as downtown improvements unrelated to housing.

Instituting an inclusionary housing program will not, of course, eliminate the competition for available CDBG funds from other directions or necessarily establish a political constituency for use of CDBG funds in support of the inclusionary housing program. Furthermore, it is possible that in some communities there may be reluctance to use these funds in a manner that suggests that they are benefiting a developer rather than in "cleaner" ways, such as direct loans to low-income homeowners or construction of a playground in a low-income neighborhood. CDBG funds, however, remain the only substantial resource, other than direct appropriations from the municipal budget, by which municipalities can overcome financial barriers standing in the way of making an inclusionary housing program work. If the municipality adopting the inclusionary program is an entitlement community, it should certainly set aside a reasonable share of its CDBG funds for this purpose; if it is in a position to apply for Small Cities funds, it should certainly do so.[28]

(3) *Tax Abatement*: Many states have enacted statutes whereby municipalities can offer tax abatement to residential developments meeting certain criteria. Typically, a statute may provide that the owner of a rental development may pay a fixed percentage of project income in lieu of property taxes annually; this is known as a payment in lieu of taxes (PILOT), and can be set at different levels, usually by action of the municipal governing body.[29]

Historically, suburban communities have been reluctant to grant tax abatement to lower-income housing developments, with the exception of senior citizen housing where it was anticipated that the cost of providing municipal services to the residents would be minimal. Fears of family-oriented developments triggering dramatic increases in school enrollment, while generally unfounded, tended to discourage the granting of tax abatement. The granting of tax abatement in support of inclusionary housing programs may be further hindered by the state of enabling legislation in this area; most state statutes tend to restrict tax abatement to developments financed with public funds or being undertaken in conjunction with urban renewal projects, or to other particular circumstances more characteristic of the development environment twenty years ago than that of the present day. As inclusionary housing programs become more widely implemented, it is not unreasonable to expect that state legislatures may adopt legislation making tax abatement, under reasonable ground rules, available as a tool in support of inclusionary housing efforts.[30]

(4) *Use of Municipally-Owned Land*: We have noted the use, in a number of jurisdictions, of CDBG funds to acquire land which is then made available to developers who will construct lower-income housing. Many municipalities, through various means, have come into ownership of vacant or underutilized land parcels suitable for residential development. In other cases, the municipality may be in a position to obtain land at present in state or federal ownership for housing development on behalf of a developer.[31] Such land may be made available for the construction of lower-income housing simultaneously with construction of more expensive housing elsewhere; in some cases, sites may be situated so that they can provide additional acreage for a site subject to an inclusionary housing program.[32]

Such opportunities are likely to be less readily available in suburban than in urban communities, since during recent years many urban jurisdictions have come into ownership of large tracts of land, often as a result of tax foreclosure or urban renewal. Many suburban opportunities are likely to exist, however: housing programs have taken advantage of underutilized parkland[33] and school buildings no longer required for educational purposes.[34]

(5) *Use of Municipal Funds*: The notion that a suburban municipality would actually appropriate funds raised by local taxes to support lower-income housing is abhorrent to most suburban residents; even the court in *Mount Laurel II* did not go so far as to mandate the spending of municipal funds, while warning that "satisfaction of the *Mount Laurel* obligation imposes many financial obligations on municipalities, some of which are potentially substantial."[35] Suburban residents, with few exceptions, perceive themselves as heavily taxed and overburdened by the costs of simply providing the basic services and facilities that they have come to consider necessary for their health and welfare.

While *some* suburbanites may be overburdened by local taxes, many are not.

The effect of the wave of state legislation of the 1970s freezing tax rates, or establishing "caps" on property tax increases and the like, coupled with the dramatic drop in school enrollments in most parts of the United States, has created an environment in which tax burdens on suburban homeowners have largely stabilized and in many cases declined. Under these circumstances, many suburban communities could readily provide the level of financial support that would make low- and moderate-income housing feasible without a significant impact on the average resident's finances. This arguably represents only a modest extension of the financial obligation assumed by most communities for the progressive extension of infrastructure and public facilities, an obligation which is generally acknowledged despite repeated efforts to shift those costs onto whichever developers may be available at any point. Locally generated tax revenues have been used to foster lower-income housing development, in ways similar to those for which CDBG funds have been more widely used, in a handful of communities, including Fairfax County, Virginia and State College, Pennsylvania.[36]

Good Faith

In the final analysis, much, if not all, of the foregoing discussion comes down to the issue of good faith. Having adopted an inclusionary zoning ordinance and framed an inclusionary housing program, is the municipality acting in good faith to see that it brings about the desired result; i.e., the production of housing that is indeed affordable to, and occupied by, lower-income households? The idea of good faith in this context, however, is more than the passive forbearance which is often associated with the idea. In a context wherein the obligation to achieve results is equally shared between the municipality and the developer, the concept of good faith is an affirmative one, grounded in the proposition that *a municipality acting in good faith to implement an inclusionary housing program must take whatever affirmative steps are reasonably available to it to bring about its success.*

That proposition can be considered an ideal. One would be unconscionably naive to believe that it is the rule among suburban jurisdictions, or anything more than an occasional, heartwarming, exception to general practice. Many inclusionary housing programs have been undertaken with little commitment to that goal by the jurisdiction involved; motivations have included the need to satisfy a court order and a variety of political considerations falling well short of a community-wide consensus. In some cases, after adoption of an inclusionary ordinance, the municipality has failed even to enforce the minimum conditions of the ordinance, let alone take affirmative steps beyond the letter of the ordinance. The Camden Regional Legal Services office brought a lawsuit on behalf of a number of lower-income households to compel the Township of Cherry Hill to enforce the terms of its inclusionary ordinance with regard to development applications that were before the municipality.[37]

The actions of the Township of Franklin, New Jersey, make an even more instructive example. The township adopted an inclusionary zoning ordinance in 1976, governing at that time four large vacant tracts zoned for planned development. Two years later, a developer submitted an application for approval under these provisions. Upon request of the developer in subsequent years, he was granted periodic extensions of time in which to submit his plan for provision of low- and moderate-income housing as required by the ordinance; finally, in 1982, the municipality waived the inclusionary requirement governing this project in its entirety. By this time, as a result of subsequent rezoning, two of the initial planned development tracts were no longer subject to an inclusionary requirement, and the township was making every effort to thwart the efforts of the owner of the fourth site to develop his land, despite that owner's public offer to provide the low- and moderate-income housing required by the township ordinance.[38]

Few municipalities would appear to have engaged in the sort of systematic gradual nullification of an inclusionary zoning ordinance that took place in Franklin Township. The inconsistency that characterized the administration of the Petaluma, California, inclusionary program, as described in one study, is equally indicative of lack of good faith.[39] In this case, the motivation for enacting the program appeared to be a desire to provide a legal "cover" for a stringent growth control program rather than any particular interest in lower-income housing.[40] Comments have been previously made with regard to a number of New Jersey ordinances equally lacking in overt good faith, although also lacking the blatant bad faith of the Franklin Townships of the world; the Bridgewater and East Windsor Township ordinances, on their face, would appear to fall into that category.[41]

Another variation on the same theme, but on its face more reasonable, is the ordinance adopted by Mount Laurel Township after the township decided not to appeal the New Jersey Supreme Court decision to the United States Supreme Court. The ordinance adopted at that point stated:

> All new developments which consist of ten or more residential units which is [sic] brought before any approving agency of the Township of Mt. Laurel, will be required to set aside mandatorily twenty percent (20%) of the dwelling units for the construction of low and moderate income housing governed by the provisions as are set forth below.[42]

The balance of the ordinance sets forth both physical standards for low- and moderate-income housing and occupancy standards generally consistent with the language of the *Mount Laurel II* decision. The deficiencies of this approach fall largely into two areas: first, the arbitrary nature of the ordinance, which fails to distinguish in any meaningful way among locations, housing types, and existing conditions; and second, the underlying and pervasive premise that by having adopted such an ordinance the municipality has fulfilled its obligation in its entirety, and that from this point on, low- and moderate-income housing is exclusively the responsibility of the developer. The ordinance contains extensive provisions dealing with the manner in which developers failing to fulfill the inclusionary requirements may be punished, but no language whatsoever even suggestive of any positive or affirmative municipal role in the matter. The township would appear to believe that it has been able, in this manner, to wash its hands of the entire subject.

The contrast between the above examples and the behavior of the local jurisdictions in those communities where inclusionary housing programs have been most successful is marked. In Orange County, California, and in Montgomery County, Maryland, local government has acted consistently and sometimes at measurable cost to the local taxpayer to encourage, support, and facilitate the construction of lower-income housing under their inclusionary housing programs.

Montgomery County has established an administrative agency within county government exclusively to provide support for their inclusionary program, known as the Moderately Priced Housing Program. The agency takes full responsibility for maintaining waiting lists, screening prospective buyers or renters of moderately priced units, and administering resale controls on moderately priced sales units, as provided by county ordinance. Furthermore, in order to facilitate the production of such units, at different times during the past ten years, the county has:

- Actively solicited available federal and state subsidies and housing funds;
- Leased county-owned land to developers participating in the program;
- Issued tax-exempt bonds through the County Housing Opportunities Commission (HOC), an entity analogous to a housing authority;
- Undertaken to administer its own housing subsidy program financed through a 4 percent tax on the sale of converted condominium and cooperative units.

The county is also reported to be considering using county funds to initiate a land acquisition program. As a result of these efforts, between 1976 and 1982 the county was able to bring into being nearly 2,000 moderately priced housing units under this program, units which are available, according to a county estimate, at prices of 60 percent or less of the average selling price of a conventional townhouse unit in the county.[43]

Orange County, California, has also provided a variety of incentives or benefits in order to facilitate production of low- and moderate-income housing, including:

- Modification of zoning standards;
- Improved processing procedures and processing assistance;
- Tax-exempt revenue-bond financing;
- Use of Community Development Block Grant funds to write down land and off-site improvement costs;
- Technical assistance in obtaining other federal and state subsidies.

By the end of three years, the county had approved developments containing a total of 5,767 affordable housing units, of which 2,122 were occupied or under construction. Toward that end, the county had issued $229,135,000 in tax-exempt housing revenue bonds.[44]

It can be argued, not without reason, that both Orange and Montgomery Counties are atypical. Both are large, affluent jurisdictions with a highly sophisticated and extensively staffed county governmental apparatus; both were able to take advantage of an unusually strong premium housing market which made developers actively interested in building within the jurisdiction. As a result, it can be argued that these two counties were more readily capable of taking affirmative steps and had a more receptive developer community with which to work than most jurisdictions. While this is undoubtedly true to some degree, it does not mean that more modestly endowed jurisdictions cannot act affirmatively and responsibly within their means. East Brunswick, New Jersey, has acted both to expedite its processing of development applications under its density bonus program and to assist in seeking and obtaining federal and state subsidies for lower-income units. For a number of years, the township, which is neither particularly large or particularly affluent, has employed a full-time housing specialist within the planning department to facilitate the inclusionary program and other housing improvement efforts being undertaken within the township.[45]

In short, for a local jurisdiction to carry out the provisions of an inclusionary housing program in good faith requires more than simply adopting an ordinance and placing matters in the hands of the developers active in the community. It requires a series of affirmative steps which lead to a form of partnership between the municipality or county and the developers, formed in order to make production of lower-income housing possible. While some actions carried out by Montgomery County, such as the issuance of tax-exempt bonds or the adoption of local dedicated taxes, may be beyond the ability of many communities, most of the incentives and benefits described in this chapter are not beyond even communities of modest size and resources.

The Role of the Developer

While the municipality must establish the ground rules for an inclusionary housing program and has an obligation to act affirmatively in support of developers' efforts to build under those ground rules, the developer is, after all, the one who will or will not build the low- and moderate-income housing which an inclusionary ordinance seeks to provide. The development industry, as a rule, has been unenthusiastic about the establishment of mandatory inclusionary housing programs, and the California Building Industry Association (CBIA) adopted a formal position in 1979 in opposition to "mandatory inclusionary housing or zoning programs, whether state- or locally-imposed."[46] Broadly held sentiment within the development industry could be summarized as encompassing first, a recognition that more affordable housing is widely needed; second, that the imposition of extensive and excessive government regulations, delays, fees, and growth controls have forced the price of housing up, and that the deregulation of the industry would provide substantial amounts of affordable housing; and third, that in any event, it is unfair and unreasonable to place the responsibility for meeting a general societal need on the back of the building industry.

While there is no doubt that relaxation of regulations, growth limits, and the like would make possible substantial reduction in housing costs,[47] there is also no reason to believe that those reductions would even approach the cost differences between the going market and the price of the units produced under inclusionary housing programs in Orange County or Montgomery County. It is equally clear that few, if any, builders will produce units that conform to the *Mount Laurel II* standards in the absence of explicit regulatory standards and conditions. Furthermore, it is apparent that despite the oppositional stance generally taken by the industry, many builders have in practice been able to operate successfully under inclusionary housing programs. A study conducted for the California Building Industry Association, an organization strongly opposed to inclusionary programs in tone and philosophy, nonetheless acknowledged that numerous builders in the four case studies included in this study had positive feelings about the inclusionary programs under which they operated, concluding with the somewhat self-evident proposition that "developers who have been successful in dealing with these housing programs hold the most positive attitudes, while those builders who have not been successful (or have even left the jurisdiction) hold negative attitudes."[48] A similar conclusion was reached by an extensive study of the Orange County inclusionary housing program.[49]

Since a substantial number of builders appear able to make inclusionary programs work, their philosophical position notwithstanding, it becomes significant to explore what factors among builders and developers appear to be related to their ability to succeed in producing housing under inclusionary programs. At least three separate factors appear to emerge from the experience to this point: the type of developer, the size of the developer, and the attitude with which the developer approaches the project, in particular the lower-income housing element within the project.

Developers are not a homogenous group. On the contrary, they are diverse with regard to their size, their organizational structure, the nature of the product that they build, and many other features, The typical developer is conservative; having become accustomed to producing a particular housing product, he will rarely deviate significantly from that model, except under duress. This is not only a matter of technical limitations; *Professional Builder* quotes one builder who notes that he has

> a reputation for building a certain calibre of housing and would not want to downgrade that image by building "affordable" housing.[50]

Even where image is not a problem, it is not generally feasible for the builder of an expensive, limited volume product to shift to the production of affordable or lower-cost housing. The difference between the two products from the technical perspective is almost so great as to suggest that two different industries are involved. The same lines divide developers on the issue of participation in, and cooperation with, government programs and agencies. It is not a significant exaggeration to state that the typical builder sees himself in an adversarial posture toward "government"; the great majority of builders have little or no interest in participating in available governmental subsidy programs.[51] This is in part a reflection of a generalized attitude, reinforced by developer folklore; it is, however, often a reflection of the very real difficulties developers have experienced in trying to take advantage of government housing programs.

Many of the differences in making inclusionary programs work are reflected in the difference in size among builders. The building industry today is more and more divided into a large number of small builders, and a small number of large builders who are responsible for a larger and larger share of total housing production. Small builders are arguably at a significant disadvantage in seeking to participate successfully in inclusionary housing programs. The discussion in one study is worth citing in its entirety:

> Small developers perceive a greater risk in building moderate-priced units and are less able to afford the cost of innovative design or technological changes. Therefore, they are less likely to build a project with affordable units on-site. Because their projects are small (on small parcels) they are less able to separate affordables from market-rate units, an action they perceive as necessary to reduce the negative effect of the lower-priced units on market-rate units. They are much less able to take advantage of scale efficiencies to cut costs, and in fact are more likely to experience increased learning costs in constructing new model types (affordables). In addition, small builders are less likely to be able to take advantage of the incentives offered by the county. In Orange County the $100 million bond issue was used to provide several large builders with below-market-rate financing; no small builders benefited. The small builder cannot make use of the density

bonus if he/she finds the construction of on-site affordable units to be too risky. Finally, small builders do not have large enough staffs to employ a permit specialist. This fact places them at a disadvantage in jurisdictions with complex regulatory schemes, such as Orange County.[52]

In contrast, a small number of large builders in Orange County were able to take full advantage of the incentives offered by the county and produce developments that were in their entirety or in large part made up of affordable housing, as defined by the county. This in turn enabled them to sell credits to other, typically smaller, developers, thereby making a substantial cash return on their production of lower-income units. The fact that small builders were willing to spend $15,000 or more per credit, which appears to be substantially more than the loss taken by the larger builders on the production of these units, suggests (1) that the pricing of conventional units in the Orange County marketplace was capable of absorbing a substantial "tax" of this nature; and (2) that their resistance to actually building lower-income housing was so strenuous that they were willing as an alternative to pay a "tax" substantially in excess of the likely direct cost to them of producing the required affordable housing.

A corollary to the above point is that a mandatory inclusionary program must be sensitive to the differences between developers, by type and by size, and express that sensitivity by offering a variety of means by which to meet an inclusionary requirement. A requirement across the board that each development contain a set percentage of lower-income housing, without exceptions or alternatives, may turn out to be unworkable for a substantial number of builders active in the community, which, in turn, could easily lead to the objectives of the program being frustrated.

A third distinction, and perhaps the most important one, although the hardest one to define with precision, is that of the *attitude* with which the developer approaches the inclusionary housing condition to which he is subject. It is apparant that many developers perceive the provision of lower-income housing to be a burden totally different in degree and in kind from other obligations and conditions that they must meet, such as site and off-site improvements. In a similar vein, it appears that many developers, treating lower-income housing as an "add-on" rather than an integral part of the development, prepare financial plans which do not include the lower-income units, *and then* superimpose the costs of the lower-income units on the financial plan. Such an approach, even if the results are tolerable, reinforces the perception that the inclusionary requirement is an arbitrary burden rather than being integral to the project. By contrast, any responsible builder will determine the extent of his off-site improvement costs on a given parcel before preparing a financial plan for the site; it would be considered irresponsible to prepare a plan *as if* there were no off-site improvements, and then treat the off-site improvements as an externally dictated loss factor.

The successful developer under an inclusionary housing program is the developer who fully meshes the planning of the low- and moderate-income housing with the overall planning of the development. To such a developer, whatever his personal or ideological leanings, the low- and moderate-income housing units, *in the context of his development planning*, are little more than one additional unit type, or price range, which is to be incorporated into the development and for which appropriate arrangements must be made in terms of financing, construction, and marketing, and, if appropriate, continued management or monitoring. Such a developer understands that there is little if any fundamental difference between the many steps that he must take to make a development of any kind "work," and the steps that must be taken to make low- and moderate-income housing "work" equally well.

Approaching the development of low- and moderate-income housing through inclusionary housing programs in this manner de-emphasizes, and may indeed undervalue, the significance of the social and economic innovations which are being made in such a program. This is both appropriate and desirable. Developers are not social or economic philosophers, visionaries, or, for the most part, radicals. They are practical individuals with a capacity in one specific, relatively narrow area: the production of housing. From their standpoint, the more the development of lower-income housing under an inclusionary program can be routinized, i.e., can be encompassed as a part of their normal routine activities rather than a departure from those activities, the better. The same is true of the residents of the housing. With few exceptions, people — especially those making a major financial commitment in the form of a home purchase — do not want to think of themselves as experimental subjects or as pioneers in the socioeconomic frontier. To the degree that inclusionary housing programs are encompassed within the scope of the normal and not the exceptional, they will be more successful.

NOTES

1. 83 NJ 76, 415 A.2d 1147 (1980). See the discussion of this case at 2-8 to 2-9.

2. Clearly, this is the ideal case. In reality, there are many cases in which the relationship is more one of bargaining from an equal starting point than one in which the municipality has the initiative; in others, the municipality lies largely dormant until a developer presents a plan and demands the appropriate zoning to conform to his objectives.

3. Bridgewater Township, N.J. Zoning Ordinance; cited in New Jersey Department of Community Affairs, *Affordable Housing Handbook*, Preliminary Draft (Trenton, N.J., 1981).

4. Cherry Hill Township, N.J. Zoning Ordinance #76-71, Art XIII, Sec. 1302.4.

5. Board of Supervisors, San Diego County, California, Policy I-75, *Inclusionary Housing Policy* (San Diego, 1979). It should be noted that the ordinance that was adopted subsequent to the adoption of this policy statement did not contain this provision.

6. City of Santa Cruz, California, Ordinance 81-05, Section 24.56.020(b).

7. Schwartz, Johnston & Burtraw, *Local Government Initiatives*, at 32.

8. There are many additional examples, some of which tend to become technical in the extreme. An interesting case is the Cranbury ordinance (see note 10 below) which requires that any rental unit

meeting the low- and moderate-income housing requirement must be maintained as rental housing for a minimum of 20 years. This is not unreasonable on its face; the ability of a developer, however, to sell the depreciation on such a project as a tax shelter, which is important to the economic feasibility and rent levels of the project, may be severely hindered, if not completely eliminated by this provision.

9. East Windsor Township, New Jersey, Zoning Ordinance, Secs. 20-16.0000 through 20-16.0600.

10. Cranbury Township, New Jersey, Land Development Ordinance, Article IX (adopted July 1983).

11. Ibid., Article IV, Sec. 150-16. This is an average, or estimate, derived from a complex procedure set forth in the ordinance for determining the number of development rights that can be derived from any particular farmland parcel. In essence, the transfer of development rights procedure results in the farmland being preserved for farming uses alone, its development rights having been transferred to another parcel, a concept similar to the "air rights" transfer permitted in New York City and some other communities. See Norman Williams, Jr., *American Land Planning Law* (Chicago: Callaghan & Co., 1974), Vol. 5, pp. 380-384; also, Jerome G. Rose, ed., *Transfer of Development Rights* (New Brunswick, NJ: Center for Urban Policy Research, 1975).

12. Discussion with Carl Bisgaier, Esq., indicating that asking prices for raw land in the agricultural zone were in the area of $10,000 to $15,000 per acre. The township attorney, William Moran, Esq., in discussion with the author, however, asserted that prices should not exceed $3000 to $5000 per acre.

13. Ibid., Article IX, Sec. 150-30. Net density is defined as density on the site less common open space and collector streets.

14. See U.S. Department of Housing & Urban Development, *The Affordable Community: Growth, Change and Choice in the 80s* (Washington, D.C. 1981), p. 38. Numerous large-scale multifamily developments have been constructed in Orange County, California, at densities of 25/acre to 45/acre; see City of Newport Beach, *Housing Element* (1981), p. 34.

15. Cranbury Land Development Ordinance, Art. XVI, Sec. 150-78.

16. Described in Mary Brooks, et al., *Housing Choice* (New York: Suburban Action Institute, 1980), pp. 129-130.

17. Ibid., p. 130. This conclusion is not particularly implausible; much Section 8 development was highly profitable to developers sophisticated enough to take full advantage of the opportunities in that and similar federal programs.

18. Town of Lewisboro, Land Development Ordinance, Sec. 324.12. This ordinance was amended in December 1979; the earlier ordinance provided an even more generous bonus, up to a maximum increase of 60% in gross site density.

19. *New York Times*, May 22, 1983, for description of project; and New Brunswick, N.J. *Home News*, February 20, 1983 for comment by township attorney. The units were to sell for a price of $58,000.

20. Schwartz, Johnston & Burtraw, *Local Government Initiatives*, pp. 15-18.

21. Ibid., pp. 13-15.

22. The author is particularly appreciative of the thoughts and comments of John Nolon with regard to this approach.

23. County Improvement Authorities Law, New Jersey Statutes Annotated (N.J.S.A.)40:37A-44 et seq., 40:37A-79.

24. See, e.g., the New Jersey Housing Finance Agency Law, N.J.S.A. 55:14J-1 et seq., Sec. 6(b).

25. Land acquisition programs using CDBG funds in conjunction with private developers have been implemented in communities such as Knox County, Tennessee; Orange County, California, and Skokie, Illinois. See Brooks et al., *Housing Choice*, pp. 55-72.

26. This has been done as a part of the Orange County, California, Inclusionary Housing Program.

27. See Brooks, et al., *Housing Choice*, pp. 73-107.

28. Other federal programs, which may be available to some but not all suburban communities, include the Urban Development Action Grant (UDAG) program to leverage private investment in housing and economic development, and the new Sec. 17 capital grant program for rental housing, discussed more fully in chapter eight.

29. New Jersey has a variety of such statutes permitting tax abatement, including the Housing Fi-

nance Agency Act, which allows the municipality to set the PILOT percentage at any rate from zero to twenty percent of project annual gross revenue; *id.*, Sec. 30(b). Other statutes provide for a flat rate PILOT at 15 percent of gross revenue; Limited-Dividend Nonprofit Housing Corporations or Associations Law, N.J.S.A. 55:16-1 *et seq.* During the 1960s, the city of New York customarily abated 50 percent of the taxes on new projects constructed under the city Mitchell-Lama middle income housing program. A similar program, under which entities receiving tax abatement make payments to the state which then returns the amount to the municipality, is the Chapter 121A program in Massachusetts

30. It can reasonably be assumed that the adoption of Proposition 13 in California, which limited property taxes to 1 percent of market value, has defused the pressure that might otherwise have come into being for legislative action in this area to parallel the other inclusionary housing statutes enacted in the California legislature.

31. In Newport Beach, California, the city and the state have cooperated in making available a parcel owned by the State Department of Transportation (Caltrans) to be developed subject to an inclusionary housing requirement.

32. While the author is not familiar with any such case in a suburban jurisdiction, or in the context of a formal inclusionary program within the scope of this study, municipally-owned sites have on a number of occasions been made available to developers in urban areas in order to complete an assemblage of land for a development considered beneficial to the municipality. A number of housing sites were assembled in this manner in Atlantic City, New Jersey, after the onset of casino gaming. At least one rental development now under construction as a result of this assistance will contain 15 percent of its units affordable to low-income households. This provision was mandated, however, by the Federal Mortgage Bond Tax Subsidy Act, and was opposed by city officials, who reluctantly acceded in order to allow the project to go forward.

33. A well-known case is that in which the city of Englewood, New Jersey, as an outgrowth of a major racial integration effort in the late 1960s, provided a section of undeveloped public parkland in a largely white area for the construction of moderate-income housing by a nonprofit organization. This action was challenged and eventually led to the landmark New Jersey Supreme Court case *De-Simone v. Greater Englewood Housing Corporation*, 56 NJ 428 (1970), affirming the legality of the project, a major pre-*Mount Laurel* decision in support of lower-income housing.

34. E.g., in Huntington, New York, a vacant school was converted into a Section 8 housing development. Many, even most, suburban communities are finding themselves with unneeded school buildings; even where the building may not be suitable for reuse, the grounds may be suitable for development.

35. 92 N.J. at 265.

36. Brooks, et al., *Housing Choice*, pp. 46-48, 69-70.

37. Discussion with Marcia Soast, Esq., Camden County Regional Legal Services, Camden, New Jersey.

38. Township of Franklin (Somerset County), New Jersey Land Development Ordinance, Sec. 1212. Conversations with David Frizell, Esq., attorney for Franklin Fields PUD and Jack Field, developer.

39. See Schwartz, Johnston & Burtraw, *Local Government Initiatives*, pp. 13-15.

40. Ibid., p. 13. This arguably had some bearing on their successful defense of their growth control program in a major federal court test, *Construction Industry Association v. City of Petaluma*, 522 F.2d 897 (9th Cir. 1975). See discussion of this case in Ellickson, *op. cit.*, at 169. Given the history of federal case law in this area, e.g., *Belle Terre* and *Tiburon*, it is hard to believe that a gesture in support of lower-income housing would be dispositive.

41. See discussion at pages F1-F3 & F4 above.

42. Ordinance No. 1983-15, Sec. 1803 (adopted May 2, 1983).

43. Montgomery County, Department of Housing & Community Development, Fact Sheet (3/2/83).

44. Orange County, California, "Orange County's Inclusionary Housing Program at a Glance" (11/10/82).

45. See in particular, New Brunswick, N.J. *Home News*, February 20, 1983.

46. Cited in Ward Connerly & Associates, *The Implications of Inclusionary Housing Programs* (study conducted for the CBIA), foreword (1979).

47. See Professional Builder, *Affordable Housing Ideas*, pp. 192-217.

48. Connerly & Associates, *Implications of Inclusionary Housing Programs*, p. 87; see generally pp. 79-87. The four communities studied were Davis, Petaluma, Palo Alto, and Marin County, all in California.

49. Schwartz, Johnston & Burtraw, *Local Government Initiatives*, p. 33.

50. "Affordable Housing Survey," *Professional Builder*, May 1980.

51. Ibid. This survey found that 55 percent of builders interviewed would not take advantage of government programs, if they were available, to produce less expensive housing.

52. Schwartz, Johnston & Burtraw, *Local Government Initiatives*, p. 48.

6

Creating and Maintaining Lower-Income Occupancy in Inclusionary Housing Programs

The essence of the practical discussion up to this point has been the *production* of lower-income housing through inclusionary housing programs, that is, the considerable effort that is needed to produce housing units that will be affordable to a lower-income homebuyer or renter. Once a program has produced a number of such units, significant and difficult questions immediately arise. First, to what degree should one ensure that these units are indeed occupied by lower-income households; and second, if one should do so, how best can it be done? Furthermore, since the initial occupants of these units will inevitably move on over time, should these units be maintained for lower-income occupancy; and if so, in what manner, and over what length of time? A failure to arrive at responsible answers to these questions — answers which are both philosophically sound and capable of being put into practice without unreasonable difficulty — will make the entire enterprise of only limited, even dubious, value.

There is substantial disagreement about the appropriate degree of intervention in ensuring and maintaining lower-income occupancy of housing units created through inclusionary housing programs. There is little disagreement, however, with regard to the threshold issue; namely, that if one has gone to great lengths to provide a unit that is *affordable* to a lower-income household, however defined, it should at least initially be *occupied* by such a household.

Although there is no evidence of a philosophical disagreement on that point in the literature, there are at least a handful of cases in which low- and moderate-income housing has been provided and sold with no effort to ensure that the buyers would be households of low- and moderate-income rather than more affluent

133

households in the market for a bargain. Two such examples are those of Petaluma and Davis, both in California and both cases in which the inclusionary requirements were outgrowths of growth-control schemes rather than explicit objectives of the community in and of themselves. In the case of Petaluma, the lack of any controls on the buyers of the units was consistent with the apparent lack of seriousness with which the program was conducted;[1] in the case of Davis, one writer who studied that community's program in detail commented:

> The reluctance of the city council to screen buyers and control resales seems to be the result of a vague desire not to get involved in more government interference, a dubious rationale in a city that limits the number of building permits.[2]

Leaving aside the lack of credibility in this particular case, concern about excessive intrusiveness is not limited to the Davis city council. As will be discussed in more detail below, much of the concern tends to focus primarily on resale controls; i.e., the means used to ensure continued low- and moderate-income occupancy of owner-occupied lower-income housing units created through inclusionary programs. Since such controls work by limiting the potential equity appreciation available to the initial lower-income homeowners, they can easily be perceived as challenging fundamental American principles and values; Hagman notes that "the [California Association of Realtors] alleges that denying a low or moderate income person the right to equity appreciation in a purchased unit is to condemn that person to continued low income status."[3] While such a formulation is preposterous, it reflects a widespread concern. This concern, coupled with a number of thorny legal and technical issues, has resulted in some jurisdictions deciding not to impose resale controls (although carefully limiting initial occupancy), and others deciding to limit the controls to a relatively short period after initial occupany.

Any effort to ensure that units constructed under inclusionary housing programs be and remain occupied by lower-income households requires a considerable level of public intervention, both in the form of initially framing and adopting detailed regulations and standards as well as in terms of ongoing monitoring and administration for the duration of the period during which the units are to be occupied by lower-income households. That this should be so comes as no surprise to those familiar with federal subsidized housing programs. A very large number of the actors dealing with inclusionary housing programs in both public and private sectors, however, have had little or no such experience. Furthermore, builders and developers may well have been reluctant to participate in the past in federal housing programs specifically because of the paperwork or bureaucracy involved.

Intervening to the extent necessary in the marketplace, and doing so without creating unmanageable bureaucracies and incurring unreasonable expenses, requires highly effective administrative machinery. It requires, as well, a level of continuity which few developers, however well intentioned, can provide. As a result, the most successful programs have been characterized by a high level of governmental involvement, either directly or through nonprofit entities, in performing the necessary functions to ensure continued lower-income occupancy.

As the following discussions will demonstrate, considerable progress has been made during the past few years toward resolving the legal and technical problems that have arisen in this area. Inclusionary housing programs are such a recent phenomenon, however, that today's solutions must still be considered provisional; it is not yet known, with anything approaching certainty, what techniques and mechanisms will best serve for the long term.

Selecting Lower-Income Homebuyers and Renters

The first step after completion of construction is the selection of appropriately qualified occupants, be they prospective buyers or renters. While there is little argument that such selection should take place, there is considerable variation in the manner in which it takes place and the degree to which conscious effort is made to establish a particular character for the prospective tenant or owner population.

It is generally accepted and understood that all buyers or renters should be households whose incomes fall within the class defined as eligible by the ordinance or program under which the housing has been produced. It is often simplest to leave matters at that, for example, to hold an unlimited lottery among the members of the pool of prospective buyers or renters meeting the income qualifications in order to identify the occupants of the development.

A wide variety of other considerations, however, argue against limiting one's scrutiny to the income qualifications of the household. At least three separate factors appear to motivate communities to go beyond simple calculation of qualifying income: a desire to prevent abuses, a desire to ensure that benefits are provided to the most "deserving," and a desire to promote other, related, community objectives. Even in Orange County, California, where the program has been informed by a conscious effort to minimize the level of screening and public involvement in buyer selection, the agency responsible for screening the prospective buyers—the Orange County Housing Authority—seeks (a) to screen out potential speculators, and (b) to give priority to households not currently owning a home.[4] The first can be characterized as an effort to prevent abuse of the program, while the second is clearly based on a not unreasonable judgment of which households are more deserving of the particular opportunity being provided. A similar consideration, which appears in many programs, is a limitation on household assets in addition to household income as a condition of eligibility.[5] Again, the objective is to ensure that households which are capable of obtaining sound housing without the intervention of the inclusionary housing program do not benefit from the program.

Priority Categories

Beyond simply eliminating those households from consideration whose participation could arguably be considered an abuse of the program, many communities have established priority categories for occupancy of lower-income units which reflect community policies regarding the appropriate distribution of the benefits being provided. Priority categories typically reflect a desire to provide units to households which have a relationship to the community, either in terms of residency or employment.

A priority ranking scheme linked to employment has been enacted by the City of Irvine, California, as follows:

- First Priority: Households whose primary wage earner, i.e., the individual earning the highest annual salary or wage in a given household, is employed in the city
- Second Priority: Households whose secondary wage earner is employed in the city
- Third Priority: General public[6]

These priority categories are established within a population that has already been screened on the basis of income and asset limitations. Since even within the priority categories the number of applicants consistently exceeds the number of units, lotteries are then used to select the actual prospective buyers.[7]

Priority rankings associated with employment within the community are perhaps the most common form of priority found in inclusionary programs; a proposed inclusionary housing development in Bedminster, New Jersey, provides for priority to be given to households in which a member works in the vicinity of the project, *and* the household either (a) lives in substandard housing; or members (b) commute an excessive length of time to work.[8] The initial plan for the Orange County, California, inclusionary program called for use of a "distance to work" priority ranking, although it appears to have been dropped in the subsequent execution of the program.[9]

The process of setting priority categories, however, can become more extensive and complex, and in the process raise a number of issues of housing policy. Before discussing the policy issues themselves, a few examples of more questionable priority ranking schemes can be provided. The Borough of Lincoln

Park, New Jersey, created a zone limited to the provision of low- and moderate-income housing financed by a state or federal agency, subject to the following priority designations:

First Priority :	Lincoln Park senior citizens
Second Priority:	Senior citizens who are parents of Lincoln Park residents
Third Priority :	Senior citizens who have resided in Lincoln Park within the past three years
Fourth Priority :	Senior citizens residing within Morris County
Fifth Priority :	Senior citizens residing in counties contiguous to Morris County
Sixth Priority :	Low/moderate-income families (as defined by U.S. Department of Housing & Urban Development or N.J. Housing Finance Agency)
Seventh Priority:	All others[10]

A still more baroque structure, which has been noted earlier in this book, has been erected by the Town of Lewisboro, New York, in order to establish priority for occupancy of the small number of units being provided through that town's inclusionary housing program. A total of 40 lower-income units are either built or planned to date in the town. This scheme provides for eight separate priority categories, each of which is divided into between three and five separate subcategories, for a grand total of thirty-three ranks. The illustration below provides the subcategories only for the first two categories, in the interest of brevity.

1. Town of Lewisboro municipal employees
   a. residents of the town of Lewisboro
   b. cumulative length of service
   c. cumulative length of residency
   d. date of application
   e. lottery
2. Town of Lewisboro School District employees
   a. resident of the town of Lewisboro
   b. cumulative length of service
   c. cumulative length of residency
   d. date of application
   e. lottery
3. Residents of the town of Lewisboro (3 subcategories)
4. Other persons employed in the town of Lewisboro (4 subcategories)
5. Relatives of residents in the town of Lewisboro (immediate family) (4 subcategories)

6. Other residents of Westchester County (4 subcategories)
7. Other persons employed in Westchester County (4 subcategories)
8. All others (4 subcategories)[11]

The elaborate Lewisboro priority categories raise serious policy issues: given that the units are a limited resource and that there are likely under almost all circumstances to be more candidates for the units than there are units available, how is such a limited resource to be allocated? In particular, to what degree should a community limit the benefits of an inclusionary housing program to those whom it characterizes as "its own," be they the community's ill-housed residents or its employees?

The desire to ensure that residents of a community be, to the degree feasible, the beneficiaries of the community's efforts to provide lower-income housing has been a constant theme throughout all suburban subsidized housing programs. This has led to an ongoing tension between political and civic leaders in suburban communities and civil rights activists, who have argued that the availability of lower-income units should be in relation to need without regard to whether the prospective beneficiary is a resident of the community, an adjacent suburban community, or a nearby core city.

While there is no apparent legal bar in the framing of inclusionary ordinances to providing *some* preference for local residents, excessive targeting of units for local residents would appear inconsistent with the underlying legal doctrines in most states in which exclusionary zoning ordinances have been struck down. In New York, for example, in the leading case, *Berenson v. Town of New Castle,* the Appellate Division held:

> In enacting a zoning ordinance, consideration must be given to regional needs and requirements. It may be true, for example, that New Castle already has a sufficient number of multiple dwelling units to satisfy both its present and future populations. However, residents of Westchester County as well as the larger New York City metropolitan region may be searching for multiple family housing in the area to be near their employment or for a variety of other social and economic reasons.[12]

The position of the New Jersey courts in *Mount Laurel II* has already been noted.[13] In similar vein, the California statutes require each municipality to plan for each "locality's share of the regional housing needs,"[14] as determined through a fair share plan adopted by the area council of governments, or, in the absence of such a body, the State Department of Housing & Community Development.[15]

In the final analysis, however, it is most probably unrealistic to expect that many communities will do other than give preference to local area residents. Even if formal priority categories are not established, simple proximity to information often results in a disproportionate share of units being occupied by local area residents, particularly where a "first come first served" selection approach is adopted. Although Orange County did not adopt any formal preference for local residents, 88 percent of all occupants of the units built through the county affordable housing program were prior residents of Orange County.[16]

Selection Procedures

The machinery that is established within a community to implement the policies that have been adopted with regard to selection of buyers or renters varies widely. Again, the variation reflects local preferences with regard to the degree of public intervention in the process. It is generally accepted, however, that at some point in the selection process some entity other than the developer of the units must, at a minimum, review the qualifications of prospective buyers to prevent misuse of the program. It is not maligning the homebuilding industry to suggest that, left to his own devices, a developer may often have a compelling interest in stretching, if not violating, any restrictions established on occupancy of units built under an inclusionary program.

Among programs with an established history of producing units, the level of intervention varies widely. Irvine, California, provides no screening of applicants prior to their selection by the developer of the project in question, but only a post-selection review to verify that the selection made by the developer falls within the criteria established by the municipality. The screening is done by the members of a nonprofit community organization, who receive limited staff support from the city, but have no staff of their own.[17]

More common is pre-screening by a public agency, which improves the efficiency of the process, but requires that there be an administering agency with staff and continuity. In both Orange County and Montgomery County, Maryland, the two largest inclusionary housing programs in the nation, a county public agency has established a countywide pool of qualified applicants. With certain exceptions, developers *must* select the purchasers of their units from within these pools. In Montgomery County, the county Department of Housing & Community Development maintains a pre-screened waiting list, and notifies households on the waiting list when a unit appropriate to their income and household size is available. Households so notified have the exclusive right to buy or rent newly available units for a period of 90 days after the unit first goes on the market. The developer, however, "may decide how to process the eligible persons seeking the available units provided that he complies with all applicable fair housing legislation."[18] In addition, the county Housing Opportunities Commission, the county housing authority, has the right to buy or lease up to one-third of the units in any development or to assign that right to low- or moderate-income households eligible for federal, state, or local housing programs.[19]

In Palo Alto, California, where the inclusionary housing program is characterized by more intensive intervention, a nonprofit corporation acting under contract to the municipality both maintains a pre-screened waiting list and acts as a *de facto* broker for the sale of the housing units created under the inclusionary program. Based on a priority ranking within the waiting list established by a lottery, the Palo Alto Housing Corporation (PAHC) identifies a limited number of potentially qualifying households, contacts households individually to determine that their income and assets still fall within qualifying limits, provides them with information about the available unit or units, encourages them to visit the unit, and then conducts a more detailed qualifying evaluation of each household. Only at that point is any household referred to the developer. One household is referred to each unit at a time, although the corporation screens "back-up" qualifying applicants in the event that one or more of the initial applicants is disqualified or fails to complete the transaction for any reason.[20]

The three models described briefly above — post-selection verification, pre-screening, and selection by a public body — reflect both differences in the philosophy of the various communities involved as well as differences in the staff resources available. The Irvine program is designed to provide the minimum intervention consistent with the basic objectives of the program in view of the extremely limited staff resources available within the community for this task as well as a distaste on the part of the city council for public sector involvement in the program — a position which is more significantly reflected in that community's position on the subject of resale controls. Both Orange County and Montgomery County, large and affluent jurisdictions, have extensively staffed departments or agencies capable of carrying out screening and selection functions without apparent difficulty. Although Palo Alto is a relatively small city, with a population smaller than that of Irvine, the Palo Alto Housing Corporation is an active and well-staffed organization, supported in part by Federal Community Development Block Grant funds, and actively committed to the program in a manner unusual in any community. Furthermore, since Palo Alto is a largely developed community, the volume of applicants that must be reviewed by the PAHC is a modest fraction of that of Irvine. In a typical year, the PAHC will process 15 to 25 units, including resales of units already within the program.[21] By comparison, the Irvine program, in a rapidly growing "new town," is generating hundreds of units subject to inclusionary program restrictions each year.[22] Given the fiscal constraints under which local governments operate, particularly in California since Proposition 13, it may be unrealistic to expect a small community to establish the necessary infrastructure to carry out a Palo Alto-style program at high volume levels of construction.

Although there is no experience to speak of to date, there may be serious problems during the coming years in this area among New Jersey inclusionary housing programs. The typical New Jersey suburban jurisdiction on which the bulk of the *Mount Laurel II* fair share obligation falls has little or no professional staff capability, indeed, substantially less than the typical California city of comparable size and development character. Furthermore, given the fact that the inclusionary requirements are coming about as a result of a court order, New Jersey municipalities are likely to be less supportive of such programs than are communities enacting inclusionary programs more or less of their free will. As a result, except where an existing and active nonprofit housing organization (which are rare in suburban areas) can fill the vacuum, there may well be serious difficulties ahead in successfully implementing the *Mount Laurel II* provisions, more so after the lower-income units have been constructed than in making their construction possible in the first place.

Preserving the Lower-Income Housing Supply —
The Complicated Issue of Resale Controls

One of the most complex and controversial issues associated with inclusionary housing programs arises after the unit has been sold to its initial buyer: specifically, the issue of whether to control the resale of that unit, and if so, in what manner. The rationale for imposing some form of control is readily apparent. It is grounded in the concern that if a unit has been made available to a lower-income household at a price substantially below the market price, to allow that household immediately to sell the unit at market price would first, provide the household with an unjustified windfall and second, result in the loss of that unit from the pool of housing affordable to lower-income households. A good statement of this rationale, grounded in an evaluation of the experience in a number of California jurisdictions, appears in the study by Schwartz and others, which has been mentioned previously:

> If affordable housing programs are to be directed at long-term goals of increasing supply and providing benefits to the largest number of moderate-income housholds, resale controls are essential. Without resale controls, the first buyer gains a windfall benefit but subsequent buyers receive little benefit. Because the unit will probably appreciate more rapidly than market-rate units, it is likely to be lost from the moderate-priced housing supply after the first owner sells it. Furthermore, any subsidies from buyers of market rate units and the community at large will be lost in the form of windfall to the first buyer. For reasons of both equity and program effectiveness, resale controls must be required. Without them, only a small fraction of the total number of units in the jurisdiction at any one time will be moderate in cost. With resale controls, the percentage will rise over time toward the percentage required in new developments.[23]

While scattered objections to the above rationale appear, most of those who object to the imposition of resale controls do not challenge the underlying rationale. They argue, however, that the purposes to be served by the imposition of resale controls do not justify the invasion of property rights, the level of intervention in the marketplace, and the sheer difficulty and expense of enforcing such controls.

Resale controls take a variety of forms, and much of the variation reflects the differences between the two elements of the rationale set forth above; namely, the prevention of speculation, and the long-term preservation of the lower-income housing stock. The prevention of speculation can often be adequately discouraged by requiring the purchaser to maintain the unit as his or her principal residence for a given period; controls have been established in various communities for periods of one to five years.[24] Prior to establishment of a more extensive resale control program, Orange County imposed an unusual antispeculation control, described as follows:

> The mechanism would be in the form of a trust deed [second mortgage] equal to 15% of the purchase price. If the house was resold within the first year from original sale, the full 15% would be due and payable to the county or its designee. If the home was resold during the second year, there would be a 20% reduction; i.e., 12% of the original price would be paid. Each year there would be a 20% reduction until after the fifth year. The home could be sold for the market value at any time, as long as the provisions of the trust deed were complied with.[25]

Other antispeculation measures are discussed in more detail in a later section.

Resale controls to preserve lower-income housing on a long-term basis, while subsuming antispeculation controls, go well beyond such controls. Typically, long-term resale controls are set for extended periods, ranging from ten years[26] to perpetuity. In the latter case, in Palo Alto, the resale control until recently was in the form of a deed restriction lasting 59 years, which period started anew with each transaction.[27] The likelihood of any one homeowner remaining in the unit for more than 59 years is remote enough for this provision to be considered a *de facto* perpetual control.

A brief overview of the most common approach is appropriate. The most common approach, which is found among other locations in Orange County (until recent changes), Palo Alto, and Montgomery County, is two-faceted. It provides first, for a limitation on the amount of appreciation on the unit, in order that the price of the unit continue to be affordable to a lower-income household; and second, for a means to ensure that the new buyer of the unit is also a lower-income household similar to the seller. Such programs to be most effective require not only ongoing monitoring of prices and sales transactions, but also maintenance of a pool of qualified buyers who can be referred in timely fashion as units become available. In the three cases cited above, the same agencies that screen initial buyers also monitor the resale controls. Where appropriately qualified and staffed agencies are not present, however, any difficulties that may arise with the initial screening procedures are compounded when applied to the issue of resale controls. To administer a long-term resale control program, the agency must not only have the necessary personnel and expertise, but must be at least reasonably confident that it will continue to exist and maintain that expertise for the life of the resale control provisions.

Before discussing the technical issues associated with the various approaches to resale controls, however, it is appropriate to focus on the central issues which have made this subject a bone of contention; first, the legal issues associated with resale controls, and second, the social and economic issues which are at the heart of the dispute.

Legal Issues Associated with Resale Controls

A number of legal issues of a technical nature dealing with antitrust considerations and restraints on alienation have been raised with regard to resale controls. Although a detailed exposition of these issues is beyond the scope of this book, a brief discussion is appropriate, inasmuch as they tend to recur in the literature and can be expected to arise in the future in jurisdictions (unlike New Jersey and California) in which the law governing inclusionary housing programs is relatively unsettled.

Antitrust law pursuant to the Sherman Act prohibits price-fixing agreements generally, including resale price agreements in which a buyer and seller agree to sell a product at a particular price.[28] Under the doctrine set forth by the United States Supreme Court in *City of Lafayette, Louisiana v. Louisiana Power & Light Co.*, public agencies may be subject to scrutiny under the antitrust laws.[29] This case — and various others stemming from it — has been argued to be a barrier to the imposition of resale controls under inclusionary housing programs.[30]

In opposition to this argument are a number of points. It has been noted that the generally held interpretation of *Lafayette* is that it applies to "the proprietary enterprises of municipalities,"[31] and not to municipal action generally. Furthermore, that same decision holds that a municipal action is exempt from antitrust liability when the state "directs or authorizes its instrumentalities to act in a way which, if it did not reflect state policy, would be inconsistent with the antitrust laws."[32] In view of the extensive body of policy statements, statutes, court decisions, and the like in almost every state setting forth the provision of low- and moderate-housing as an important public policy goal, it is more than likely that this argument would take resale controls when instituted for the purpose of preserving lower-income housing out of the realm of antitrust concern.

A second issue is that of restraints on alienation, or restrictions on the use of property by its owner. While courts generally have held that such restrictions are undesirable as a general rule, the courts have also recognized the existence of exceptions to the rule. Compelling arguments have been made to support the proposition that resale controls, enacted for the purpose under consideration here, would not be overturned. Under California law, a preemptive right establishing a condition that an owner will not sell a piece of property without first offering it to a designated person is generally considered valid, even where the preemptive right is based on a fixed price, substantially below market value,[33] although the law holds that the "price the preemption fixes should be reasonable under the circumstances."[34] Reasonableness is determined by (a) the purpose of the restraint; (b) the duration of the restraint; and (c) the method of determining the price.[35]

There can be no serious issue raised about the legitimate purpose of resale controls as a restraint as a means to preserve low- and moderate-income housing. Furthermore, where the restraint is limited in duration (typically, the administering agency has 60 to 90 days in which to find a buyer under such programs, failing which the seller can sell the unit freely) and the resale price is based on a rational method of adjusting the initial price over time, it is unlikely in the extreme that such a restraint will be overturned by the courts. Under New Jersey law, the standard is simpler, being a straightforward judgment of reasonableness. Given the considerations discussed above, it should be clear that New Jersey courts as well would be unlikely to invalidate a soundly drafted and administered resale control provision.[36]

In any event, the California legislature has since enacted statutory language which can reasonably be construed as providing explicit statutory authority for the imposition of resale controls. The California statute providing for density bonus and other incentives for the development of affordable housing provides that,

> Where there is a direct financial contribution to a housing development pursuant to Section 65915 through participation in cost of infrastructure, writedown of land costs, or subsidizing the cost of construction, *the city, county, or city and county shall assure continued availability for low- and moderate-income units for 30 years.*[37] [Emphasis added.]

Where such a contribution is made and low- or moderate-income housing units result, the imposition of resale controls or the equivalent is *mandated* by the act. Such controls can therefore be assumed to be permitted under other circumstances, inasmuch as the above statute changed not at all any of the various provisions which might have been argued to have stood in the way of local authority to enact resale control provisions.

In New Jersey, the *Mount Laurel II* decision dealt with the issue in its characteristic forthright manner:

> As several commentators have noted, the problem of keeping lower income units available for lower income people over time can be a difficult one [citations omitted]. Because a mandatory set-aside program usually requires a developer to sell or rent units at below their full value so that the unit can be affordable to lower income people, the owner of the development or the initial tenant or purchaser of the unit may be induced to re-rent or re-sell the unit at its full value.
>
> This problem, which municipalities *must* address in order to assure that they continue to meet their fair share obligations, can be dealt with in two ways. First, the developer can meet its mandatory quota of lower income units with lower cost housing, such as mobile homes or "no frills" apartments, which may be affordable by lower income families at close to the units' market value. The other, apparently more common, approach for dealing with the resale or re-rent problem is for the municipality to require that re-sale or re-rent prices be kept at lower income levels.[38]

The first alternative will indeed be rare, particularly with regard to the "low income" category defined by the court in *Mount Laurel II*. Furthermore, even if the *price* need not be controlled, which is unlikely, selection of the future tenant or purchaser may still require controls to ensure that the intent of the court is carried out. In short, the effect of the above language is to mandate the imposition of resale controls as an integral part of future inclusionary housing programs in New Jersey. The practical implications of this course and some concerns about the ultimate feasibility of such an imposition will be discussed below.

Social, Economic, and Political Issues Associated with Resale Controls

It should be apparent that legal problems, while perhaps not trivial, are not of such magnitude as to render the subject of resale controls a particularly difficult one. The objections lie, rather, in the social and political sphere. Leaving aside for the moment the technical difficulties affecting implementation of such controls, it appears, however, that most of the "practical" objections to resale controls on social or economic grounds are trivial or even patently unreasonable.

Relatively few separate such objections have been identified. They include the argument that the imposition of resale controls condemns lower-income households to permanent lower-income status,[39] that it acts to discourage the household to maintain their housing unit,[40] and that it deprives local governments of tax revenues.[41] Each of these arguments can be dealt with summarily given the premise that resale controls, with no exceptions known to the author, do allow *some* appreciation, generally keyed to the increase in the consumer price index or the area median household income.

The notion that the opportunity to make disproportionate profits on the sale of a home is the only route to middle class status in America is, simply stated, a bizarre notion that one imagines is held only by realtors and at that, hardly any realtors except those in California. Indeed, most families that have moved out of units developed through inclusionary housing programs have done so because their income rose, making it possible for them to buy a larger or otherwise more desirable home.[42] One assumes that their economic status improved in the conventional fashion; namely, a higher salary or a better job.

With regard to poor maintenance of units subject to resale controls, there is no evidence whatsoever to support this argument. Furthermore, even if it were potentially true, it is counteracted by the widespread practice of allowing some upward adjustment in the permitted resale price for documented capital improvements made by the owner, thereby providing an incentive for improvement of the property.[43]

The city of Palo Alto has gone further. After experiencing a single case of property destruction by an owner (which experience has never been repeated),[44] a provision has been added to the resale control deed restriction providing that in such eventualities the cost of bringing the property back to reasonable standards is deducted from the allowable resale price.[45]

Finally, there is little argument that a unit may provide less tax revenue to a municipality over time if its value is controlled in a manner that keeps it below the market value of the unit. That notwithstanding, three points should be made. First, the effect of such a reduction on the overall municipal fisc is almost certain to be negligible. Second, the disparity between the tax revenues collected from such units and "full taxes" is likely to be significantly less than the disparity resulting from any other means of providing lower-income housing, such as tax abatement or subsidized rental housing. Third, and most importantly, barring those communities in which property values are accelerating at significantly greater rates than the rate reflected in the consumer price index or in regional income growth, *the property tax disparity does not arise from the resale controls, but from the disparity in the initial selling price relative to market value.*

There is no evidence to date of serious unhappiness or distress on the part of program participants with regard to the limitations imposed on the appreciation of the unit they are buying. A survey of affordable housing occupants conducted in Orange County found that 74 percent of the households, or roughly three-fourths, felt that resale controls were "fair" or "somewhat fair." Of the total respondents, 83 percent felt that their home was fairly priced and that its controlled value had kept up with inflation, suggesting the presence of a core group (under 10 percent) who may object to resale controls on grounds of principle, whatever the practical effect of the controls on the value of their home.[46] Informal comments supported this conclusion both in Palo Alto and Orange County. Interestingly, an executive of a major developer of affordable housing in Orange County commented that no buyers, to her knowledge, had refused to buy because of the resale control, but that "one father looked at his kid's mortgage, and refused to help him [because of the resale controls]."[47] It would appear that, for most lower-income households, the present opportunity to buy a home that they could otherwise not afford far outweighs the future potential loss of windfall benefits. In any event, such future benefits by the mid 1980s had begun to appear far more uncertain than was the case in the late 1970s.

It seems clear that the crux of the opposition to resale controls lies not in the practical consequences of such controls, but in the issue of principle or ideology that they represent. From the standpoint of those individuals concerned with what they perceive as the free market, resale controls represent an intolerable intrusion by public regulation into the exercise of a fundamental and closely held property right. The potential danger seen as implicit in the imposition of resale controls may be more serious than the controls themselves; to many opponents the controls are a foot in the door, opening it wider to progressively more governmental controls and restraints on traditional property rights. In the words of a "high secondary mortgage market official" quoted in an article in the *Los Angeles Times:*

> "We are experiencing government by intimidation and coercion. This is the beginning of no one knows what," he said, predicting that soon government will be dictating room size. "This is clearly an infringement of rights and freedoms."
>
> To argue for controls on the basis of public investment is coercion, he said. "The value of real estate historically is in its bundle of rights," the biggest of which being the right to use it, to sell it, and enjoy the profit or suffer the loss.
>
> "Once we do this [accept resale controls], God knows what will happen. This is a very dangerous precedent and I am going to fight it as far as I can. It's time for all to stand tall or we might as well live in Russia."[48]

While the language is perhaps more melodramatic than is appropriate to the subject, the perception of resale controls as being violative of fundamental property rights is clearly the central concern. The same concern was expressed by the principal opponent of resale controls on the Orange County Board of Supervisors, Supervisor Roger Stanton, who submitted an alternative proposal to the Board in 1981, grounded in the objective of allowing "the free market to determine the resale price of the unit."[49] According to other local officials in Orange County, the same theme was central to the continuing campaign mounted by the real estate industry in opposition to the inclusionary program generally, and resale controls in particular, from the inception of the program in 1978 and 1979.[50]

It is not clear how one is to evaluate these concerns. Although the untrammelled free market is clearly a thing of the past in the realm of housing and land development, as demonstrated by building codes, zoning and subdivision regulations, environmental regulations, fair housing laws, and the like, the notion of governmental regulation of the price at which a property changes hands between a willing buyer and willing seller can not unreasonably be perceived as an intrusion of a more direct nature. While that intrusion has in all inclusionary housing programs been the second part of a *quid pro quo* — i.e., the outcome of an initial positive intrusion by the public sector in order to make the unit available at lower price to the lower-income household[51] — opponents of the controls could not unreasonably argue that that relationship was by no means inevitable, and that once the idea of price controls had been accepted, it would sooner or later be extended to housing which had not necessarily benefited from governmental intervention.[52]

Looked at from another perspective, however, the problem may well be the explicit nature of the social objective being served by resale controls and the fact that they operate directly on the price of the unit rather than indirectly through such means as land use controls. It has long since been recognized that many land use and zoning provisions are little more than roundabout techniques of price manipulation in order to ensure both the construction of expensive housing in the first place and the "maintenance of property values" in the long run — in other words, an intrusion into the marketplace in order to keep prices up rather than down.[53] Such regulations, however, can be distinguished from resale controls in two significant ways. First, they provide a land use "fig leaf" to cover the economic intent of the regulation; and second, they act to reinforce or increase private fiscal gain rather than to constrain it.

The political opposition to resale controls may have been particularly strong in Orange County because of the particular local circumstances. Leaving aside the right-wing political reputation of the county which has been, in any event, exaggerated, the real estate market in that county had become by the late 1970s a major arena for land speculation. During the latter half of the 1970s, real estate prices rose dramatically in the county at a rate far greater than the prevailing rate of inflation. Between 1975 and 1980, the average home price in Orange County increased by 142 percent.[54] In this context, particularly to those active in the real estate industry, it is arguable that the *purpose* of housing units came to be perceived more as investment and speculation than as shelter.

Finally, resale controls, which must be recognized as intrusive to some degree whether or not one argues that they are justifiably so, can become targets of attack in a political climate oriented toward the deregulation of the private sector and the general dismantling of governmental controls. Deregulation was not only a central theme of the national administration in the early 1980s, but became a major state and local political issue, particularly where it was widely perceived that regulation — and especially environmental and growth control regulations — exceeded reasonable levels during the 1970s. In California, the most significant thrust of land use legislation in the early 1980s was the rolling back of regulations generally enacted in the 1970s which became perceived as intrusive and as hindering the production of housing and the economic growth of the state.[55] One by-product of this climate was the repeal of the statutory language giving the California Coastal Commission the authority to carry out an extensive inclusionary housing program, and the transfer of the responsibility for carrying out affordable housing policies in the coastal zone to local government.[56] In a survey conducted roughly a year after responsibility had been transferred to local government, nine of 23 municipalities had yet to take steps toward compliance with the new mandate, while an additional seven had carried out some preparations or drafting but had yet to adopt any ordinance or regulation in conformity with the law.[57]

One need not agree with the objections to resale controls, as this author by and large does not, to recognize that they are powerful, at least from a political standpoint. In Irvine, which has one of the largest inclusionary programs, the City Council has consistently rejected staff proposals to institute resale controls in the program for reasons which, although containing some practical considerations, have had largely to do with the political or philosophical grounds discussed above.[58] In Orange County, after setting up a resale control system and beginning to implement the controls on resale transactions, the program was in the process of being dismantled by 1983, an outgrowth of a change in the political complexion of the County Board of Supervisors. A lawsuit has been filed challenging this action.[59]

Still, if the purpose of inclusionary housing programs is to create a long-term stock of housing affordable to lower-income households rather than a one-time infusion of less-expensive housing into the marketplace with an attendant one-time windfall for a small number of lower-income households, it is hard to justify *not* establishing such controls. A frequently cited example of the impact of not having controls is the experience with the Woodbridge Village project in Irvine. This project was built with Section 235 interest subsidies and sold to low- and moderate-income buyers in 1976 at prices from $31,000 to $34,000, the result of considerable effort at cost reduction. By 1979, roughly 20 percent of the units had changed hands, the units selling at prices between $60,000 and $75,000.[60]

If one holds an absolute view of the inviolability of property rights, resale controls cannot be found to be acceptable. Similarly, neither can zoning ordinances, building codes, nor a host of other generally accepted regulations.[61] In the context, however, of reasonable trade-offs between costs and benefits, which is the realistic context of development regulation in the United States, and given the compelling social purposes served by the controls, the philosophical arguments that have been raised in opposition fall well short of a legitimate basis for failing to use this essential tool in the preservation of the affordable housing stock being created through inclusionary housing programs. Whether the difficulties of implementation and administration of such controls are severe enough to raise serious questions about the feasibility of implementing resale controls will be addressed in the following section.

The Mechanics of Resale Controls

The establishment of any resale control program requires two elements: the adoption and execution of legal documents embodying the controls, and the establishment and ongoing operation of an administrative mechanism to carry out the public responsibilities associated with these controls. The latter is particularly important. It is unrealistic to imagine that resale controls can ever be effectively self-administering.

In theory, a self-administering resale control system would appear to be possible. Assuming a unit is subject to a covenant restricting sale to a household meeting certain income qualifications, at closing the title company would require evidence of the buyer's qualifications before providing title insurance on the unit. In practice, enforcing resale controls in this manner places an unreasonable burden on the seller. The seller has the entire burden of ensuring that the household to which he or she proposes to sell the unit meets the necessary qualifications, not only making the selling period substantially more extended (because the seller will have to eliminate many prospective buyers from consideration), but also placing on the seller the burden of verifying the prospective buyer's income, a duty for which most sellers are not likely to be qualified. If a buyer, under such a scheme, misrepresents his or her income, is "passed through" by the seller, and the discrepancy is determined at closing, the seller is harmed despite his or her innocence in the matter.

The notion that a system can be "self-administrating," in the final analysis, is a delusion. *Somebody* must carry out the tasks associated with enforcement of the covenants or deed restrictions that have been built into the initial transaction. Since the purpose of resale controls is to benefit the public interest and to promote equity and the achievement of the greatest possible benefit from the use of public resources, it is appropriate that the responsibility for their administration lie with the public, in an appropriate manner. To shift the burden to the seller, who may have benefited from the unit initially but is clearly not benefiting from the resale controls as such, is unreasonable.

Typical Systems of Resale Control. In the typical resale control program, the legal mechanism for enforcing the control is a document that becomes a part of the deed to the unit, whether termed a deed restriction (Palo Alto), a covenant (Montgomery County), or an Attachment to Grant Deed (Orange County). All of these are the same type of document. Under the Montgomery County program, for example, a covenant is attached to the deed of any unit sold under the county's Moderately Priced Dwelling Unit (MPDU) program. The covenant provides that

> For a period of ten years from _____ [the date of the original sale of this property] or such other period as established by law, the improvements hereon and those that may be subsequently made to the subject property shall not be sold for an amount in excess of the maximum sales price established by written regulation of the County Executive from time to time and in accordance with [applicable provisions] of the Montgomery County Code, 1972, as amended.[62]

Additional provisions of the covenant prohibit the buyer from renting his or her unit except if a waiver is granted by the county for sufficient cause. Controls on the actual sale of the unit are imposed through administrative regulations, which provide the following:

1. The county establishes the resale price;
2. The county notifies qualifying households on their waiting list of the availability of the unit, immediately after determining the resale price;
3. Those families so notified have the exclusive right to contract for the unit, for a period of sixty days;
4. Thirty days after the determination of resale price, the owner of the unit may *also* offer the unit to the Housing Opportunities Commission (Housing Authority) or its assigns. The HOC shares the exclusive right with the families notified as above for the remaining thirty days of the option period.
5. If no contract has been entered into with any party at the end of the sixty days, the owner may offer the unit to the general public *at the price determined by the county.*[63]

The provisions of the covenant itself, it should be stressed, are not waived or released—only the administrative provisions outlined above.

In Montgomery County only the bare essentials of the resale controls are embodied in the covenant attached to the deed. Most provisions, including the determination of the maximum resale price, are embodied in administrative regulations adopted by the county and referenced in the covenant. In contrast, the Orange County program incorporated the entire scope of the controls, to the degree feasible, into the deed in a document entitled *Attachment to Grant Deed:*

Grant of Preemptive Right to Purchase to the County of Orange.[64] This four-teen-page document sets forth all of the resale provisions in detail, including the basis on which the resale price is established, the structure of resale transactions taking place under the control provisions, notice requirements, and penalties for failure to abide by the control provisions over and above such self-administering penalties that would emerge at closing.

In addition to its greater specificity and detail, the Orange County program differed from that of Montgomery County in a number of substantive respects. First, it should be stressed that the resale controls in Orange County applied only to those units financed under the county's tax-exempt bond mortgage program, although more limited antispeculation controls did apply to other units resulting from the inclusionary housing program. Second, certain features of the resale controls themselves were designed to reduce the extent to which they would be considered intrusive of the owner's property rights.

All sellers were offered at the time of resale a *conditional waiver of option*, under which the county waived its sixty-day option, allowing the seller to sell the unit directly, but only to a buyer meeting the income qualifications previously established for the unit. Income verification was to be done either by the Orange County Housing Authority (acting as agent for the county), or the lender, where the mortgage was to be assumed by the new buyer. There is, however, little evidence of sellers taking advantage of this provision, which, in the final analysis, could be considered of little or no objective benefit to the seller of a controlled unit.[65]

The Orange County resale controls provided, furthermore, that if the county had not assigned its option within the sixty-day period — i.e., found a buyer for the unit — the option was lost and the property released from the provisions of the Attachment to Grant Deed in its entirety. In other words, the seller was then free to sell the unit on the open market at the market price.

The differences between the two programs and between either program and the Palo Alto program are substantially less than the similarities. Price is controlled on the basis of a reasonably predictable formula — i.e., the formula is predictable, although, as will be discussed below, the outcome is not. A purchase option for a fixed period is provided to a public agency. In Montgomery County, the governmental entity legally responsible administers the program; in the other cases, the responsibility is contracted to a different public entity or to a nonprofit entity. In each case, the responsible public agency maintains waiting lists, qualifies prospective buyers, and seeks to ensure a flow of potential purchasers to each unit. Finally, in each case, if the agency is unable to match the unit with a buyer, the seller is freed after a non-excessive length of time to find a buyer on the open market. In Montgomery County, the sale is on the open market but at the controlled price level; in Orange County, the entire transaction takes place under open market conditions.[66]

The Complexities of Price Control Systems. As a result of a series of both unusual and unfortunate circumstances affecting the Orange County inclusionary
program, *of the first 70 units subject to resale controls resold, 48 or nearly 70
percent were released from the deed restrictions, and sold on the open market.*[67]
The circumstances, although exceptional, illustrate the potential pitfalls in a resale control program. The calculation of maximum resale price provided that it
would be determined by increasing the base price (the initial purchase price) on
the basis of the increase in the median household income for Orange County determined by the U.S. Department of Housing & Urban Development, from the
date of the initial transaction to the date of the resale.[68] This index, however,
turned out to be remarkably volatile in Orange County, with an average annual
increase since 1976 of 12.2 percent.[69] Even more seriously, and immediately
before the first substantial number of resales under the program occurred, HUD
increased the median by 30 percent from 1980 to 1981 as a result of a compensation for discrepancies between prior estimates and the information available from
the 1980 census.[70] This took place at the same time (late 1981 and 1982) that
mortgage interest rates were rising precipitously. As a result, moderate-income
buyers could not, because of income constraints, either (1) assume the tax-exempt bond mortgage, because the down payment was beyond their means; or (2)
refinance with a new mortgage, because the debt service payments would be beyond their means. As a result, only a limited number of units remained under the
county controls. As determined by a county evaluation study, the differences
between the two categories were significant:

• The units remaining under the controls were significantly less expensive than
  the units released — 15 percent less for one-bedroom units, and 24 percent
  less for two-bedroom units;
• The units remaining under the controls had been held a substantially shorter
  period than those released — an average of 14-15 months compared to 20
  months.[71]

The same evaluation noted that more than a third of the units sold by the Housing
Authority under the resale controls were sold before the precipitous rise in median income took place in September 1981.

The problems of the Orange County program stem from two unrelated sources:
first, the risk of tying appreciation to an index whose future performance is un-
predictable, and second, the lack of any consistent relationship between the price
of a unit and its affordability. As was discussed in an earlier chapter, affordability is the sum of a variety of factors, most significantly the interaction between
price and mortgage interest rate.

Pricing problems arise from the inconsistency between the various purposes
which the system is designed to serve: to provide for as "automatic" as possible

a process of price adjustment, to be "fair" to the initial purchaser, who becomes the seller upon resale, and to ensure that the units remain affordable to lower-income households over an extended period. The first two purposes, if not carefully evaluated in the context of the ultimate objective of a resale control program, can easily frustrate the final, or more fundamental purpose. *Given the lack of complete consistency between price and affordability, any single formula for price adjustments, if adhered to rigidly, will sooner or later create inconsistencies harmful to the objectives of the program.* The inconsistencies are not likely often to be as extreme as those experienced in the Orange County study, but will occur nonetheless. No responsible agency, therefore, can expect to put a formula in place and expect it to "work" indefinitely into the future.

The question of what is fair to the initial purchaser is more complex. It is clear in the Orange County study that many, if not all, of the sellers reaped windfall profits; the authors of the assessment noted that "owners of units subject to the Attachment who resold at the option price have realized greater appreciation than owners of 'market rate' units during the same time period." [72] Although it is impossible to tell with certainty, it would appear that the average owner at a minimum doubled, and often tripled, his or her down payment investment within less than two years. This massive profit was made possible by virtue of a formula which allowed a percentage increase far greater than that taking place in the private market during the same period, thereby allowing the owners of units purchased at below-market prices to bring them up to market levels on resale.

Appreciation to this degree is clearly inimical to the objectives of an inclusionary housing program. Even if in some manner the price adjustment formula provided that the appreciation was at the *same* rate as the market so that the relationship between the price of the unit and the market price remained the same, the inconsistencies between price and affordability could end up yielding the same result, although perhaps less drastically than in Orange County. If a unit, for example, were made affordable to a moderate-income household in the first place as a result of a tax-exempt bond mortgage or a mortgage buydown program which were not available to the purchaser on resale, the affordability of the unit would be less, even if mortgage interest rates generally had not risen. The only ways, realistically, to ensure continued affordability of units through resale controls are either (1) to set the rate of appreciation *substantially below* the market-rate increase, so that the "price" component of affordability declines relative to income; or (2) to establish a formula keyed directly to affordability with the resale price being an outcome of affordability rather than a direct adjustment of the initial, or base, price.

The former approach is now in effect in Palo Alto. As a result of the problems experienced with a formula keyed to increases in the consumer price index, the deed restrictions governing the program were amended early in 1983 to provide that future adjustments would be on the basis of one-third of the increase in the consumer price index, rather than the full amount of the increase. [73] According to officials of the program, this change has not generated any complaints among the program's clientele.[74]

Although no program has adopted a standard keyed directly to affordability, it has been suggested by one commentator, as follows:

> Since every person allowed to buy an inclusionary unit must be screened for eligibility in some way, one must know the income of that buyer and what buyers at that income can afford. Say buyer X, whose income is 89 percent of average income, buys a unit based on that ability to pay. When X later sells, he would be allowed to sell at the lower of market or what buyers with 89 percent of the then average income are then able to pay. If a 93 percenter is allowed to buy, the surplus could go to a pool which would be used to reimburse whatever agency is administering the inclusionary housing program when it has to pay the seller a bonus to put; e.g., an 85 percenter in an 89 percenter unit. The suggested scheme avoids any base value plus consumer price index or inflation aberration and avoids the need to make predictions about how much of their budget persons in the future will pay for housing.[75]

This appears to be an eminently reasonable approach, and would be well worth trying. It suffers, however, from the fact that an owner would be unable to estimate at any time prior to the price determination what the resale value of his or her unit might be.

Neither of these approaches guarantees the owner a rate of appreciation equal to that of market rate units in the same area, nor is it clear why "fairness" dictates that a formula should do so. Arguably the only unassailable rock-bottom standard of fairness is that *an owner should be entitled to appreciation of his or her investment in the unit–i.e., down payment and closing costs–not less than that available from alternative non-speculative investments.* Precisely which investments should be considered alternatives for comparison purposes can be debated, but based on recent years' experience, a reasonable annual rate of return would appear to be between 10 and 12 percent. Thus, if the buyer's investment were equivalent to 15 percent of the house price (10 percent down payment and closing costs equal to 5 percent), an appreciation of house value equal to 1.5 to 2 percent per year would be adequate to meet the "fairness" threshold.

In summary, the objective of simplicity in having a straightforward formula which automatically determines the resale price with a minimum of intervention cannot be allowed to outweigh the more important goals for which price controls are being established. The most appropriate one balances the underlying purpose of maintaining the units affordable to lower-income households with the need for fairness to the homeowner, bearing in mind that the purpose of providing this housing is shelter and not the creation of speculative windfalls.

Recapture as an Alternative to Price Controls. A variation on the "typical" re-

sale control approach described above is that of subsidy recapture. Under a subsidy recapture approach, the owner of the unit is free to sell the unit at the market
price, and by extension, to a buyer of his or her choosing, but must make a payment back to a housing agency or authority over and above the mortgage indebt-
edness from the proceeds of the sale. The amount subject to recapture would
typically be the difference between the market value of the unit and the actual
cost of the unit to the purchaser under the inclusionary program.[76] Such a recapture scheme, where the amount subject to recapture was framed as a second
mortgage (or a second trust deed, in California terminology), was used briefly as
an antispeculation control in certain Orange County projects, as noted earlier on
pages 136-142. While in this particular case the second trust deed diminished and
disappeared after five years, such a provision could run as long as the agency
administering the program saw fit, as is the case with resale controls.

The intent of the recapture approach is to blend the free market and continued
affordability approaches. No price controls or third-party selection of buyers are
imposed, but the housing agency, at least in theory, still ends up with the funds
needed to maintain affordable housing. The rationale of the program is that of
substitution: one unit may be lost to the program, but another, subsidized in some
manner with the funds obtained from the second mortgage recapture, takes its
place.

There does not appear to be any case in which such a recapture scheme has
been consistently implemented despite the discussion of the approach that has
taken place. There appear to be two notable drawbacks to such a scheme when
compared to the more representative resale control approach described previously. First, *there appears no way to ensure that the funds obtained from the recapture program will be sufficient to produce another unit of comparable affordability at the time the resale removes the initial unit from the affordable housing
stock.*

That problem is itself a combination of two problems. To begin, it is extremely
difficult, if not impossible, to calibrate the amount of the recapture payment so
that it will be certain to fill the gap between the market price of housing and the
desired affordability level at the time the resale takes place. Exhibit 1 illustrates
the problem. It is based on relatively conservative assumptions: For a hypothetical unit "worth" $60,000 and selling to a lower-income household for $50,000
and thus with a second mortgage due on resale of $10,000, we have assumed that
(1) the second mortgage will carry an interest rate of 10%; (2) the house will appreciate at a rate of 8% per year; (3) incomes will rise at a rate of 6% per year;
and (4) a moderate-income household can afford a unit selling for two times
family income. As the exhibit shows, there is a constant shortfall between the
affordability that the housing agency makes possible with the recapture payments
and the initial affordability of the unit. Furthermore, the shortfall increases as the
years pass and is nearly $10,000 by the eighth year after the initial transaction.

EXHIBIT 1
Example of Second Mortgage Recapture Program

Year	A Market Value	B Recapture Amount on $10,000 2nd. Mort.	C Lowest Substitution Price (A-B)	D Target Income Level	E Maximum Affordable House Price (2 × D)	F Shortfall (C − E)
INITIAL	$60,000	$10,000	NA	$25,000	$50,000	NA
1	64,800	11,000	$53,800	26,500	53,000	$ 800
2	69,980	12,100	57,880	28,090	56,180	1,700
3	75,580	13,300	62,280	29,780	59,560	2,720
4	81,630	14,600	67,030	31,560	63,120	3,910
5	88,160	16,100	72,060	33,460	66,920	5,140
6	95,210	17,700	77,510	35,460	70,920	6,590
7	102,800	19,500	83,300	37,590	75,180	8,120
8	111,050	21,400	89,650	39,850	79,700	9,950

Note:
This example is based on the following assumptions:
1. Unit has initial market value of $60,000, sold at $50,000 with second mortgage due on resale of $10,000, increasing at 10% compounded annually.
2. House market value assumed to increase by 8% per year.
3. Median income (target income) assumed to increase at 6% per year.
4. Maximum house price affordable to household at target income assumed to be twice target income.

While it is theoretically possible to vary this particular example to eliminate the shortfall, it is unlikely that any formula will work consistently.

Furthermore, even assuming there is no paper shortfall, there may not be a comparable unit available at the time of resale with which to make the substitution given the uncertainties of the housing market. It is foolhardy to assume that substitutable units will invariably be available at all times over an extended future. This leads to the second problem. *Since the housing agency cannot assume that suitable units will be available, it must be prepared and able to produce them or else lose a unit permanently from the affordable housing stock.* As a result, an approach which was intended to simplify matters actually makes them far more complex. Under typical resale controls, the administration of the controls, although requiring a certain commitment of manpower and mastery of technical and mechanical detail, is fundamentally straightforward. It is a matter of establishing a mechanical system which is capable of being administered on a largely clerical level with only modest and occasional intervention of more sophisticated managerial or professional personnel. Administering a recapture program is far more complex since it hinges on the ability to use funds creatively to produce housing units. That, of course, is the most complicated task of all associated with inclusionary housing programs.

As we will see in the next chapter, few communities have the professional and technical resources to utilize effectively the funds which have been given them by developers in lieu of providing lower-income housing. The same problem, but compounded by the fact that the funds will not become available except in small increments many years hence, applies to the recapture alternative to resale controls. It does not appear to be a sound alternative except, perhaps, in rare and unusual circumstances.

Rental Housing and the Problem of Conversion

In view of the significant public policy issues raised, the new technical questions that must be addressed, and the fact that most units built under inclusionary programs tend to be offered for sale, the discussion above has focused on maintaining lower-income occupancy in owner-occupied housing. It is likely, however, that at least some of the units generated through inclusionary housing programs will be rental units. Where this has happened in Orange County and elsewhere, the rental units have generally been built under federal or state subsidy programs. Such programs generally embody their own institutionalized controls. New developments constructed under the federal Section 8 program build in over a period of 20 years or more extensive and detailed controls on occupancy, tenant selection, rent levels, and the like. The premise that subsidized housing projects should be subject to regulation of occupancy and rent level is generally accepted, and a host of agencies and companies exist with the qualifications and experience necessary to administer such regulations.

Any rental housing development constructed in an inclusionary program without federal or state subsidies and thus not falling under an existing regulatory scheme, should have no difficulty borrowing or adapting one such scheme to its purposes. As a result, there appear to be no major threshold issues of policy or substance raised by the idea of regulating both initial and continued occupancy, as well as the rent levels, in rental housing constructed to be affordable to lower-income households. There are some potentially problematic economic issues, however, which make the provision of affordable housing through rental developments, in the absence of federal or state subsidies, a potentially uncertain proposition.

The first problem is that of maintaining affordability over time, not from the regulatory standpoint, but from the economic. The charm of the Section 8 program from the landlord's perspective is that the tenant pays whatever he or she can pay, and up to some reasonable level, the federal government makes up the difference. Thus, any cost increase in excess of the increase in tenant incomes is simply passed on to the federal government. A project built without outside subsidies does not have that luxury. Where a project is initially operating at a break-even level with a rent structure oriented to lower-income tenants, it may not be able to continue to do so indefinitely. Unanticipated increases in maintenance costs, repairs, or taxes could easily create circumstances under which the rents were no longer adequate to provide the necessities of maintenance and operations. Raising the rents would render the development out of reach of the existing tenants as well as future lower-income occupants; failing to raise the rents would bring about the deterioration and possible foreclosure of the development. Every federal housing program other than Section 8 has had to confront this problem, and the only answer, as was the case with both the Public Housing program and the Section 236 program, was an increase in Congressional appropriations to "bail out" the projects.[77]

There is no broadly applicable answer that can be suggested to this potential problem. Under some circumstances, developers or owners can utilize Section 8 existing housing certificates as a back-door way of participating in the Section 8 subsidy program.[78] In other cases, projects can be sold to investors seeking the tax shelters associated with the depreciation on the project. The proceeds of what is termed the "syndication" of the project can then be used, at least in part, to create rainy-day reserves against future shortfalls. In the latter case, it is always possible to levy the investor-limited partners for deficits as they arise; they have little recourse, since to allow the project to go into foreclosure would eliminate their tax shelter, but it is a course of action generally frowned upon and is clearly not fiscally prudent.

A second problem arises from the sale of projects as tax shelters to investors. This is often necessary in order to make the project financially feasible in the first place. The only financial impetus today for construction of rental housing, for the most part, is the sale of the depreciation, which is valuable enough to provide the developer with an attractive return on his initial investment. The actual operating cash flow from the project in all but unusual cases is not enough to serve as a financial incentive to a rational developer or investor.

While there is no inconsistency as such between ownership by wealthy investors and lower-income occupancy, ownership by such investors triggers an imperative arguably inconsistent with the objectives of inclusionary housing programs; namely, the sale of the project within only a few years after initial occupancy. Since enactment of the 1981 Tax Reform Act by Congress, which provided for sharply accelerated depreciation schedules for rental housing generally and low-income rental housing in particular, the typical investor exhausts the greater part of the available depreciation in the first 7 to 10 years after initial occupancy.[79] At that point, the rational investor gets little or no benefit from the property and seeks to sell it, and if possible, convert it to condominium ownership. Conversion is likely to offer the potential of substantially greater appreciation than would sale for continued rental operation.

Again, no ready answer is apparent. There has been some discussion of establishing constraints on such conversion — e.g., requiring that sale prices upon conversion be such that the unit will be affordable to lower-income buyers — but that does not represent a clear answer. If the purpose of providing the development in question is to provide *rental* housing opportunities, then nothing short of prohibiting conversion for an extended period can suffice.[80] Such a prohibition could make the development so unattractive to investors that it would be unable to raise any funds through the syndication process, thereby reducing affordability. Since it appears likely that many rental developments cannot be made affordable to lower-income households without application of a substantial portion of syndication proceeds to offset operating or debt service costs, failure to syndicate a project successfully can easily mean that the project simply cannot be built.

One can argue that the underlying problem which has led to the above contradictions is the irrationality of public policy with regard to the provision of rental housing, or alternatively, the economic no-man's-land into which rental housing has fallen in the United States as a result of the homeownership boom of the 1970s. It is absurd that even the most modest developer cannot obtain a cash flow from a newly constructed rental development comparable to alternative investments and must depend on tax shelters to provide an economic justification for the project. It does not lie within the means of either the developer, however, or the local government with which he must deal to resolve such issues. In the meantime, rental housing is likely to remain a smaller part of the inclusionary housing project than the distribution of housing needs would objectively justify.

A Note on Public Intervention

A recurring theme in this chapter is the importance of effective, competent, public sector intervention in the process of ensuring and maintaining lower-income occupancy of housing constructed under inclusionary programs. Such programs are not self-administering, and all efforts to make them so have diminished the program benefits as a result. Not only do they call for a certain level of competent management, but they ask that the management also be sensitive to the complexities of what it is undertaking, and above all, committed to the objectives that it is serving. The success of Palo Alto and of Montgomery County is a tribute to the quality of program management and the commitment which the managers bring to the program. In Orange County the inclusionary program was a success as long as such a commitment was present. As one former official in the program commented, "we made it work."[81]

This should not be surprising; indeed, it would be surprising if it were otherwise. The conduct of any program designed to serve social policy goals is almost certain to require a substantial commitment of time and resources by the public sector, if only to ensure that the beneficiaries of the program are those for whom it is intended. In an era, however, which is characterized by deregulation and Proposition 13, one finds considerable resistance to this position. Programs such as those in Irvine and Petaluma are instructive. Massive expenditures, largely by builders, result in substantially less long-term social benefit than would be possible with only a modest additional expenditure on the municipality's part for long-term program administration.

Irvine, notwithstanding the protestations of local officials, is almost certainly large enough to be able to absorb the needed administrative functions within its governmental structure without great difficulty. Other smaller communities may have more difficulty; unless the nucleus of the management system is present, it is hard to justify imposing the additional costs of setting up such a system on the developers on whom one relies to provide the affordable housing units, often below cost. It is for this reason that the most successful programs, such as those in Orange County or Montgomery County, have been implemented by large, heavily populated jurisdictions in which a substantial level of technically competent personnel was already employed by the county or the county housing authority to carry out not dissimilar functions.

One alternative is to encourage regional, or even statewide, structures for the management of inclusionary housing programs. In California, a number of small local jurisdictions contract with county housing authorities to carry out tenant or homebuyer screening or the administration of resale controls. In New Jersey, officials of the state Department of Community Affairs are considering offering their services to developers and local governments in the same area.[82] Such approaches have two clear advantages: The costs are spread across a base wide enough to absorb them without serious difficulty, and the program is insulated, to some degree, from the vagaries of local political change.

The process of giving careful consideration to the nature and duties of the administrative machinery is as much a central element in framing an inclusionary housing program as is drafting the regulations and requirements with which builders and developers will be confronted. Without a means in place through which the necessary managerial functions can take place, it is unlikely that an effective means of ensuring and maintaining lower-income occupancy will be established; without such means, the credibility of the program is inevitably called into question.

NOTES

1. Schwartz, Johnston & Burtraw, *Local Government Initiatives*, p. 19; see also, Brooks, et al., *Housing Choice*, pp. 46-48, 69-70.
2. Schwartz, Johnston & Burtraw, *Local Government Initiatives*, p. 18.
3. California Association of Realtors, Local Government Relations Committee, Inclusionary Housing Statement (April 10, 1979), quoted in Hagman, "Bootstrapping Low and Moderate Income Housing," p. 24.
4. Schwartz, Johnston & Burtraw, *Local Government Initiatives*, pp. 26-27.

5. See, e.g., city of Santa Cruz, California, Exhibit A to Ordinance No. 80-06, "Income, Asset and Housing Cost Guidelines," which sets forth in detail the allowable amount of assets as well as household income, and a detailed definition of "assets" to be applied to potential tenants and homebuyers.

6. Described in memorandum from Pam Sheldon, City of Irvine, to Carolyn Burton, California Department of Housing & Community Development, "Revision of Description of Irvine's Inclusionary Housing Program," September 23, 1980, p. 6.

7. Ibid., p. 6.

8. The Hills Development Company, Bedminster, New Jersey, "Statement of Policies, Procedures and Organization of the Bedminster Hills Housing Corporation," October 1983.

9. County of Orange, Environmental Management Agency, *Principles and Guidelines for an Inclusionary Housing Program* (Santa Ana, CA: 1978).

10. Borough of Lincoln Park, New Jersey, *Zoning Ordinance*, Sec. 28-44(a 2).

11. Town of Lewisboro, Housing & Community Development Committee, "Additional Selection Priorities," adopted March 25, 1980.

12. 38 N.Y. 2d 102 at 110.

13. Although the *Mount Laurel II* court is explicit about the regional nature of the fair share obligation, the decision points on a number of occasions to the discrete existence of an "indigenous housing need" within each community, leaving open the possibility that a municipality within an overall fair share program could arguably provide some priority or preference to local resident households in need of better housing.

14. California Planning & Zoning Law, Sec. 65583(a)(1).

15. Ibid., Sec. 65584.

16. Orange County, Environmental Management Agency, *Orange County's Inclusionary Housing Program Assessment* (Santa Ana, CA: Nov. 1982), Table 4.

17. Interview with Peggy Schneble, Planner, City of Irvine.

18. Montgomery County, Office of the County Executive, *Executive Regulation 44-81*, "Administrative Procedures and Requirements for the MPDU Program," October 15, 1981, Sec. C(2).

19. Ibid., Sec. C(3) & (4).

20. Interview with Valerie Glassford, Palo Alto Housing Corporation.

21. Ibid.

22. The author estimates that since 1978, when the Irvine inclusionary housing program first started producing a significant volume of units, through 1984 (based on units now under construction), an average of nearly 400 units per year will have been produced, including both the affordable sales program and the Sec. 8 rental housing program in the city.

23. Schwartz, Johnston & Burtraw, *Local Government Initiatives*, p. 41.

24. Where tax-exempt bonds are used to provide mortgage financing, units by federal law must remain occupied by the mortgagor for the period the mortgage is outstanding.

25. County of Orange, Environmental Management Agency, *History, Rationale Implementation and Alternatives Regarding the Anti-Speculation and Continued Affordability Policies for Affordable Housing* (Santa Ana, CA: 1981), p. 9.

26. Montgomery County, Office of the County Executive, *Executive Regulation 44-81*, Sec. C(5).

27. *Model Deed Restriction*, prepared by City of Palo Alto. The length of the control has recently been reduced to 30 years, starting anew with each transaction.

28. 15 U.S.C. Sec. 1 *et seq.* (1890).

29. 435 U.S. 389, 98 S.Ct. 1123 (1978).

30. The only case in which, to the author's knowledge, this issue was actually raised in other than an academic context was in post-trial hearings on proposed remedial action in the exclusionary zoning case of *Allan-Deane Corporation v. Township of Bedminster*, New Jersey Superior Court, Law Division — Somerset County, Docket No. L-36896-70. P.W. L-28061-71 P.W. Attorneys for the defendant township argued that, although "Mr. Raymond [the court-appointed master] was of the opinion that any mandatory set-aside for sales units would be worthless unless such controls were implemented. . . ." he "advised the Township that there were significant problems under the anti-trust laws of New Jersey and the United States as to the control of prices of condominiums. . . . on resale" (letter to the court, May 22, 1980). The issue was not resolved by the trial court at that time and has now been rendered moot by the *Mount Laurel II* decision.

31. Concurring opinion by Chief Justice Berger, 98 S.Ct at 1123, 1141.

32. Ibid. at 1138. The author is indebted to Kenneth E. Meiser, Esq. for his assistance in the foregoing discussion of the antitrust issue.

33. Witkin, 3 *Summary of California Law*, Sec. 318, p. 2026, cited in Legal Division, California Department of Housing & Community Development, opinion memorandum "Legality of Deed Restrictions," Dec. 19, 1978, p. 3.

34. 4 *Restatement of Property*, Sec. 413, p. 2441 (1944), cited in ibid., p. 3.

35. Ibid. See also Lake S. Trout, Esq., Loeb & Loeb, legal memorandum "Lost Cost Housing — Resale Controls," March 15, 1979, from Southern California Association of Governments, papers for Inclusionary Zoning Conference, September 1980.

36. See Lewis Goldshore, Esq., legal memorandum, April 27, 1981, p. 12.

37. California Planning and Zoning Law, Sec. 65916 (added by Stats. 1979, Ch. 1207).

38. Slip opinion at 112-113.

39. California Association of Realtors, cited in Hagman, "Bootstrapping Low and Moderate Income Housing," p. 24.

40. Connerly & Associates, *Implications of Inclusionary Housing Programs*, p. 37.

41. Ibid., p. 37.

42. This point was made separately in interviews with officials familiar with the characteristics of program participants in both Palo Alto and Orange County.

43. See, e.g., Montgomery County, *Executive Regulation 17-82*, "Administrative Procedures and Requirements for the Resale of MPDUs," June 28, 1983, Sec. A.5.b; County of Orange, Environmental Management Agency, "Anti-Speculation and Policies for Affordable Housing," p. 7; City of Palo Alto, *Model Deed Restriction*, pp. 2-3. It should be noted that inasmuch as most units built under inclusionary programs and offered for sale are condomimium flats the opportunities for significant property improvements are very limited.

44. Interview with Valerie Glassford, Palo Alto Housing Corporation.

45. City of Palo Alto, *Model Deed Restriction*, pp. 3-4.

46. County of Orange, "Affordable Housing," p. 7. There were 253 respondents to the survey. The interpretation in the text is that of this author, not that of Orange County officials.

47. Interview with Lila Lieberthal, Financing Director, The Carma-Sandling Group, Irvine, California.

48. Unidentified "high secondary mortgage market official," quoted in *Los Angeles Times*, "California Government Moves Toward 'Affordability' Shelter Price Limits," August 10, 1980.

49. Supervisor Roger R. Stanton, "Supervisor Stanton's Home Resale Plan for Orange County's Housing Revenue Bond Program Mortgages," Presentation to Orange County Board of Supervisors, July 7, 1981.

50. Interviews with Judith Swayne, Orange County; and Steven Mabs, California Department of Housing and Community Development (formerly with Orange County).

51. William Olson, (then) Manager, Information and Housing Development Office, Orange County, quoted in *Los Angeles Times*, August 10, 1980.

52 In the above-mentioned *Los Angeles Times* article, the following phrase appears, "Bettencourt [exclusion director of the Orange County Chapter of the Building Industry Association], along with many others predict that price controls will eventually have to be imposed on everyone's home." It should be added that from the free market perspective, it is likely that such controls are perceived as *significantly* more intrusive than rent controls in that they directly affect one's ability to dispose of one's property, an action with no overt consequences for anyone but oneself and the willing buyer. Thus, the consumer protection rationale that more or less justifies rent control does not apply.

53. The use of large lot zoning, minimum floor area requirements, and the like to mandate expensive house construction is too well known to require further comment. There have been occasional experiments in local land use ordinances with explicit minimum price regulations, but these have not, as a rule, been welcomed by the courts; see Williams, *American Land Planning Law*, Vol. 2, pp. 610-615, who notes that (as of 1972), the Federal Housing Administration recommended restrictive covenants setting minimum house prices, ibid., p. 615. For a discussion of zoning to maintain property values, see ibid., Vol. 1, pp. 315-325.

54. Southern California Association of Governments, *Costs, Causes and Consequences of the Housing Shortage* (1981), p. 16.

55. Interview with Ruth Schwartz, California Department of Housing & Community Development.

56. Senate Bill 626 (Mello, 1981), Ch. 1007, Statutes of 1981. At *California Public Resources Code*, Sec. 30500.1.

57. Seymour I. Schwartz, Robert A. Johnston, Geoffrey Wandesforde-Smith, and Kirk Savage, *The Implementation of SB 626 in Southern California: A Summary of Findings* (Davis, CA: Institute of Governmental Affairs, 1983), Table 1.

58. Interview with Peggy Schneble, Planner, City of Irvine.

59. Interviews with Judith Swayne and Steven Mabs; also Crystal Sims, Esq., Orange County Legal Aid Society.

60. City of Irvine, "Low and Moderate Income Housing in Irvine, California A Status Report," 1979, p. 14.

61. For an interesting statement of the absolute position on property rights which bears, of course, no relationship to any past or present reality, see Roger Pilon, "Property Rights and a Free Society" in M. Bruce Johnson, ed. *Resolving the Housing Crisis* (San Francisco: Pacific Institute for Public Policy Research, 1982).

62. Montgomery County, *Executive Regulation 44-81*, Sec.C(5).

63. Paraphrase of Montgomery County, *Executive Regulation 17-82*, Sec.A(5)(f).

64. County of Orange, adopted by County Board of Supervisors by Resolution 80-1127, July 9, 1980. This was subsequently amended on May 4, 1982 to provide (a) for a reduction in terms from 30 to 20 years, and (b) for a Conditional Waiver of Option provision.

65. See note 62. It would appear that the only circumstances under which this waiver would be attractive to a seller would be where the seller was hoping to carry out a non-arms length sale to a relative or acquaintance who was, however, income-qualified.

66. An interesting variant on this approach is being developed for the Bedminster, New Jersey, inclusionary housing program in which, if the agency cannot sell the unit, the homeowner may sell the unit to whomever he or she pleases, *but* (a) at the formula resale price already set by the agency; *and* (b) subject to continuing resale controls. This way, although the new buyer may not be a lower-income household, the program has the opportunity to restore the unit to the ranks of lower-income housing at the *next* resale transaction. Thus, the unit is not lost permanently from the lower-income housing stock.

67. Orange County, Environmental Management Agency, *Orange County's Inclusionary Housing Program Assessment* (Santa Ana, CA, November 1982)) unpaged.

68. *Attachment to Grant Deed*, Sec. 5. Strictly speaking, the provision provides that the resale price will be the lowest of (a) the increase based on increase in median income; (b) the market price; or (c) a price negotiated between the seller and the County.

69. *Assessment*. During the same period, median household income nationally increased by an average of 7.0% per year.

70. Ibid.

71. Ibid.

72. Ibid.

73. Palo Alto Housing Corporation, *Semi-Annual Report January-June 1983*, p. 2.

74. Interview with Valerie Glassford and Marilyn Zatz, PAHC.

75. Hagman, "Bootstrapping Low and Moderate Income Housing," pp. 25-26

76. An alternative, which was embodied in a proposed modification of the Orange County program brought forward in 1981 by County Supervisor Stanton, an opponent of the program, was to establish a second trust deed recapture program keyed to the amount of the interest rate subsidy obtained by a buyer who received financing under the county tax-exempt mortgage bond financing program. It is unclear, from the subsequent history of this proposal and Supervisor Stanton's subsequent positions, whether the proposal was seriously intended or not.

77. This was particularly notable with regard to the Section 236 program. This program was enacted in 1968 and provided a moderate subsidy in the form of interest rate reduction to an effective rate of 1%. All other costs were expected to be borne by the tenantry. In the various economic circumstances of the 1970s, particularly the 1973-1974 recession, that assumption turned out to be invalid and a large number of projects went into default.

78. Section 8 Existing Housing certificates are designed to be provided to individual low-income

households to be used in the existing housing stock without being linked to any particular housing unit. Under some circumstances, particularly where existing moderately priced rental housing is in short supply, arrangements have been made to tie these certificates to specific newly developed rental housing. Although inconsistent with the program rationale, it often is required if these certificates are to be used at all.

79. Under the Accelerated Cost Recovery System (ACRS) provision established in 1981, the depreciation schedule for low-income rental housing allows 13% of the value of the property to be depreciated in the 1st year, and so forth. At the end of 7 years, 65% of the value has been depreciated, and at the end of 10 years, 80% of the value has been depreciated. The remaining five years from 11 to 15 allow only 4% of the value to be depreciated each year.

80. There is a strong public policy argument that inclusionary programs should include rental housing, as a substantial number of the lower-income households that are designed to benefit from such programs, especially under the New Jersey income standards, are not likely to be able to purchase a home, either by virtue of poor credit history, earning instability, or lack of downpayment funds.

81. Interview with Steven Mabs, California Department of Housing and Community Development.

82. Interview with Sidney Willis, Assistant Commissioner, New Jersey Department of Community Affairs.

7

Housing Trust Funds and Payments in Lieu of Housing Production

The basic model of an inclusionary housing program is one in which developers construct lower-income housing as a part of a larger development built for the private marketplace. In a variation on that theme, a developer is provided with alternatives either to build or to make a payment in lieu of building lower-income units. A substantial number of the inclusionary housing programs initiated by California municipalities contain provisions under which a developer may pay such an "in lieu" fee, either at his discretion or at the discretion of the municipality.

A different approach, which is substantially further removed from the basic inclusionary model, is one in which the exaction of payments from developers becomes the essence of the program rather than being an option intended to have only limited applicability. The purpose of such programs is to establish a fund, often termed a housing trust fund, which can then be used by the public sector to further the objectives of providing housing affordable to low- and moderate-income households. This approach is attractive to many municipalities where the physical inclusion of lower-income units is unrealistic, as is the case with most non-residential development, particularly high-density downtown office development. In the best-known program, the San Francisco Office/Housing Production Program, funds are obtained from the developers of downtown office buildings and used to support a variety of low-income housing undertakings throughout the city.

The application of the inclusionary approach to the urban scene is especially interesting. In cities like San Francisco or New York, the high density and high cost of most private market residential development does not lend itself readily to the economical inclusion of lower-income households. Furthermore, in those cities, the volume of residential development of *any* kind is so limited that local governments are reluctant to discourage what little is taking place. In this context, the San Francisco approach is very attractive. Most urban municipalities, unlike most suburban communities, have plans and strategies waiting to be used to meet lower-income housing needs and have some professional staff trained to carry out those plans. Trust fund programs enable urban governments to tap the only source of development investment to which they are particularly attractive and create a source of funds over which the governments have broad discretion and little accountability other than that dictated by local political realities.

For many developers, both urban and suburban, a cash payment appears to be an acceptable alternative. It is a clearly-defined cost of doing business, uncomplicated by the potentially difficult social and economic issues associated with the development of lower-income housing units. It is likely to be perceived as a further extension of customary local government demands for money, whether for parks and recreation, sewer and water hookup charges, or dozens of other costs. Where given the choice, even developers who are realistically in a position to provide lower-income housing units will most often choose to pay even a considerable fee in lieu of doing so.

Despite the appeal of this approach, it raises many questions in both its suburban and urban variations. From a legal standpoint, to the extent that the public objective has become one of raising funds from developers rather than securing a particular type of land use, the question of exactions becomes more significant and the relationship of the program to conventional zoning law more and more tenuous. Beyond the legal issues lie significant issues of public policy, of fairness, and of reasonableness. Finally, and more importantly, it remains to be seen whether this approach is really an effective means of achieving its objective, namely, improving the housing conditions of lower-income families.

After a discussion of the legal issues associated with the trust fund or in lieu payment approach, the suburban and urban variations of the approach are each discussed, the latter in greater detail. In view of its unique character and features, a section of this chapter has been devoted to the San Francisco Office/Housing Production Program.

Housing Payments and the Problem of Exactions

We have argued, following the lead of the New Jersey Supreme Court in *Mount Laurel II*, that inclusionary provisions requiring a developer to build a given percentage of units in a development to be affordable to households of a given income level are a direct extension of the land use regulations governing the zone in which he is building.[1] As such, inclusionary housing is encompassed within a broad, but not unreasonable, definition of the zoning power. The exaction of fees by the municipality to be used for some public purpose, however, clearly falls beyond the zoning power. An extensive body of case law, which has been briefly alluded to in chapter two, has come into being in an effort to delineate the distinctions between reasonable and unreasonable or permissible and impermissible exactions.

The general principle, held to with varying degrees or rigor by the various state courts, is that an exaction in order to be permissible must bear a reasonable relationship or a rational nexus to the needs generated by the development or the harm created by spillovers from the development.[2] Typical exactions that have been allowed by the courts have been park dedication or in lieu fees,[3] fees for expansion of water and sewer systems,[4] and drainage improvements.[5] While most state courts, with the notable exception of the Illinois courts, appear to allow some exercise of judgment on the part of local officials where they determine that a particular improvement is associated with a particular development, many are careful to scrutinize efforts to extract cash from developers to ensure that the amount of money exacted bears a clear relationship to the improvement for which it substitutes.[6]

If we argue that the basic inclusionary model is not an exaction at all and that a program such as the San Francisco Office/Housing Production Program, in all probability, *is* an exaction, there is, nonetheless, a substantial middle ground in which a particular program may or may not fall into that category. Each major category of program or regulation must be separately scrutinized in this light.

The first version is an inclusionary program in which a developer is given a choice between constructing lower-income housing units or paying a fee in lieu of such construction, *under circumstances in which construction is, nonetheless, a realistic alternative.* The short answer would appear to be that if the builder is indeed given the choice and is free to select the option he considers preferable, and it has already been clearly established that building the units is not an exaction, neither should an in lieu payment be under these circumstances.

That may well be the case. If, however, the rationale for the inclusionary requirement is that it is part and parcel of the use permitted on the site, then the mere offer of a waiver of the requirement in return for a fee raises questions. To begin, it calls into question whether the inclusionary requirement is as closely tied to the use of the site as has been previously argued; in other words, if it is an intrinsic part of the use, how can it be waived in return for payment of a fee? If it can be waived in return for a fee, then it is more likely to be an improvement for the benefit of the community — such as a park or drainage system — and must therefore be considered an exaction. Alternatively, if it is not an exaction, it is open to question as a form of "contract zoning," a practice which is considered dubious in most, if not all, states.[7]

It is unlikely that this particular issue will be the subject of a serious challenge since, whatever the legal ramifications, the fairness and reasonableness of offering the developer the choice, under circumstances where the municipality *could* reasonably simply require production of units, is considerable. That notwithstanding, it should be noted that it is unlikely that the typical suburban inclusionary housing program, seen as an exaction, would satisfy anything but an extremely liberal interpretation of the "rational nexus" argument. Leaving aside special and unusual cases, it is hard to argue that the typical suburban housing development either creates a harm to lower-income households that must be mitigated in some manner, or generates a significant increased demand in the community for lower-income housing. We have noted earlier that the argument that the construction of middle- and upper-income housing in a community by virtue of increasing the demand in that community for goods and services, which in turn creates added lower-income employment, thereby increasing the demand for lower-income housing, will rarely be supportable by rigorous economic analysis.[8] Similarly, except in cases involving displacement of lower-income households, it is hard to establish a connection between any suburban housing development and the reduction of lower-income housing opportunities which will withstand careful scrutiny.[9] In short, the nexus appears to be tenuous, if not nonexistent.

While this may not be a serious problem under those circumstances where the developer can realistically construct lower-income housing units in a particular development, it may become a serious issue in those cases where the parties involved all recognize that the basic inclusionary model is inappropriate. An example of the latter would be the construction of a luxury high-rise building in a particularly high-density and high-demand area such as the Atlantic City boardwalk or midtown Manhattan. Although it is clearly not *impossible* to incorporate low- and moderate-income housing units into such a building, the cost and nature of the product clearly dictate that such a course would be extremely burdensome to the developer in intangible ways as much as in direct dollar losses.

In an effort to further their inclusionary housing policy under precisely these circumstances, the New Jersey Division of Coastal Resources, which has imposed inclusionary requirements on suburban developments in the Atlantic City area, has imposed different requirements on luxury high-rise developments in Atlantic City. These requirements, which are written into the development permit issued under the New Jersey Coastal Area Facilities Review Act, provide that such developments "contribute" in an appropriate manner to meeting lower-income housing needs in the Atlantic City area.[10] In one case — that of a particularly expensive oceanfront high-rise condominium development — the contribution that was approved included the underwriting of an affordable condominium development in a nearby mainland community and a commitment to support future housing rehabilitation efforts in Atlantic City.[11] The policy appears to be one of negotiating specific contributions on a case-by-case basis with each development subject to this requirement, which can provide either for support of lower-income housing elsewhere or the making of a cash contribution. Since the Division of Coastal Resources has been particularly eager to entertain off-site proposals and since no local entity appears to be an appropriate potential recipient of any funds that might be contributed, no contributions have been required or made to this point.[12]

While from a social policy perspective it may be reasonable to require developers who are benefiting from the economic growth of Atlantic City to share a part of the benefit with those who are being harmed by that growth,[13] the legal basis upon which the State of New Jersey imposes these requirements appears tenuous. There is no argument being made that these luxury developments are the cause of the deterioration in lower-income housing conditions in Atlantic City, or that the impacts being mitigated by these "contributions" are those created by the developments. In essence, developers of luxury housing are being required to contribute to mitigating the impacts that have been generated by the casinos. This issue was not addressed in the only court case arising from the CAFRA regulations, the *Egg Harbor Associates* case, in which the requirement was a more conventional inclusionary requirement, and in which the court chose not to deal with the issue of exactions.[14] Although, if the issue ever reaches the courts, it is likely that the New Jersey courts with their social policy commitment to lower-income housing will find a way to approve such "contributions," this may well not be the case in other states.

Imposing payment conditions on luxury residential development in central cities, where the demand for that housing has been generated by economic growth in the downtown business district, is subject to the same considerations as the Atlantic City example described above. Such payments are likely to be viewed as a tax imposed to further social policy goals; the only apparent rationale for linking that tax to luxury housing development is that the development of such housing represents a large, stationary target.

The one plausible exception to the pattern could be where there is a clear relationship between the particular development and the displacement of lower-income households. This may well be the case where expensive housing is being constructed or produced through substantial rehabilitation in urban neighborhoods characterized by the upward mobility sometimes termed "gentrification." In such cases, displacement could be either a direct outcome of the development, where a building previously occupied by lower-income households is being converted to more expensive occupancy; or an indirect, but still closely related, by-product. Here, the generally accepted theory that a developer may be required to contribute to mitigate the harm created by his actions is available to support the exaction of a contribution to a housing fund, or similar purpose.[15]

Another approach, recommended by Kleven, who recognizes the same problem that has been addressed above, is that compensatory measures be included in the program; e.g., that the contributions be exacted only as a *quid pro quo* for particular concessions, such as density bonuses, and only in proportion to the value of the concessions, rather than as a condition of development.[16] The object of such compensatory measures is to provide additional economic benefits to the developer over and above the benefits available to him by right, which are at least equal to the level of contribution to be exacted. Then,

> If subsidy costs are not imposed; i.e., if no economic loss results from having to comply with the inclusionary requirements, then the unfairness claim is undercut. Nor, since the purpose of the nexus test is to discover whether there has been unfairness, should a community then have to show any nexus at all between new development and the need for low cost housing.[17]

A current New York City proposal calls for the creation of a housing trust fund financed by developer contributions in return for approval to develop additional square footage.[18] Assuming that such programs can be designed to avoid the "contract zoning" issue, they should be able to withstand a legal challenge on the question of exactions.[19]

The above discussion has concentrated on the issue of exactions applied to *residential* development. The same issues arise with the imposition of contribution requirements on non-residential development, such as in the San Francisco program. Here, however, there does appear on its face to be a relatively straightforward rationale for the exaction, arguably falling within the rational nexus framework. The relationship hinges on the not unreasonable presumption that an increase in employment creates a demand for additional housing within close proximity of that employment. Furthermore, less obviously but still compellingly, when that employment growth takes place in the center of a fully-developed community such as San Francisco, constraints on the ability of the private market to produce additional housing in close proximity to the growth center will result in pressure being placed on the existing housing stock. Thus, the price of the existing housing stock will be bid up with attendant harm to lower-income households. This is stated explicitly at the beginning of the program guidelines issued by the city of San Francisco:

> Findings from the EIRs (Environmental Impact Reports) show that the construction of new office buildings create a demand for new housing in excess of the supply provided by the current market. Therefore, the City Planning Commission has adopted a policy of imposing housing requirements, where appropriate, on proposed office developments to mitigate said adverse impact.[20]

While the relationship claimed certainly does exist, it implicitly stretches the definition of public harms and benefits beyond that generally contemplated by the law of exactions. Typically, exactions were designed to mitigate burdens on the public system, e.g., parks, sewer and water systems, and the like. The assumption implicit in the San Francisco program and in its imitators around the nation is that housing for lower-income households is a form of public service and that overburdening low-income housing is at least as much a general public concern as is the overcrowding of schools and parks, or the overutilization of a public sewer system. This premise is not unreasonable; indeed, it is a part of much of the doctrine of rent control that emerged in a number of states, particularly New Jersey, during the 1970s.[21] Still, it does represent an extension of traditional notions of the scope of exactions, and should be recognized as such.

Furthermore, if one is relying either on the law of exactions or on the rationale that the contribution is designed to mitigate negative environmental impacts, a question of linkage arises; should not there be some close relationship, either geographic or functional, between the office/commercial project and the housing activities for which it is being required to contribute? As one commentator on the New York proposals notes, "to what extent may developer contributions paid for increased floor area of Manhattan office buildings be used to finance housing in Queens?"[22] Similarly, some of the funds exacted under the San Francisco program have been used to rehabilitate vacant public housing units for senior citizen occupancy.[23] If the rationale for these exactions is the need for worker housing created by the growth in employment opportunities, an argument can be made that only activities directly supporting the provision of such housing can be considered appropriate uses of funds collected on this basis.[24]

In the final analysis, it is difficult to escape the conclusion that the exaction of contributions from developers for housing trust funds, in circumstances in which development of lower-income housing by those developers is not a realistic option, is much more a tax or special assessment than it is truly an exaction. As a tax, it has reasonable justification: wealth is being created through the development process, and it is not inappropriate to tax that wealth in order to benefit the public weal, either generally or in a manner in which the funds are earmarked to a particular public purpose — that of providing lower-income housing.[25] One can argue, as has Ellickson, that it is not a particularly efficient tax from the standpoint of classical economics;[26] appropriately enacted, however, it would clearly be a legal tax. As a general rule, however, taxes cannot be enacted in the United States by local jurisdictions without enabling legislation from state government; in some jurisdictions, the matter is further complicated by constitutional limitations such as California's Proposition 13. Thus, it appears inevitable that any court concluding that a required contribution to a housing trust fund was indeed a tax would then most likely find that enactment of such a tax without appropriate enabling legislation would be *ultra vires*, and therefore illegal.

Such an outcome is by no means certain. As suggested earlier, it is quite possible that a number of courts, attracted by the strong public policy arguments in

support of housing trust funds, may accept the exaction or environmental mitigation rationales put forward by their proponents in order to uphold these programs.
It is possible that other rationales may be found, such as that suggested by one
commentator, of social recapture of land and development value increments
created by zoning or other public intervention.[27] In the final analysis, however,
these arguments represent a difficult effort to unearth a legal rationale in existing
law for a desired public policy objective.

Payments in Lieu of Housing Production: The Suburban Approach

The typical suburban program under which funds earmarked for lower-income
housing have been collected from developers has been one in which the payment
into a fund has been framed as an option and an alternative to the developer
building affordable housing units.

Two fundamentally different models under which such options are available
exist: in one, the developer is given a choice of building units or paying an "in
lieu" fee; and in the second, the option of paying the in lieu fee is available under
limited circumstances and exercised at the discretion of the municipality or
county administering the program.

In most cases it would appear to be preferable from the standpoint of the public
interest to obtain affordable housing units directly rather than funds which may or
may not be adequate to secure comparable units. Given a free choice, however, it
would appear that most developers will choose to pay the in lieu fee, thereby
providing the municipality administering the program with the less desirable outcome. As a result, it is widely held that the determination of whether an in lieu
fee should be allowed should lie with the city or county, as is the case in Palo
Alto; furthermore, it is held that in lieu fees should be permitted only (a) in
small-scale developments where the provision of units is not feasible; and/or (b)
where a clear finding of hardship has been made. The Model Inclusionary Ordinance issued by the California Department of Housing & Community Development suggests the following language:

> In developments of 20 units or less where, due to the extreme cost of de-
> velopment, the planning commission deems that the provision of inclu-
> sionary units will constitute extreme hardship, the developer may pay an in
> lieu fee instead of providing inclusionary units.[28]

This language is designed to make clear that the opportunity to pay a fee in lieu of
producing lower-income housing units is a special opportunity and one offered
only in extremely unusual circumstances.

Having established the circumstances under which it is considered appropriate
to allow a developer to pay an in lieu fee, the city or county must determine an

equitable way of setting the fee. This is particularly important in cases where the jurisdiction, rather than the developer, retains the power to determine whether an in lieu fee will be entertained. If the developer has the choice, he will, one assumes, choose the option that is less expensive to him. Where he does not have the choice, a legal issue of unfair burden could arise if it cannot be shown that the cost of the in lieu fee is reasonable compared to the cost associated with providing the required number of lower-income housing units.[29]

The Model Inclusionary Ordinance proposes a formula as follows:

> The amount of the fee shall be determined by the following formula: estimated average sales price of a newly constructed 1200 square foot unit in the jurisdiction (such estimate to be made by the appraisal section of the county assessor's office and be updated on quarterly basis) minus the median income times 2.0, times the number of inclusionary units required in Sections E-1-a and E-2-a.[30]

Sections E-1-a and E-2-a, which apply to rental and sales developments respectively, require a 15 percent set-aside of lower-income units for developments of less than 50 units; since the above provision applies only to developments of 20 units or less, we can assume a hypothetical 20-unit development, in which the inclusionary requirement would be three units. Assuming, then, that the market value or sales price of the model 1200-square-foot unit is $100,000, and the median income in the area $32,000, both reasonably representative California figures, the amount of the developer's in lieu payment would be as follows:

$$(\$100,000 - \$64,000) = \$36,000 \times 3 = \$108,000$$

That amount translates into $5,400 for each conventional unit built in the development.

It appears clear that the drafters of the Model Inclusionary Ordinance sought to approximate the level of subsidy that a developer would have to provide if he were building the required number of affordable housing units. Realistically, though, a developer who is building a unit to sell for $64,000 will not spend as much as he will spend on a unit to sell for $100,000. The unit will be smaller, will contain less expensive fixtures and finishes, and so forth. As a result, the formula will consistently overstate the level of subsidy actually involved, therefore making the in lieu payment more costly than the production of units.[31]

The inclusionary program of the city of Livermore, California, by comparison, requires that developments of five or more units contain 10 percent of their units affordable to households earning 80 percent of the area median income or less; or that the developer pay an in lieu fee to the city. The amount of the in lieu fee is established through a formula based on the fair market value of residential land zoned at a density of three units per acre. For each unit in the development (not low-income, but total units) the developer must pay, where V represents fair market value:

$$(V \div 3) \times .10 = \text{In lieu payment}$$

Based on an adjustment early in 1983 the fair market value of one acre of vacant land so zoned has been set at $25,000 and the in lieu fee would be calculated as:

$$(\$25,000 \div 3) = \$8,333 \times .10 = \$833 \text{ per unit.}$$

Thus, the hypothetical developer of 100 units would have the choice of providing 10 units of lower-income housing or of making a contribution of $83,300 to the city of Livermore.[32] From 1979 until early 1983 the fee was $443 per unit.[33] This formula, which assumes implicitly that the developer's subsidy is limited to the land cost, may well understate the amount of subsidy involved in producing lower-income units, and provide a positive incentive to developers to choose the in lieu payment alternative.

In Livermore, perhaps for reasons related to the above factor, the majority of developers have chosen to pay the fee rather than produce the units, although the increase in the size of the in lieu fee apparently was enough to convince one developer to change his mind and build lower-income units, a change which is anticipated to result in 20 lower-income units being built during 1984.[34] By the fall of 1983, the city had collected approximately $180,000 in fees[35] — fees which under the Livermore General Plan must be used "for the implementation of the [city of Livermore] low-income housing program."[36]

Although the city has been collecting fees since 1979, by the end of 1983, with the exception of some funds that were expended for administrative costs, no use had yet been made of the fund established with the in lieu fees. Planning for the first such use, however, was relatively far along; specifically, the city was seeking to leverage $50,000 from the fund with $100,000 from private sources to create an investment pool, the proceeds of which would be used to subsidize rents down to the level of the HUD Fair Market Rents, so that families holding Section 8 Existing Housing certificates would be able to rent the units.[37] Based on a projected yield of roughly $15,000 per year, it was anticipated that this project would make 15 to 20 two-bedroom units accessible to low-income households.[38] Assuming this project takes place, over $100,000 would still remain in the fund with no concrete plans for its use.

Livermore is one of at least ten California municipalities in which the option of an in lieu fee is offered, excluding those jurisdictions in which transfer credit provisions, which are significantly different, are in effect. In some cases similar fees are levied as a condition of approval of condominium conversion, a related but somewhat different issue. Many of these communities have accumulated substantial dedicated funds as a result of the imposition of these fees: the city of Novato and the county of Marin had each collected $400,000 or more by mid-1983.[39] In most cases where these fees are collected, the funds tend to accumulate because of the difficulty local officials find in spending the money.[40]

One exception is in Palo Alto. Unlike most programs in which it is the developer's option to choose housing production or payment of an in lieu fee, the Palo Alto program provides that the city decides whether or not to allow the developer to "buy out" of his lower-income housing production obligation. In addition, Palo Alto has an ongoing housing program, which includes a number of activities such as rental rehabilitation, Section 8 subsidies, and the like in addition to the inclusionary housing program. As a result, funds have not accumulated but have been applied directly to ongoing programs, particularly for the purpose of land acquisition.[41]

Although it may appear strange, the problems in most communities with spending the funds collected in this fashion are very serious. Small suburban jurisdictions tend to have limited technical capabilities, particularly in a complex area such as this; the options, particularly those which clearly demonstrate that the community is not wasting its money, are relatively few. In addition, a cautious municipality with limited expertise will be reluctant to explore risky options, such as land purchase or acquisition of housing units and buildings. Finally, fear of the consequences of failure in a politically volatile area like this becomes a further constraint on action.

In a suburban setting, the political constraints can become paralyzing. Once the municipality has begun to collect funds through in lieu payments from developers, it has become responsible for taking action in an area often politically attractive in the abstract, but highly unattractive when translated to specific sites or buildings. A community may support the idea of a residential rehabilitation program, but may object strenuously when the municipal housing agency proposes to purchase large Victorian houses in middle-class areas and convert them to lower-income multiple occupancy.

The same issues can arise in central cities. One aspect of the proposed New York City inclusionary program, discussed later in this chapter, is for the use of funds collected through in lieu payments by Manhattan office and luxury residential developers to assist lower-income housing projects in the outer boroughs, a proposal that has already generated considerable opposition by Manhattan housing activists, who have argued that any such funds collected in Manhattan should stay in Manhattan.[42] Although in central cities the intensity of the needs and the number of competitors for the available resources sooner or later dictate that any funds raised will somehow be spent, the same is not true, as has been established in California, in the suburbs. Far less attention has been paid to these problems than is necessary by the framers of programs which provide for payments in lieu of lower-income housing production, or simply require developer payments into a housing trust fund. There is not yet a single successful example of a housing trust fund, as such, created through developer payments under an inclusionary housing program. In San Francisco, as will be discussed below, developer payments have been effectively channeled to lower-income housing projects, but only because of an unusual series of circumstances. Furthermore, in San Francisco there is no "trust fund" as such; the city acts as a broker, making the connection between developers with housing obligations and an existing network of public agencies and nonprofit organizations with a substantial backlog of unfunded but sound housing projects.

When a municipality begins to accept in lieu payments and deposits them in a restricted fund, it has assumed a heavy responsibility for meeting the housing needs of its citizens. This is a responsibility that many municipalities, particularly suburban jurisdictions, may not be ready to accept in unequivocal fashion. In the context of the difficulties described above, the establishment of such a fund can become as much of a problem as an opportunity for a community. The greater the chain of actors and decisions before housing production can take place and the more closely tied housing production becomes to the political arena, the more likely it is that delays and obstacles will arise. The combination of the technical difficulties of implementation with the potential for intense politicization of the issue can easily result in outcomes far less attractive than those contemplated by the framers of the program.

The Orange County Credit Transfer Program

An approach which appears to resolve some of the problems associated with in lieu payments is the mechanism incorporated in the Orange County inclusionary housing program which provides for the transfer of excess affordable unit credits between projects and between developers. The provision is described by one commentator as follows:

> Developers who build more than the required 25 percent of their units in the affordable range receive credit for each unit above the 25 percent requirement. They may then apply those credits to other developments of their own, or they may sell them to other developers. Each unit credit is used to reduce by one the number of affordable units in the other (receiving) development.[43]

In order to prevent overconcentration of affordable housing units, the county must approve each transfer of credits across Community Analysis Area lines,[44] which approval is granted subject to a determination that:

1. The transfer will not lead to a significantly greater concentration of affordable

units in the CAA (Community Analysis Area) from which the transfer is made;

2. The transfer will tend to place affordable units as near or nearer to jobs, public transportation, shopping, and other community facilities and services than if such units were provided on-site.[45]

The institution of the credits transfer simultaneously provides that the number of affordable units sought by the county is actually built, while providing each individual developer with a choice of building or purchasing transfer credits. As importantly, the price of transfer credits, in contrast to the level of in lieu payments, is set by the marketplace and should automatically align itself to reflect the price relationship between constructing conventional housing and the affordable housing required by the inclusionary housing program.[46]

Furthermore, since the non-dollar burden of providing lower-income housing can be expected to vary widely from builder to builder, those builders who choose to purchase credits are likely to place a greater negative value on these non-dollar burdens than are those builders who are oriented toward the affordable housing market. From this *it logically follows that the former group, the purchasers, will pay the sellers more for each credit than it costs the sellers to produce it.* As far as can be determined, this is precisely what took place. During 1981, purchasers of credits were spending between $10,000 and $15,000 per credit, a cost substantially higher than the apparent dollar loss being taken by the builders of excess affordable housing units.[47] As a result, the production of excess affordable units became a major element of the business strategy of a number of area builders, whose profitability was apparently enhanced as a result.[48] Although the purchasers of credits would undoubtedly have preferred not to do so, there is no evidence that the effect was unduly burdensome on them. Certainly, the market in credits was a brisk one.[49]

The credit transfer scheme appears to have been a substantial success in Orange County, and is well worth considering elsewhere.[50] The circumstances which led to its success in that jurisdiction, however, suggest that it is not automatically replicable. First and foremost is the scale of development in Orange County, a single jurisdiction within which transfers of credit take place. During the three-year period after initiation of the program, Orange County approved a total of 135 separate developments containing over 18,000 dwelling units.[51] This scale and diversity of development activity provided reasonable assurance to developers that there would be a market for any excess affordable housing units they could create. Without a large scale of development activity providing a potentially large number of buyers of credits, the incentive to create the credits is significantly reduced. If a developer must wait more than a short period to dispose of his credits, the incentive is further reduced.[52] In a typical growing northeastern suburban jurisdiction, for example, annual development activity is unlikely to be consistently more than 150 to 300 units. Such a volume does not, in all probability, provide the opportunity for the rapid turnover of credits necessary to make the program work.

The scale and diversity of the county was important in other ways. The size of the market encouraged developers of affordable housing to maximize efficiency, constructing large numbers of inexpensive units simultaneously. The large number of active builders in the area ensured that there would be an adequate "mix" of builders of different scale, different housing type, and different quality to provide a balance between potential users and potential suppliers of the credits. Finally, the strength of the demand for expensive housing in Orange County ensured that it would be worth the while of custom and small-scale builders to buy the credits, even at a substantial cost.

One alternative in smaller jurisdictions, where no one community appears large enough to sustain a transfer credit program, would be to establish a regional program, based on a compact or other agreement between a number of suburban municipalities. It does not require much imagination to anticipate some of the difficulties that would be involved, given the politically sensitive nature of lower-income housing, but they could be overcome with an adequate incentive to do so. One can speculate that perhaps in New Jersey the *Mount Laurel II* decision might provide that incentive.

Inclusionary Zoning Moves Downtown:[53]
Housing Trust Funds and Urban Redevelopment

While the initial impetus for inclusionary housing programs was clearly suburban in nature, recent developments in America's central cities have created a new form of inclusionary program, grounded in the linkage between downtown office and commercial development and the rise and fall of the surrounding urban residential neighborhoods. In this new approach, for which the San Francisco Office/Housing Production Program has been a model, developers of downtown office and commercial projects are required to contribute funds to assist in the development and preservation of affordable housing, including but not limited to the need for affordable housing triggered by the growth and development of the downtown. By the end of 1983, such a program was underway in San Francisco, was the subject of detailed plans and proposals in Boston and Seattle, and was under serious consideration in New York City, Honolulu, and Santa Monica. Other communities had begun to explore the idea.[54]

The imposition of exactions on office and commercial development to support the development and preservation of lower-income housing has its roots in two parallel considerations: first, the growing awareness of the relationship between the redevelopment of central city downtowns and the pressure on the affordable housing stock in nearby urban neighborhoods, triggering gentrification and displacement; and second, the more opportunistic desire to tap a major source of private investment in order to address serious housing problems in view of the drastic reduction in the traditional source of funds for that purpose — the federal government.

Whether or not opportunistic, which is not in itself necessarily a bad thing, the idea has clear attractions. Despite some suburbanization of major office employment, it is clear that major central cities continue to possess certain unique attributes prompting large corporations, banks, and similar entities to locate there. As long as that is the case, it appears economically feasible for those cities to capture part of the benefit obtained by developers from those attributes. Furthermore, it is arguably more effectively redistributional, should that be the objective, than most alternatives, including most more conventional inclusionary programs; to the degree that the developer passes the cost of the contribution on to his tenants, they will be large corporations or similar entities, rather than individual homebuyers or renters. Although, in the broadest sense, it is not inconceivable that some of that cost is in turn passed on to consumers, it is nonetheless likely to retain a substantially redistributional character.

Before pursuing this and similar issues further, it is appropriate to turn to a description of the San Francisco program, which is, as has been noted, the only such program which has been in effect for any length of time and about which it is possible to draw any conclusions.[55]

The San Francisco Office/Housing Production Program (OHPP)

The San Francisco program was initiated informally in 1981 and formally adopted early in 1982 when program guidelines were issued. The impetus for the program came from a combination of pressures for affordable housing, exacerbated by the loss of federal programs, and ongoing controversy involving downtown office development.[56] In recent years, not only has San Francisco become one of the most expensive urban residential communities in the United States, but there has been continued widespread opposition to the pattern of downtown office development, a pattern which has been characterized as the "Manhattanization" of downtown. Although referenda that would have significantly reduced the amount of downtown development and imposed stringent height restrictions on new construction have failed, such movements have elicited widespread support and contributed to a political climate in which exacting housing contributions from office developers was an attractive option. As one writer commented,

> The policy has the added blessing of a simple populist appeal of socking it to the rich — fueled in San Francisco by xenophobic stories of Hong Kong, Canadian and Texan money flowing into downtown.[57]

In addition to the OHPP, the city is seeking to exact funds from downtown development to support public transportation,[58] and has recently presented a proposed downtown master plan designed to exert an exceptional level of design and site planning control over future downtown development.

The OHPP is not an ordinance, or a plan, but a "policy," grounded legally in the California Environmental Quality Act, and characterized as one of the implementation strategies dictated by the San Francisco General Plan and Proposition K, a ballot initiative passed by the city's voters in 1980 which called for construction of 20,000 housing units by 1985.[59] While the soundness of this legal basis was never actually challenged,[60] the position of the city is that recent amendments to the California Environmental Quality Act have significantly reduced its utility as a legal basis for the OHPP, and efforts are underway to draft an ordinance to carry the program forward.[61]

The basic premise of the program is straightforward. The development of office buildings creates a need for housing, which need must be met by office developers in direct relationship to the number of square feet of office space proposed. Developers can either build housing, provide financial aid to a specific housing project built by others, or participate in a citywide mortgage write-down program. The number of units that must be provided is based initially on a formula derived from the following assumptions: (a) one worker is added for every 250 square feet of office space; (b) 40 percent of office employees in San Francisco live in San Francisco; and (c) 1.8 working adults occupy each housing unit. Based on those assumptions, the housing requirement is as follows:

$$\text{gross square feet of office space}/250 \times 0.22 = \text{housing requirement}^{62}$$

Thus, a developer constructing a 500,000-square-foot office building has a "housing requirement" of 440 dwelling units. As will be discussed below, the nature of a housing requirement can vary widely from project to project.

The requirement applies to housing generally, and a few developers have built luxury housing to meet their obligation. The program does provide, however, a substantial incentive scheme to direct investment to lower-income housing as follows:

- two-for-one credit for facilitating production of lower-income housing under governmental rental or operating subsidy programs;
- three-for-one credit for units affordable to *moderate*-income households without governmental rental or operating subsidies;
- four-for-one credit for units affordable to *low*-income households without governmental rental or operating subsidies.[63]

In practice, between this incentive and informal pressure exerted during negotiations between city staff and developers, most of the funds have gone to support lower-income housing development.

The timing of the program, in that it was initiated at a point where significant new projects were being proposed for downtown San Francisco, was excellent. Within roughly a year and a half after initiating the program, the city had secured nearly $19 million in housing investments.[64] Leaving aside those projects that developers chose to build on their own, investments tended to fall into three categories:

- Financial support to the San Francisco Housing Authority for the purpose of rehabilitating vacant substandard public housing units;
- Financial support in order to make Section 8 new construction and substantial rehabilitation projects feasible within HUD cost limits; and
- Contributions to the citywide shared appreciation mortgage investment pool.[65]

The last program is a program administered in conjunction with a tax-exempt mortgage revenue bond issued by the city. Under the program, the funds in the investment pool are used to write down the interest rate on mortgage loans to low- and moderate-income home buyers who cannot afford otherwise to buy a house in San Francisco, even at the lower interest rate provided by the tax-exempt bonds. At the end of 30 years or when the property is sold, the investors in the pool receive the investment back with accrued interest or half of the appreciation on the property, whichever amount is less. A contribution of $6,000 into this pool has been established by the city as being equivalent to one credit, or one unit of the housing requirement.[66]

The use of these funds to facilitate Section 8 developments may have been the most effective activity so far under the OHPP. Early in 1982, the city realized that it might not be able to take advantage of a substantial number of Section 8 subsidy allocations available to it, because the cost of construction or substantial rehabilitation in San Francisco was considerably higher than the maximum mortgage amounts that HUD would permit under the program. Funds from the OHPP were used, in a number of cases, to bridge the gap between project cost and the maximum mortgage allowed, thereby enabling the city of San Francisco to utilize its full allocation under the Section 8 program prior to the program's demise.[67]

In addition to these activities, funds have been used to finance student housing and privately financed moderate-income housing projects. Based on information provided by the city which is current through the middle of 1983, an impressive total of 2586 units have been constructed or rehabilitated, or in the case of the citywide mortgage pool, made affordable to low- or moderate-income households as a result of the program. A tabulation of these units, by category, is provided in Exhibit 1.

EXHIBIT 1
Low- and Moderate-Income Housing Units Generated
Through the San Francisco OHPP Program

New Construction	**UNITS**
1. Family Section 8 Housing	301
2. Senior Citizen Section 8 Housing	85
3. Student Housing (Hastings School of Law)	282
4. Private Low-/Moderate-Income Housing	39
5. Private Moderate-Income Housing Project	60
6. Private Moderate-Income Housing Project	228*
Rehabilitation	
1. Family Section 8 Housing	82
2. Senior Citizen Section 8 Housing Project	81
3. Senior Citizen Section 8 Housing Project	73
4. Public Housing Rehabilitation (Yerba Buena)	305
5. Public Housing Rehabilitation (Scattersite)	450
Citywide Mortgage Pool	600
Total	2,586

Note: *Tentative: may include mix of market-rate and moderate-income units, with number of moderate-income units to be determined.

Source: City of San Francisco, *OHPP Commitments to Housing Developments*, February 1, 1983. Analysis and classification by the author.

By any frame of reference, this is an impressive record for a program that has been in effect less than two years. One commentator, in his paper on the subject, concludes "clearly, the OHPP has worked."[68] There has been some criticism, however, much of it focused on issues arising from the fact that despite the presence of published guidelines, a great deal of the program continued to be grounded in an *ad hoc* negotiated framework.

Two substantial concerns with implications for other communities entertaining similar programs are first, the disparity in the level of contribution required of different developers; and second, the extent to which the projects carried out are reflective of deals, either between developers, between developers and non-profit organizations, or between developers and the city, rather than being grounded in an overall housing policy or body of priorities. Both concerns are logical outgrowths of the informal negotiating process that characterizes the program.

With the exception of the citywide mortgage pool, where the city established a flat contribution amount per housing credit, the test of the amount that a developer must contribute has been grounded in the fiscal needs of each specific project. If a Section 8 project could be made to work with a cost of $5,000 per Section 8 unit, for each of which a developer receives two credits, that developer will satisfy his obligation for $2500 per unit of housing required under the formula, in contrast to $6000 for those participating in the mortgage pool. The cost per formula unit of one contribution cited by Sedway was $3833.[69] According to Brooks, the level of contribution of some developers participating in Housing Authority rehabilitation projects was as low as $1000 per credit.[70] There are two separate issues involved here: first, the question of fairness and equity in the treatment of different builders; and second, whether the level of contribution is as high as it should be. Local housing advocates have proposed that the contribution be established at $20,000 per credit.[71] On its face, that appears burdensome. Returning to the earlier hypothetical case of a 500,000-square-foot office building with a 440-unit housing requirement, at a cost per unit of $4000 to $6000, which appears representative, the cost impact on the project (assuming development costs in the area of $150 to $175 per square foot) is between 2 and 3.5 percent.[72] A cost of $20,000 per credit would increase the cost to the developer by 10 to 12 percent, a level that is likely to exceed what can be passed on to the office rental market or absorbed within a reasonable profit margin.

The absence of clear-cut priorities is a legitimate issue. It appears that the city staff members responsible have been ambivalent about how active a role to play in the choice of projects. At times, it appears clear that city officials have intervened in directing contributions to specific projects, such as a 400-unit housing development in Hunters Point sponsored by the Redevelopment Agency.[73] At other times, it appears that the city's role was more passive and responsive to proposals initiated by developers or crafted between developers and non-profit organizations. With the exception of the Housing Authority's public housing rehabilitation program,[74] the substance of the projects financed with the contributions (given the premise of the program) have not been seriously criticized. The process, however, and the apparent lack of public participation or accountability in the informal negotiations between developers and city officials, is problematical. In the review of the program now taking place and the drafting of an ordinance for the OHPP, it is likely that the procedure will be tightened, although it is unclear whether that will result in more public participation. Consideration is also being given to having the program administered by an independent third party rather than the city.[75]

A further inconsistency appears between the ostensible premise of the OHPP — that it is a general housing program — and the acknowledged efforts by the program's administrators to target the funds for low- and moderate-income households. Clearly, if the issue is one of adherence to a formula, it would not be impossible to estimate the percentage of downtown San Francisco workers who live in low- and moderate-income households.[76] The issue is not technical, but political or philosophical. The city of San Francisco clearly perceives at least part of their charge being to expand the housing stock generally, while providing some preference through incentives for low- and moderate-income housing. A substantial part of the housing built through the OHPP is not low- and moderate-income housing; Brooks notes that only one-quarter of the units made available through the citywide mortgage pool will be low- and moderate-income households.[77] Given the need to set priorities on such limited resources, it is at least worth serious consideration to limit use of contributions to programs and activities that provide housing affordable to low- and moderate-income households whose needs are demonstrably greater than those of the well-to-do and whose choices are far more limited.

Notwithstanding the above criticism, it is hard to quarrel with the positive conclusions that have been noted above. The program has delivered in a remarkably short period a substantial number of low- and moderate-income housing units, most of which may well not have been produced in the absence of the OHPP. The timing of the program was not only fortunate from the standpoint of the pace of downtown office development, but also from the standpoint of a body of more or less "ready-to-go" housing activities that were being frustrated due to lack of funds. That existing pool of projects, coupled with an energetic and dedicated staff working with apparently strong support from the city's mayor, produced the results that are evident. The degree to which this is replicable, and furthermore, the degree to which San Francisco can sustain the level of activity that characterized the first two years of the OHPP, are open to serious question.

The Future of Downtown Inclusionary Zoning

The search for new revenues for affordable housing development coupled with the success of the San Francisco experiment has prompted the development of similar programs in other communities. By late 1983, serious planning was under way for the establishment of housing trust funds financed through office and commercial developer contributions in Seattle and Boston. In New York, a more ambitious trust fund proposal combining a wide variety of financing sources into a single whole was being developed by a body of civic and academic organizations although it had not yet received formal public support from city or state government.

The proposed Boston and Seattle programs are not unlike the San Francisco OHPP. The Boston program, as proposed, would require a contribution of $5 per square foot paid over a twelve-year period from developments subject to the program. Those would include downtown office and commercial developments larger than 100,000 square feet as well as those large industrial and residential developments resulting directly in a reduction in the supply of low- and moderate-income housing.[78] The program is anticipated to raise between $37 and $52 million over a ten-year period, which funds will be directed through a proposed Neighborhood Housing Trust to expanding the supply of low- and moderate-income housing as well as to related activities in the city's neighborhoods.

While the Boston program calls directly for a fee to be paid by commercial developers to further housing activities, the Seattle program proposes that developers either build "accessory housing," or pay a fee to a housing trust fund in lieu of producing the necessary housing units. The proposed formula is that all downtown office and commercial development would have to provide 300 square feet of housing for every 1,000 square feet of commercial space or contribute a fee of $5 per square foot of commercial space.[79] The targets for use of the funds collected have not been determined with specificity, but city projections estimate that the program could create 4,000 to 5,000 units over the next twenty years principally affordable to moderate-income households.

The two programs are different in underlying purpose. The Seattle program, similar to the San Francisco program, is grounded in the concern for housing pressures triggered by downtown office development. As such, the city believes that the legal authority for the program can be secured through the downtown plan and accompanying land use regulations.[80] The Boston plan, although sharing this concern, is much more of a program to redistribute resources from the Boston CBD to the city's neighborhoods. For that to take place, it is anticipated that state-enabling legislation will be necessary.[81]

The New York City proposal is, as befits that community, far more ambitious. The proposal, which is being developed by a team made up principally of the Pratt Institute Center for Community and Environmental Development and the Queens College Center for Metropolitan Action, is for the creation of a $200 million housing trust fund financed from a wide variety of levies on both commercial and residential developers with additional public sector support. While the proposal includes a number of ingenious approaches to taxing various steps in the development process including real estate transfers, cooperative filing fees, building department fees, and the like,[82] the core of the program lies in the exaction of contributions from commercial developers and in an inclusionary requirement for the developers of luxury residential projects. The funds collected from all sources would be administered by a body under the direct control of the New York City Board of Estimate, would be earmarked for low- and moderate-income housing development and rehabilitation, and would be targeted in a way to ensure that low-income neighborhoods would be the recipients of the greater part of the disbursements from the fund.[83]

A variety of legal and equity issues arise when programs such as the above are considered — issues which have been discussed in the preceding pages. Assuming that the equity issues are resolved and the programs are determined to be legally permissible, economic issues remain. Is it sound economic policy for cities to undertake the sort of redistributional program characterized by the San Francisco OHPP or the proposed New York City trust fund?

One question is that of the effect of these exactions on the production of downtown office buildings in central cities. Although some advocates of these programs tend to make light of this concern,[84] it may not be insignificant. As the San Francisco experience shows, where the market is particularly strong and the excess costs can be readily passed along to tenants, housing trust fund fees will be paid. As the market weakens, the marginal cost of these fees is likely to have a progressively greater impact on the developer's decision to build, potentially resulting in relocation of facilities to other, typically, suburban locations. While in the long run market upturns may bring back development of prime office space, substantial secondary space, such as corporate "back office" facilities, may be permanently lost to central cities. While it may never be possible to establish how much of this space would be lost to the suburbs in any event, it may not be sound policy for a city to impose burdens on projects for which it does not have unique attributes and which are capable of moving elsewhere.

This may be taking place in San Francisco where, according to one writer, secondary office facilities are leaving the city for suburban and satellite city locations.[85] Furthermore, there is evidence that the CBD office market in San Francisco, after a number of boom years, is significantly weakening. Rentals are declining, vacancy rates are rising, and the number and scale of future office projects "in the pipeline" has been substantially reduced.[86] As a result, it appears likely that the future ability of the city to extract funds at the levels of prior years for the OHPP is questionable; as one writer points out, "several developers claim the rule [the OHPP] adds from 2 to 3 percent to overall costs — a small sum in boom times when a tenant may be willing to pay, but an obstacle when the market is less secure."[87] Two to 3 percent may appear trivial from the outside, but it is a substantial amount in a tenants' market, particularly where the CBD office space onto which it has been added is intrinsically more expensive than suburban office space of similar quality. The proposed fee scale in the Seattle program is estimated to add 3 to 5 percent to the cost of development.[88] This can be expected to have similar effects.

In essence, the policy choice becomes one of balancing risks and rewards. In San Francisco, given the degree to which the city is ambivalent about the extent and scale of CBD development, the balancing process may well work in support of the OHPP exactions. It is possible that the city would accept the risk of reduced office development in the future as a fair trade-off for the funds obtained for housing programs, since maximizing CBD development is not necessarily a priority objective of the community. Furthermore, as core cities go, San Francisco is a relatively affluent one without as pressing a need for tax rateables as many less favorably situated communities, such as Boston, for example. Cities in which maximizing tax rateables and employment opportunities through attractive private non-residential investment is a high priority may find that the balancing of risks and rewards from a housing trust fund program financed by commercial development suggests a different conclusion than that of San Francisco.

A variation of this theme which may be appropriate in some cities is to impose the fees only in those parts of the CBD in which the demand for office space is particularly intense or to impose them only in return for a *quid pro quo* such as additional square feet of floor area. In New York City, for example, it might be appropriate to impose the housing trust fund fee only on office developers building within the central areas of lower and midtown Manhattan. These are areas in which there is substantial question whether further maximizing the intensity of development provides more benefits than costs, but in which the demand for office space appears to continue despite high costs and congestion. Thus, the cost disparity might encourage some office development to take place in other areas in Manhattan and in the outer boroughs where the existing intensity of land use can more readily accommodate additional development.

Most of these questions are not likely to arise at all outside of the relatively small number of American cities in which demand for office space is strong enough to support the rent structure dictated by CBD land and construction costs. As a San Francisco Chamber of Commerce official commented, "imagine what Detroit or Cleveland would do for these developers. They'd probably give them tax breaks and bring out the brass band. Here, we try to nail them for the entire city's housing problem." [89] Not only Detroit and Cleveland, but most of the small- and medium-sized cities of the northern and central parts of the United States are desperate for almost any job-generating and taxpaying development that they can attract. These cities are not likely to join a housing trust fund bandwagon, however severe their housing problems may be.

In view of these risks and in view of the importance given by most cities to the fostering of non-residential development, it is unlikely that more than a handful of cities will adopt formal policies or programs similar to the San Francisco OHPP during the coming years. An ongoing pattern of *ad hoc* negotiations for housing contributions between city officials and those developers in need of particular assistance or consideration from local government is likely to be more widespread.

The imposition of inclusionary requirements on center city residential development raises similar questions. The city of San Francisco, which had imposed a conventional inclusionary requirement on residential development some years prior to enactment of their OHPP, subsequently abolished that requirement. It was perceived by local officials that the inclusionary program was acting as yet a further disincentive to development of housing in an environment where, as a result of exceptionally high land and construction costs as well as strict regulations and strong neighborhood pressures, residential development was already exceptionally difficult. [90]

The issue is made still more complex by its relationship to neighborhood change and gentrification. A major objective of the framers of the New York City proposal is the creation of resources that will counteract the effects of gentrification of neighborhoods occupied by low- and moderate-income households, such as the Lower East Side or Clinton.[91] While the entire subject of neighborhood change raises questions far beyond the scope of this book, its link to inclusionary housing programs raises questions. It can be assumed, to begin, that a new residential development in a largely low-income neighborhood will command lower prices than a similar development in a stable upper-income section of the same city. Indeed, unless there is a perception on the part of prospective tenants or purchasers that the character of the low-income neighborhood is likely to change in the future, the development is likely to be unmarketable. Therefore, significant private investment is likely to take place only in low-income neighborhoods, and only in those perceived as likely to change, if the cost of the development is significantly less than the cost of development in the more stable and more affluent areas.[92] If exactions are imposed specifically on luxury developments in such changing neighborhoods, they are likely to reduce or eliminate the cost advantages that make it possible to develop at all in those areas. The effect, in all probability, will not be that money is raised to support low-income housing needs, but that development of luxury housing in changing neighborhoods will be discouraged. From the standpoint of those who advocate the vesting, as it were, of low-income households with rights to their neighborhoods, this may be an equally desirable, or even preferable outcome.[93]

Among central cities, New York City may be unique in its potential ability to impose substantial inclusionary requirements — particularly as a *quid pro quo* for density increases — without severely hindering development activity. Manhattan developers in recent years have shown considerable willingness to make substantial contributions in return for zoning changes or density increases; in one notable example, the developers of the massive Lincoln West project on Manhattan's West Side agreed to a package of developer-financed improvements to city facilities and lower-income housing worth $125 million.[94]

Most older central cities are as desperate to obtain private market residential investment as they are to obtain commercial or office development, and in many cases are even less successful at attracting the former. Rather than being only a matter of tax ratables, residental development is perceived by many cities as essential to their ability to retain a substantial middle class population. It is unlikely that most central cities would be willing to impose an inclusionary requirement on residential development if it meant incurring even a modest risk that some such development would as a result be discouraged. In contrast, most cities offer to the best of their ability and the enabling laws of their state a variety of inducements, including financing, tax abatement, and other support to attract private market residential development.

In conclusion, despite the undeniable success of the San Francisco Office/Housing Production Program, inclusionary zoning is not likely to "move downtown" in most American cities. That minority of central cities in which market demand will tolerate the costs of an inclusionary housing program and which can successfully navigate the complex legal issues associated with those programs in an urban context may find them to be a valuable economic tool. Even there, great care in program design is required to ensure that the program indeed raises funds for lower-income housing and does not act as a barrier to development sought by the community.

NOTES

1. See pages 36-38.

2. The case law on exactions is extensive and shows considerable variation from state to state, particularly in the holdings with regard to the degree that the exaction must be related to the needs generated by the development; the most narrow position is that of the Illinois Supreme Court in *Pioneer Trust and Savings Bank v. Village of Mt. Prospect*, 22 Ill. 2d 375, 176 N.E. 2d 799 (1961), which held that the burden must be "specifically and uniquely attributable to his activity" in order to be permissible; at 802. Many states have adopted broader positions; e.g., Florida, in *Dunedin v. Contractors & Builders Assoc.*, 312 So.2d 767 (1975), upholding sewer and water impact fees; Wisconsin, in *Jordan v. Village of Menominee Falls*, 28 Wis.2d 608, 137 N.W.2d 442 (1966), upholding school and park land dedication requirement or in lieu fee; and California, in a number of cases, notably *Associated Home Builders v. City of Walnut Creek*, 4 Cal.3d 633, 484 P.2d 606 (1971). New Jersey can be considered somewhere in the middle; see note 6 below.

3. In addition to *Menominee Falls* and *Walnut Creek*, above, note also *Jenad, Inc. v. Village of Scarsdale*, 18 N.Y.2d 78, 218 N.E.673, upholding similar requirements. There are, however, a number of cases in which courts have found specific requirements to be excessive despite the general acceptability of such dedication and/or in lieu fee requirements. See *Norsco Enterprises v. City of Fremont*, 54 Cal. App. 3d 488 (1976), and a very recent New York case, *Kamhi v. Town of Yorktown*, decided by the Court of Appeals July 7, 1983. This last case may have significant implications with regard to the potential acceptability of a housing trust fund program in New York courts.

4. E.g., *Dunedin*, see note 2.

5. *Divan Builders, Inc. v. Twp. of Wayne*, 66 NJ 582, 334 A.2d 30 (1975). While upholding the general principle that a developer could be assessed for off-site improvements to storm drainage systems, the court remanded for a further hearing to determine the precise share of the total cost of the improvements that could legally be assessed against the developer.

6. The New Jersey cases appear most notable in their attention to precise measurement of the share of benefit and, therefore, cost associated with a particular development or particular improvement. In addition to *Divan*, noted above, see also *Longridge Builders, Inc. v. Planning Board of Township of Princeton*, 52 NJ 348, 245 A.2d 336 (1968), which held that "assuming off-site improvements could be required of a subdivider, the subdivider could be compelled only to bear that portion of the cost which bears a rational nexus to the needs created by, and the benefits conferred upon, the subdivision." Ibid., at 337. The development of the state of the art of allocating costs and benefits in New Jersey since that time has been considerable. See also *Norsco*, note 3.

7. See Williams, *American Land Planning Law*, Vol. 1, pp. 585-599.

8. The key economic problems are twofold: first, the difficulty of narrowing any secondary economic impact of this nature to a single suburban community; and second, the extremely limited level of job growth associated with the level of incremental consumer demand that can be anticipated from a moderate-size development. See Mallach et al., *Social, Economic & Fiscal Assessment Handbook*, Annapolis, Md. (1976). In any suburban community other than a regional commercial and service center, such as a Paramus, New Jersey, or a King of Prussia, Pennsylvania, the greater part of what limited job impact there will be will take place outside the community.

9. In fact, one could argue that in most cases the opposite would be true, i.e., that the construction of the suburban housing development would increase filtering, thereby benefiting the lower-income housing market. On the other hand, there are some suburban areas in which the cumulative effect of

upper-income housing development has clearly reduced housing opportunities for lower-income households by bringing up the price of the existing housing stock. To link this effect to a particular development would be difficult and unreliable.

10. CAFRA permits for Tannen Towers, Atlantic City, New Jersey; and Ocean Club, Atlantic City, New Jersey.

11. Interviews with John Weingart, New Jersey Division of Coastal Resources; Albert Gardner, developer, Ocean Club.

12. Interview with John Weingart.

13. One can argue whether low- and moderate-income households have benefited more from the employment opportunities created by casino development than they have been harmed by the price escalation, speculation, displacement, and the like also triggered by casino development. There is no question, however, that substantial harm, particularly with regard to lower-income housing opportunities, has occured.

14. *In re Egg Harbor Associates*, 185 NJ Super 507, (1982) affirmed, 94 NJ 358 (1983). While the developer argued that the particular circumstances of his development made the literal application of the CAFRA inclusionary requirement impracticable and raised the issue of exactions, the court was uninterested, commenting without further explanation, "If the 'rational nexus' test of *Brazer* and like cases is to be applied, the required nexus is surely shown here. Given the size and scope of Associates' project, and the stringent limitations on large-scale development of housing in the coastal area, the 'fair share' housing requirement imposed on Associates must be said to be rationally related to the benefits and burdens created by the project itself." Ibid., at 523. This, frankly, makes no sense whatsoever. The court proceeded, however, to make clear that it was not required to reach that conclusion in the context of this particular case.

15. This can be supported either under the law of exactions or under more recent environmental impact law with the requirement that a development mitigate harmful environmental impacts created by the development; e.g., California Environmental Quality Act (CEQA), California Public Resources Code 21000-21174.

16. Thomas Kleven, "Inclusionary Ordinances and the Nexus Issue," paper presented at *Inclusionary Zoning Moves Downtown: A Legal Symposium*, New York, N.Y., November 18, 1983.

17. Ibid., p. 13.

18. See, e.g., testimony by Prof. Frank DeGiovanni, Pratt Institute, to the Mayor's Development Commitment Study Commission, New York, Sept. 22, 1983. Prof. DeGiovanni is part of a group working at Pratt Institute on plans to develop a housing trust fund to be financed largely by developer contributions in New York City.

19. New York City has a long history of providing bonuses in return for developer contributions. New York, in addition, is one of the most liberal states on the law governing contract zoning; see Williams, *American Land Planning Law*, pp. 592-593.

20. City of San Francisco, Office/Housing Production Program (OHPP), *Interim Guidelines for Administering the Housing Requirements Placed on New Office Developments* (San Francisco, January 1983), p. 1.

21. See, e.g., *Hutton Park Gardens et al. v. Town Council of the Town of West Orange et al.*, 68 NJ 543, 350 A.2d 1 at 7.

22. Ann Berger Lesk, "Theater Fund and Housing Trust Fund Issues," paper presented November 18, 1983; see note 16.

23. Interview with William Witte, Mayor's Office of Housing & Development, City of San Francisco.

24. An analogy might be drawn with more typical environmental impact mitigation, i.e., whether it is appropriate to require of a developer that he contribute to a fund that can be used for any of a variety of environmental improvement measures in the community rather than mitigating the specific environmental impacts (air quality, water quality, etc.) associated with the particular development. Few people would argue that environmental mitigation measures are fungible; e.g., that preserving a wetland area in community A substitutes for reducing air pollution in community B. The same is arguably true of housing mitigation measures.

25. There are a variety of public policy issues that arise with regard to the appropriateness of earmarking flows of funds from dedicated taxes; see Ellickson, "Inclusionary Housing Programs: Yet

Another Misguided Urban Policy?'', paper presented November 18, 1983; see note 16, pp. 7-9. His point, in essence, is that dedicating such funds for housing trust funds and the like unfairly removes those funds from the scrutiny and accountability of elected public officials.

26. Ibid., pp. 2-5.

27. Norman Marcus, "Zoning Exactions Employed to Solve Housing Problems," *New York Law Journal*, October 5, 1983. Marcus points out, however, that "once zoning takes to the value recapture high road, what is its obligation when it down-zones, designates landmarks, or otherwise lowers the value of property consistent with constitutional standards?"

28. California Department of Housing & Community Development, *Model Inclusionary Zoning Ordinance*, Section G-1.

29. See Kleven, "Inclusionary Ordinances — Policy and Legal Issues," pp. 5-6. There is some exaction case law where this issue has arisen; e.g., *Norsco Enterprises v. City of Fremont*, note 3, in which a park in lieu fee was found excessive where it exceeded the value of the land that would otherwise have to be dedicated.

30. *Model Inclusionary Zoning Ordinances*, Section G-1.

31. Leaving aside legal issues, this is not necessarily bad from a public policy standpoint. It can reasonably be argued that a developer who is providing lower-income units, particularly in a small-scale development, has intangible costs and burdens over and above the direct subsidy cost. Thus, it is not inappropriate that the direct dollar cost of the in lieu payment be higher.

32. City of Livermore, California, City Council Resolution 17-83, adopted February 14, 1983.

33. City of Livermore, Response to California Department of Housing & Community Development Inclusionary Housing Program Survey, April 1983.

34. Interview with Barbara Hempill, Senior Administrative Assistant, City of Livermore.

35. Letter from Barbara Hempill to Alan Mallach, September 21, 1983.

36. City of Livermore, *General Plan*, as amended August 1982, p. 108.

37. Interview with Barbara Hempill. Under the Section 8 program, households holding certificates are eligible to have their rents subsidized by HUD; certificates can be used only in units whose rents are at or below the fair market rents for the type of unit and geographic area determined by HUD. Typically, in well-to-do suburban areas, rent levels are often well above the fair market rent level, thus making it impossible for low-income households to utilize the certificates, even when they are made available.

38. Ibid. The Livermore Housing Authority has an allocation of Section 8 certificates available for this project.

39. This information was extracted by the author from his review of responses to a spring 1983 Inclusionary Housing Program Survey of the California Department of Housing & Community Development. Other jurisdictions with provisions for in lieu fees included Corte Madera, Del Mar (including condominium conversions), Fairfax, Long Beach (housing replacement policy), Marin County, Novato, Palo Alto, Pleasanton, and Santa Clara County. Transfer credit provisions were in effect in Orange County and Santa Cruz County.

40. Interview with Ruth Schwartz, California Department of Housing & Community Development.

41. Interview with Marilyn Zatz and Valerie Glassford, Palo Alto Housing Corporation.

42. E.g., *New York Times*, July 11, 1983, "'It is clear that my board wants the funds to stay here,'" said Edith Fisher of the Upper East Side's Community Board 8, which has pressed developers to aid the neighborhood's elderly poor. "'What you have . . . under these proposals is taxation without representation, because we would be paying the high price of extra density without an appropriate return.'"

43. Schwartz, Johnston & Burtraw, *Local Government Initiatives*, p. 25.

44. The Orange County program was designed to apply only within those Community Analysis Areas (CAAs) within the county in which county staff had determined that less than 25 percent of the existing housing stock was affordable. Developers within areas already meeting that criterion were not required to participate in the inclusionary program.

45. Orange County, California, *Inclusionary Housing Program Assessment*, November 1982.

46. This is almost a perfect example of the "invisible hand" at work. The more onerous the inclusionary requirement, the more certain builders will pay to be rid of it. The amount they pay should consistently be enough, except in extreme cases, to provide an incentive for developers oriented toward affordable housing to meet the inclusionary requirements.

47. Schwartz, Johnston & Burtraw, *Local Government Initiatives*, pp. 34-36.

48. Ibid., p. 32.

49. During the three-year period studied, 1100 transfer credits were transferred within CAAs and 263 between CAAs. Orange County, *Inclusionary Housing Program*.

50. According to information provided by the California Department of Housing & Community Development, a transfer credit program is in effect as well in Santa Cruz County, California. It was not possible to obtain information on its effectiveness or results.

51. Orange County, *Inclusionary Housing Program*.

52. In addition to the obvious direct costs of holding onto unsold credits, which may easily mean that the developer is carrying losses over an extended period, is the added risk that the program will be abolished or modified as a result of political or other changes in the jurisdiction. The Orange County program is now being phased out; the inclusionary requirement has been substantially reduced, and as a result, it is likely that the value of credits has also changed.

53. The author would like to acknowledge his borrowing of this title from the symposium organized by Paul Davidoff, director of the Metropolitan Action Institute at Queens College, New York.

54. Mary Brooks, "Lessons to Learn from Inclusionary Zoning," paper presented November 18, 1983; see note 16. Other communities noted as entertaining similar programs in this paper are Chicago, Hartford, and Denver. It should be noted as well that the mayor of Boston, Raymond Flynn, included in his campaign platform a pledge to initiate such a program.

55. A distinction should be noted. This is the only *program* in effect at present; there have been, however, a number of individual cases where municipalities have extracted contributions for housing from non-residential developers on an ad hoc basis.

56. See Mary Brooks, "The San Francisco Office/Housing Production Program," unpublished ms., August 1983, p. 1. This paper is an excellent source for more detailed information and a preliminary critical assessment of this program.

57. Marshall Kilduff, "San Francisco's Novel Scheme to Provide Affordable Housing," *California Journal*, May 1982, p. 169.

58. Ibid., p. 170.

59. Paul Sedway, "Presentation on the San Francisco Office Housing Production Program," paper presented November 18, 1983; see note 16, p. 2.

60. The CEQA language explicitly required public agencies to "consider the effects of projects on housing and a satisfying living environment," quoted in Sedway, "San Francisco Program," p. 2. Kilduf, "San Francisco's Scheme," comments that "suspicious developers feel the formula is so much city hall mumbo-jumbo, cooked up to squeeze them." Given the California courts' traditional deference to municipal action, however, it is likely that the program would have stood up to challenge. The economies of large-scale office development, furthermore, make it even harder for a developer to go to court over anything short of a total denial of a project than is the case with residential developers. If the market can support the added cost, they grit their teeth and pay it, whatever their lawyers' advice may be.

61. Brooks, "San Francisco," p. 2. Also interview with William Witte, City of San Francisco. Brooks comments without elaboration that there is considerable disagreement with the city attorney's conclusion that CEQA can no longer be relied upon as the legal basis for the program.

62. City of San Francisco, *Guidelines*, p. 5.

63. Ibid., pp. 9-10. Low income is defined as under 80 percent of the median income for the SMSA, and moderate income between 80 and 120 percent of the median income for the SMSA.

64. City of San Francisco, *OHPP Commitments to Housing Developments*, February 1, 1983.

65. Ibid., interview with William Witte.

66. Brooks, "San Francisco," pp. 6-7; also City of San Francisco, *Citywide Affordable Housing Program*, January 6, 1982.

67. Interview with William Witte.

68. Sedway, "San Francisco Program," p. 7.

69. Ibid., p. 6.

70. Brooks, "San Francisco," p. 13. This appears to be inconsistent with information provided by the city, which indicates that the cost per credit in the housing authority program varied from $2200 to $4000.

71. Ibid., p.13.

72. This is consistent with statements in Kilduff, "San Francisco's Scheme," who cites "several developers" as indicating that the cost of the OHPP adds "from two to three percent to overall costs."

73. Ibid., p. 170, Brooks, "San Francisco," p. 14.

74. Brooks, "San Francisco," p. 12. The comment on the housing authority program is worth quoting: "The San Francisco Housing Authority is apparently faced with serious rehabilitation problems with something like 1,000 units vacant at any point in time because of disrepair . . . . According to housing advocates, the entire OHPP could be taken up on rehabilitation activities of the Housing Authority, and would have to be repeated again in another year because of the inability of the Housing Authority to maintain the units. This was a 'cheap' option for the developer and one that was, reportedly, very popular with the Mayor of San Francisco. It has been criticized because it essentially undermines the basis for establishing the OHPP (regardless of the vast need for improved public housing in San Francisco) and has not been in much use recently as an option."

75. Ibid., p. 13.

76. Brooks, p. 13, cites a study that established that 60 percent of office workers in San Francisco make $24,000 or less annually, which is 80 percent, roughly, of the area median income. While this is not household income, some translation from the one to the other is methodologically possible.

77. Ibid., p. 13.

78. Brooks, "Lessons," p. 10.

79. Ibid., p. 11.

80. Ibid., p. 10.

81. Ibid., p. 10. The conflict between the neighborhoods and downtown over development priorities and the allocation of resources is perhaps the most volatile political issue in Boston today; indeed, both recently elected Mayor Flynn and his principal opponent in the election made the redirection of priorities and resources to the neighborhoods a central theme of their campaigns. This context strongly colors the proposed Boston housing trust fund proposal and raises many questions about how it is to be carried out, should it be enacted into law.

82. Testimony of Ron Shiffman, Director, Pratt Institute Center for Community and Environmental Development, to the Mayor's Development Commitment Study Commission, September 22, 1983, p. 3.

83. Ibid., p. 5.

84. An example of this occurs in the testimony of Prof. DeGiovianni, note 18. In response to one of a series of potential objections, "a surcharge on office development will stifle growth," he comments, "This didn't happen in San Francisco . . . In San Francisco, the impact of the $1/square foot/year cost to developers is equal to less than 2 % of new office rents." Given the short time period that the San Francisco OHPP has been in existence, this conclusion is at best premature, if not clearly irresponsible. It is important to note as well that a substantial number of the projects that have contributed to the San Francisco program were "in the pipeline" before the program was enacted.

85. Kilduff, "San Francisco's Scheme," p. 170.

86. See, "Office Market Outlook: San Francisco," *National Real Estate Investor*, June 1983, pp. 56-58.

87. Kilduff, "San Francisco's Scheme," p. 170.

88. Brooks, "Lessons," p. 11.

89. Quoted in Kilduff, "San Francisco's Scheme," p. 170.

90. Interview with William Witte.

91. Testimony by Phil Tegeler, Queens College Center for Metropolitan Action, to the Mayor's Department Commitment Study Commission, September 23, 1983.

92. Indeed, in most cities in which "gentrification" has taken place, the first wave of change has been the outcome of individual decisions by homebuyers to rehabilitate their units sometimes coupled with public sector support, but with large-scale private investment notably absent. Private investment, in the form of large-scale residential development, has typically lagged many years behind the initial changes in such neighborhoods, except where enticed by public sector assistance, guarantees, or subsidies. The character of the housing market, as well as the physical fabric in Manhattan, however, makes it an exception to this general rule.

93. Even when one is concerned about the effects of neighborhood change on low-income and minority households, one may still find some of the propositions of their advocates troubling; the notion, which appears in Tegeler's testimony, note 91, and elsewhere, that a particular population, de-

fined by income or ethnicity, has a "right" in perpetuity to a neighborhood, which right is to be protected with the police power, raises serious questions.

94. Estimate by city officials cited in, "A Citywide Fund to Aid Housing is Being Studied," *New York Times*, July 11, 1983.

8

The Present and Future State of Inclusionary Housing Programs

Each chapter in this book has sought to present a different facet of inclusionary housing programs, so that the reader will have a clear picture of both the underlying issues and the technical features of this particular means of providing lower-income housing opportunities. At this point, therefore, it is appropriate to turn to the actual experience of municipalities and counties around the United States with inclusionary housing programs. The object of this chapter is first, to provide an overview of that experience; and second, to speculate on the future of inclusionary housing programs. Of particular importance in the latter regard is the future of programs in New Jersey in light of the mandate for inclusionary housing programs provided by the *Mount Laurel II* decision. A section of this chapter is devoted to a description and assessment of the initial steps that have been taken in that direction in New Jersey since the *Mount Laurel II* decision was issued in January 1983.

No effort is made in this chapter to present a comprehensive or complete survey of all inclusionary housing programs in the United States in all their complexity and dimensions.[1] The only area in which some effort has been made to provide a complete picture is the state of California, which is the only state in which programs have been widespread enough and extant for long enough so that an overview can have some significance. Elsewhere, programs are scattered widely, are generally located in small jurisidictions, and are of modest scale — the most notable exception being that of Montgomery County, Maryland. In New Jersey prior to the *Mount Laurel II* decision, although there were at least thirteen programs in place, none was of a scale or character justifying detailed attention.

The first section of this chapter deals with the California experience followed by a short survey of inclusionary housing program activities in other states. The third section is devoted to the New Jersey experience, particularly with regard to the post-*Mount Laurel II* directions now emerging, and is followed by a closing section in which an attempt is made to see into the future.

The California Experience with Inclusionary Housing Programs

Although no effort was made in conducting the research for this book to arrive at a definitive list of inclusionary housing programs, in the course of the research that was conducted, a total of seventy-two separate programs were identified. Of these, thirty-eight were in California, or more than half of all of the inclusionary housing programs in the United States.[2] Indeed, a casual reader of the literature on the subject could easily get the impression that such programs are limited to California in view of the degree to which that state's activities have attracted national attention. California is clearly the only state for the moment in which inclusionary housing programs are widely enough diffused to be a major part of the regulatory landscape; nearly all of the programs which have achieved significant levels of housing production are located in California. Furthermore, the levels of production achieved are significant. It is estimated that by 1983, the total of units built, under construction, or committed for development attributable to inclusionary housing programs in California is nearly 20,000 units. It is unlikely that more than a handful of these units would have been built, or if built would have been affordable to low- and moderate-income households, in the absence of inclusionary programs.

That the program should have had so much greater an impact in California than elsewhere is not coincidental. It is, rather, the result of three closely related factors: first, the severity of the affordability crisis in California, compared to most other parts of the United States;[3] second, the enactment of a body of state law mandating local action to further lower-income housing opportunity and which is supportive of inclusionary housing programs; and third, the commitment over an extended period by state government, especially by staff members of the California Department of Housing & Community Development, to the inclusionary housing program approach and their energetic advocacy of the idea around the state.

The affordability crisis has already been noted; indeed, in the opening of the California Housing Program, the authors observe, "housing costs in California have increased dramatically since 1970. The median value of a home in California in 1981 increased by 300%, while gross rents increased by 158%. During the same period, incomes increased by 139%."[4] This plan, which sets forth an energetic agenda for state action in housing, is an outgrowth of the legislative and executive priority given housing in California in the late 1970s and early 1980s.[5]

During this period, legislation was enacted requiring municipalities and counties to adopt five-year plans to meet low- and moderate-income housing needs,[6] plan to meet regional "fair share" goals of low- and moderate-income housing as set forth by regional councils of government,[7] zone land for housing that could be built at the "least possible cost,"[8] provide coordinated processing of residential development applications,[9] and provide density bonuses and other incentives to developers providing 25 percent or more of the units in a development as low- or moderate-income housing.[10]

These new laws were vigorously promoted by the Department of Housing & Community Development (HCD). The guidelines adopted by the Department to implement the housing element provisions of the law, Sec. 65580 *et seq.*, were considered particularly strong and were the subject of considerable controversy.[11] HCD activity advocated the use of inclusionary housing programs as a means of achieving the objectives of the new statutes and disseminated widely a model inclusionary ordinance as well as legal opinions prepared by staff counsel affirming the legality of inclusionary programs in general, and deed restrictions in particular.[12] Staff counsel to the department at the time, Carolyn Burton, who was a leading figure in the development of HCD positions and policies, independently published an article strongly advocating the adoption of inclusionary housing programs.[13]

During the 1970s other state agencies with direct regulatory and enforcement powers, which HCD did not have, implemented inclusionary housing programs, often under pressure from or with the strong support of the department. Particularly notable in this regard was the California Coastal Commission, the body created along with a series of regional coastal commissions initially as a result of a ballot initiative in 1972, Proposition 20, and more permanently institutionalized as a result of the enactment of the California Coastal Act in 1976.[14] This act included strong language dealing with low- and moderate-income housing:

> Housing opportunities for persons of low and moderate income shall be protected, encouraged, and, where feasible, provided. . . . New housing in the coastal zone shall be developed in conformity with the standards, policies, and goals of local housing elements adopted in accordance with the requirement of Subdivision(c) of Section 65302 of the Government Code.[15]

The Commission interpreted this mandate broadly and adopted guidelines providing for an ambitious inclusionary housing program affecting residential development within the coastal zone. A goal that 25 percent of the units in new development were to be housing affordable to low- and moderate-income housing was established; the guidelines provided, however, for considerable flexibility in interpretation of the goal, allowing construction of units off-site, payment of in lieu fees, as well as adjustments based on findings of economic infeasibility.[16]

While there is little doubt that the Coastal Commission was able to generate a substantial number of affordable housing units, implementing the Commission's goals was made difficult by the strains of the state/local interaction associated with the program. While the commission could mandate the provision of lower-income housing, it could not offer developers any assistance or incentives to do so, nor could it ensure that zoning provisions permitted efficient development. Such matters were solely within the purview of local government. The most the commission could do was encourage local government to support its efforts. In some cases, such as in Orange County, this was often successful, but in many cases it was not. A similar problem arose with regard to the payment of in lieu fees. The commission could allow a developer to pay a fee in lieu of producing housing units, but since it was not a housing agency it could not accept the fees directly. The developer was responsible for finding an appropriate agency which would accept the fee and commit to use it in a manner designed to produce affordable housing. This, too, often made it difficult to carry out the commission mandate.[17]

The tensions associated with the Coastal Commission's definition of its housing responsibilities and its conduct of its affairs according to that definition as well as those intrinsic to the state/local relationships involved, led to the enactment of state legislation in 1981 stripping the commission of those responsibilities and giving local government the responsibility to ensure provision of affordable housing in the coastal zone.[18] While the 1981 act did not ostensibly modify the state's *policy* with regard to affordable housing in the coastal zone, the simple act of decentralizing enforcement of the policy among dozens of separate and generally small jurisdictions could be expected to reduce the effectiveness of policy enforcement. An evaluation study prepared for the Department of Housing & Community Development confirmed that this was indeed taking place.[19] Given the dramatic reduction in pressure and direction from the state that has taken place, the future of coastal housing policies is very much in question.

A further state agency which has taken actions in support of inclusionary housing programs has been the California Air Resources Board (ARB). On a number of occasions in Orange County between 1977 and 1979, the ARB has required inclusion of low- and moderate-income housing as a condition of approval.[20] The rationale for the requirement was that it was necessary to mitigate the negative impacts on air quality resulting from excessive commuting by workers, which in turn was a by-product of the absence of affordable housing in Orange County, an area of dramatic employment growth during the 1970s. The specific affordable housing features in each project were negotiated between the developer and the ARB with the assistance of HCD on a case-by-case basis. No formal guidelines other than statements of general policy were adopted, and the

program was discontinued after Orange County implemented its own inclusionary housing program in 1979.[21]

Although the activism of the state agencies undoubtedly contributed to the
climate in which inclusionary housing programs proliferated at the local level, it
would be unreasonable to characterize local actions as no more than a response to
state-level pressures. As exemplified by the wave of state housing legislation, the
feeling that affirmative steps were needed to respond to the burgeoning housing
crisis was widespread. In 1976, for example, in Orange County the Board of
Supervisors created a Housing Task Force "to examine possible solutions for
meeting housing needs in Southeast Orange County."[22] This task force submitted an extensive report in mid-1977, including among its recommendations a
proposal that an inclusionary housing program be considered in Orange
County.[23] Similar activity was taking place elsewhere, concentrated principally
in the two major growth regions of the state, Southern California and the San
Francisco Bay Area. The enactment of inclusionary housing programs by local
government was fueled, more than anything else, by a widely held conviction
that housing affordability was a major problem affecting a substantial part of the
area population and that the inclusionary approach was a rational way in which to
address the problem.

Exhibit 1 presents a survey of local inclusionary housing programs in California, compiled by the author with substantial assistance from materials gathered
by the Department of Housing & Community Development. The survey covers
the programs in effect in thirty-one different counties and municipalities, which
would appear to be the great majority of such programs around the state.

Although common themes and patterns appear, as shown in Exhibit 2, the diversity of standards and conditions within the common ground of the underlying
program approach is considerable. It would appear that the model inclusionary
zoning ordinance distributed by the Department of Housing & Community Development has not been closely adhered to, although specific features of local ordinances may show its influence. Certain key patterns that can be discerned include:

- There is no consensus regarding the appropriate percentage of lower-income
  units to be required, although nearly all communities fall within a range between 10 and 25 percent;
- There is also no consensus regarding the income groups in the population to be
  served; some programs target all units toward the low-income population, and
  some have no income conditions at all for occupancy, only price limitations;
- Slightly more than half of the communities allow developers some alternative
  to constructing lower-income units; in most cases the favored alternative is a
  payment to the municipality in lieu of producing units;
- The great majority of communities impose resale controls on the units pro-

EXHIBIT 1
Survey of California Inclusionary Housing Programs[1]
Part 1

Municipality	Program Requirements	Alternatives Offered	Income and Price Definition	Occupancy and Affordability Controls
Avalon	20% of developments over 5 DU (dwelling units)	None	Standard Income[2] Price ≤ 2.5 times median income	Price may not exceed 2.5 times median as adjusted by HUD
Chula Vista	10% of developments over 50 DU (larger percentages encouraged)	None	Standard Income	Resale controls negotiated on case-by-case basis
Corte Madera	10%-15% of developments over 10 DU depending on density	1. Offsite provision of units 2. Payment of fee in lieu of production	Standard Income	20-year deed restriction with price controls (see Marin Co.)
Cupertino	10% of developments over 10 DU and 6 DU/acre density	None	80-120% of median and asset limit	Resale controls in effect for 50 years with city option to extend 50 more years

EXHIBIT 1 – Part 1 (Cont.)

Municipality	Program Requirements	Alternatives Offered	Income and Price Definition	Occupancy and Affordability Controls
Davis	No fixed percentage. Targets keyed to growth control ordinance "points", up to maximum of 1/3 low-price and 1/3 moderate-price units	None	No income standard. Price standard in 1983 as follows: House: LOW-<$60,000 MOD-$60-$82,000 Condo: LOW-<$55,000 MOD-$55-$67,000	Two-year owner occupancy requirement. No resale controls.
Del Mar	10% low income in all developments	Payment of in lieu fee	Section 8 limits	Deed restriction in perpetuity
Fairfax	Same as Corte Madera	Same as Corte Madera	Standard Income	Same as Marin County
Irvine	Planning targets set for each section generally 10% moderate income with variable low income percentage[3]	None	Standard Income sales price 3× income, rental at 30% of income	1-year occupancy requirement; no resale controls

EXHIBIT 1 – Part 1 (Cont.)

Municipality	Program Requirements	Alternatives Offered	Income and Price Definition	Occupancy and Affordability Controls
Livermore	10% low income in developments over 5 DU	Payment of in lieu fee @ $833/DU (1984)[4]	Under 80% median	None
Los Angeles	15% (6% low and 9% moderate) of developments over 5 DU	None	LOW 0-50% median MOD 50-80% med.	Deed restriction with right of 1st refusal to city
Los Gatos	10% moderate income in all developments	None	80-120% median	Deed restriction and price control on resale
Marin County	All developments over 10 DU with density≤6 DU an acre, 10% moderate income; ≤ 6 DU an acre, 15% moderate income	Payment of in lieu fee	80-120% median	Deed restriction with price limited to lower of increase in 1. price index; 2. median income; 3. market value
Monterrey	15% moderate income in developments over 10 DU	None	0-120% median price 3x income (at present from $72,000-$99,000)	Deed restriction with resale price controls

EXHIBIT 1 – Part 1 (Cont.)

Municipality	Program Requirements	Alternatives Offered	Income and Price Definition	Occupancy and Affordability Controls
Napa	Voluntary density bonus program	None	NA	Resale controls through contract
Nevada County	Voluntary density bonus to provide 25% of lots for low- and moderate-income units	None	0-120% median	Planned but not yet established
Novato	1. Some zones mandatory 20% (5% low and 15% moderate) 2. Other areas voluntary program up to 15%	Payment of in lieu fee	Standard Income Price to be affordable to low income @ 25% income, mod. income @ 30%	City right of 1st refusal for 30-year period
Orange County	25% requirement in developments over 5 DUs in selected[5] areas	Transfer credit program	LOW 0-80% median MOD 1 80-100% MOD 2 100-120%	20-year deed restriction with right of 1st refusal on some units; other controls on other units

EXHIBIT 1 – Part 1 (Cont.)

Municipality	Program Requirements	Alternatives Offered	Income and Price Definition	Occupancy and Affordability Controls
Palm Springs	Voluntary program with density bonus	NA	No income standard Price range from $43,950 to $75,950	Covenant on resale with resale price control tied to CPI increase
Palo Alto	10% moderate income in developments over 10 DU	Payment of in lieu fee only at city option	80-120% median and asset limits	30-year rolling[6] deed restriction with resale price control and right of first refusal
Petaluma	Target of 10-15% keyed to "points", in growth control ordinance	1. Donation of land 2. Payment of in lieu fee	VERY LOW 0-50% LOW 50-80% median MOD 80-120% median	No occupancy or affordability controls
Pleasanton	25% of developments over 4 DU/ tied to growth controls	Payment of in lieu fee	NA	No occupancy or affordability controls
San Diego City	25% density bonus for 20% of units affordable to low income renters or moderate income buyers	None	See Petaluma/rents May not exceed 30% of income or 90% of market rents	Resale controls not specified

EXHIBIT 1 – Part 1 (Cont.)

Municipality	Program Requirements	Alternatives Offered	Income and Price Definition	Occupancy and Affordability Controls
San Diego County	20% density bonus for 15% of units for lower-income households	Option to provide lower income units on other site	Income standards not specified	Rental units must be reserved for lower income occupancy for 'useful life of structure'
San Francisco	Housing requirement for office/commercial developers over 50,000 square feet area	Payment of in lieu fee as determined by city	Varies with nature of project	Varies with nature of project
Santa Clara County	10% LM income in subdivisions over 10 DU with 10% density bonus	1. Deed lots to county 2. Payment of in lieu fee	NA	Not yet established
Santa Cruz City	15% of developments over 10 DU bonus to increase to maximum of 25%	1. combined site (off-site development) option 2. Transfer credit program	Standard Income with asset limit	Resale control with city right of 1st refusal for 30-year period
Santa Cruz County	15% of development over 5 DU	Transfer credit program	Standard Income	30-year resale deed restriction

EXHIBIT 1 – Part 1 (Cont.)

Municipality	Program Requirements	Alternatives Offered	Income and Price Definition	Occupancy and Affordability Controls
Santa Maria	10-15% requirement imposed on general plan amendments	None	80-120% median	NA
Santa Monica[7]	.25-.3 LM income per 1 market unit in all MF projects	Payment of in lieu fee	Subcategories in 0-120% median range to be established to reflect city distribution	Occupancy and affordability controls to be devised
Sunnyvale	10% of developments over 10 DU	None	80-130% median/price range from $34,717 (studio) to maximum of $90,486 (3+ bedroom unit)	Deed restrictions with resale price control and right of 1st refusal
Tiburon	Negotiated % in developments over 10 DU as condition of plan approval	Payment of in lieu fee	80-120% median	20-year deed restrictions

EXHIBIT 1
Survey of California Inclusionary Housing Programs
Part 2

Municipality	Priority Categories	Program Results	Incentives and Other Program Features
Avalon	NA	2 units built 7 committed	Avalon has special program under which hotels must provide rental units for lower-income employees
Chula Vista	None	235 committed	
Corte Madera	1. People working or renting in city; 2. People working or renting in Marin County	6 built 43 committed	For each two moderate-income units required, a developer may substitute one low-income unit
Cupertino	Priority for families with wage earner in Cupertino sphere of influence[8]	8 built 110 committed	City will expedite processing of inclusionary developments, and provide infrastructure and other assistance to developers who provide more than 10% of the units for LM income
Davis	None	93 built 284 committed	City is at present considering establishing income standards for program and lower sales price levels
Del Mar	None	None	1. City has accumulated $100,000-$150,000 in unspent in lieu fees paid by developers 2. City also has 10%-20% inclusionary requirement for condominium conversions

EXHIBIT 1 – Part 2 (Cont.)

Municipality	Priority Categories	Program Results	Incentives and Other Program Features
Fairfax	NA	3 units committed	
Irvine	1. Primary wage earner employed in Irvine 2. Secondary wage earner employed in Irvine 3. All others	975 low-income and 1,493 moderate-income units built; 590 low- and 545 moderate-income units proposed[9]	1. City offers various incentives, including priority processing, fee waivers, reduction of parking area and park dedication requirements; 2. City also has carried out large-scale Section 8 New Construction program, using CDBG funds for land acquisition
Livermore	None	30 built 50 committed	City has accumulated $180,000 from in lieu fees; 1st project (20 units) to use funds from this source in planning stages
Los Angeles	NA	400 units built	Program applies only where federal subsidies are available; units built have used Sec.8 and Sec.235 financing
Los Gatos	NA	4 built 8 committed	
Marin County	NA	14 built 47 committed	County has accumulated $450,000 from in lieu fees by developers

EXHIBIT 1 – Part 2 (Cont.)

Municipality	Priority Categories	Program Results	Incentives and Other Program Features
Monterrey	Priority for Monterrey residents	60 committed	
Napa	NA	NA	NA
Nevada County	NA	None to date	
Novato	Extensive priority ranking system (similar to Tiburon)	375 committed	City has accumulated $400,000 from in lieu fees paid by developers
Orange County	None	2,122 units built and 3,655 committed	1. County offers many incentives, including priority processing, reduced standards and requirements, and use of CDBG funds 2. County has issued over $200 million in tax-exempt bonds to support the program 3. Program is at present being phased out as a result of political changes and pressures
Palm Springs	NA	361 built 694 committed	Program is characterized by city as "middle income" program

EXHIBIT 1 – Part 2 (Cont.)

Municipality	Priority Categories	Program Results	Incentives and Other Program Features
Palo Alto	Families who live or work in city	65 built 40 committed	1. City sees inclusionary program as only one part of housing program; has ambitious Sec.8 and rehabilitation programs for low-income households 2. Program is excellent example of cooperation between city government and strong nonprofit corporation
Petaluma	None	456 units built 391 under construction or in planning: VERY LOW 26 LOW INC. 114 MOD INC. 176 UNSPEC. 75 TOTAL 391	Developers receive points under growth control ordinance for provision of low- and moderate-income housing; more points are offered for lower-income categories (very low/low)
Pleasanton	None	NA	
San Diego City	NA	14 built 176 committed	Developers receive a further bonus for providing "very low income" units, or for providing low-income units in upper income area
San Diego County	NA	NA	All lower-income units must be rental units

EXHIBIT 1 – Part 2 (Cont.)

Municipality	Priority Categories	Program Results	Incentives and Other Program Features
San Francisco	Varies with nature of project	2,586 units built, under construction, or committed[10]	City targets funds from office developers to various programs; Sec. 8, public housing rehabilitation, and a shared appreciation mortgage fund. See detailed discussion in chapter seven.
Santa Clara County	NA	None to date	County has $5,000 in fund from in lieu fees paid by developers
Santa Cruz City	None	121 units built	1. 120 of units built to date used Section 8 subsidies 2. City requires that any rental units must be low-income units
Santa Cruz County	None	162 units built "several hundred units" committed	County uses tax-exempt mortgage revenue bonds in support of inclusionary program
Santa Maria	None	66 approved	City participates in county tax-exempt revenue bond program
Santa Monica	NA	None to date	Santa Monica has generated some low- and moderate-income units through contributions by non-residential developers. This program is now in litigation.

EXHIBIT 1 – Part 2 (Cont.)

Municipality	Priority Categories	Program Results	Incentives and Other Program Features
Sunnyvale	Families who live or work in city	5 built 300 committed	City offers 15% density bonus
Tiburon	1. Elderly and handicapped 2. City workers 3. Long-term city residents 4. Families with children 5. People locally employed	114 built 20 committed	

NOTES:

1. Municipalities in California noted in references as having inclusionary programs, but not shown on table owing to lack of information, including Moraga, Morgan Hill, Oakland (for elderly only), Santa Rosa, Saratoga (elderly only), and Simi Valley (mobile homes only).

2. "Standard Income" on survey tables refers to municipalities that apply the (California) standard income definition of 0-80% of area median for low-income, and 80-120% of area median for moderate-income households.

3. Irvine has imposed a 5% low-income requirement in one section of the city, and a 10% low-income requirement in another. Most sections do not have a low-income requirement, although they may include low-income units under the city Section 8 program.

4. This figure refers to the fee per unit in the development, not per low- and moderate-income unit waived.

5. Orange County program applied only to areas in which county planners had determined that under 25% of the existing housing stock was "affordable."

6. A rolling restriction is one in which the time period begins anew with each resale, rather than representing a fixed period dating from the initial transaction. This was recently reduced in Palo Alto from a 59-year rolling period.

7. The provisions given for Santa Monica represent policy positions adopted by the city, which are at present being incorporated into an ordinance to be adopted in the near future.

8. The "sphere of influence" of a city, under California law, includes that city as well as whatever unincorporated area adjacent to that city is anticipated to be annexed by the city in the foreseeable future.

9. Totals include units provided through the Irvine Section 8 program, which are integrated into mixed-income neighborhoods in an appropriately inclusionary manner.

10. Total includes only the low- and moderate-income units generated by the San Francisco program; the program has also generated a modest number of more expensive units, which are an available option (although discouraged by city officials) for developers under the program.

Source: The principal source for the majority of the information in this survey is an unpublished survey by the California Department of Housing & Community Development, conducted in Spring 1983. This information was supplemented by a survey by the author, interviews by the author in a number of California jurisdictions, and written material provided by certain jurisdictions. The author is solely responsible for the interpretation and classification of the data that appears in this survey, and for any errors of fact or interpretation that appear therein.

EXHIBIT 2
Summary of Features of California
Inclusionary Housing Programs

1. *Target percentage of lower-income units*
10%	8
15%	5
20%	3
25%	3
Variable between 10% and 20%	6
Variable on other basis/negotiated	6

2. *Alternatives offered to inclusion of lower-income units*
Payment of in lieu fee	9*
Transfer of credits	2
Off-site development of units	1
Payment or off-site development	2
Payment or donation of land	2
Transfer of credits or off-site development	1
NONE	13

3. *Controls on future occupancy and affordability*
Resale controls	21
Minimum term of initial owner occupancy	2
No controls	3†

4. *Duration of controls*
1-2 years (initial occupancy)	2
20 years	3
30 years	3
Over 30 years	4

5. *Occupancy preference*
Work in community/area	2
Work or live in community/area	3
Live in community/area	1
Other priority rankings	2
NONE	10

Notes: *In two cases allowed only at option of municipality, not at developer's option
†Four additional municipalities indicated that, although they did not have provisions in place, they were going to establish resale controls in the near future.

Source: Survey of California Inclusionary Housing Program

duced under their inclusionary housing programs; where information is avai_-
able on the duration of resale controls, it appears that most municipalities seek
to have controls extended far into the future.
- Most communities do not establish priority categories for local employees
  and/or residents, although a substantial minority of the jurisdictions do so.

These points suggest the diversity of programs to be found among California
jurisdictions. That in turn — particularly the range of target populations — reflects the differences in underlying housing policy. The jurisdictions tend to fal_
into three general categories: communities which seek to benefit a *low*-income
population exclusively (Los Angeles, Livermore); communities which seek to
benefit a *moderate*-income population, largely or exclusively (Cupertino, Monterrey, Marin County); and those with no income standard or standards that vary
from project to project. These distinctions do not always reflect true policy differences; in some communities, the inclusionary program is the sole vehicle for
affordable housing, and in others, it is but one of a number of means by which
housing for lower-income households is produced. Two of the latter type, Irvine
and Palo Alto, have ambitious low-income housing programs that are separate
from their inclusionary housing programs.

Still, it is clear that what is counted as an "affordable" unit in one community
varies widely from what is considered such a unit in another. The Monterrey program permits units selling for up to $99,000 to be considered affordable to mod-
erate-income households, a price level which is three times the ceiling income for
the moderate-income category. In contrast, at least a few communities have directed serious efforts toward providing housing for low-income households; only
a few, however, have designed programs so that the needs of low-income households (80 percent or less of the area median income) are addressed where federal
or state subsidy funds are unavailable. There is widespread sentiment that this is
not feasible, particularly in areas of high land and improvement costs. A demonstration project in Orange County, however, utilizing tax-exempt mortgage
bonds from the county and benefiting from lower than usual land costs but receiving no other subsidies or assistance, was able to provide a substantial number
of units affordable to low-income households.[24]

Perhaps because of this diversity of objective, which tends to reflect local concerns and priorities, substantial numbers of housing units are emerging from
California's inclusionary housing programs. Allowing for a limited amount of
interpretation, a summary of the numbers from the survey indicates that some
7,000 to 7,500 units have been constructed under these programs and an additional 9,500 to 10,000 committed,[25] for a grand total of over 17,000 units. This
includes some, but most probably a small part, of the roughly 2,000 units of low-
and moderate-income housing that have been built or committed through the pro-

EXHIBIT 3
Year of Enactment of California
Inclusionary Housing Programs

1971 to 1974	4
1975 to 1978	2
1979	5
1980	4
1981	9
1982	1

Source: Survey of California Inclusionary Housing Programs

gram of the California Coastal Commission. Nearly 70 percent of the total, however, are located in three jurisdictions: Irvine, Orange County, and San Francisco. Part of this is a function of the scale of these communities, at least the latter two. Many of the other communities, such as Santa Cruz or Petaluma, which tend to be small suburban jurisdictions, have achieved respectable numbers of lower-income units as well. This is also significant since as shown in Exhibit 3, most of the programs are of recent vintage. Thus, with favorable economic and political climates, substantial future production of lower-income housing units can be anticipated from inclusionary housing programs already enacted.

The future political climate for inclusionary housing programs in California is uncertain. Recent developments have not been generally supportive of inclusionary programs. Two major and highly visible programs, those of the Coastal Commission and of Orange County, have been curtailed. The Department of Housing & Community Development, a strong advocate under the Brown administration, has substantially reduced its profile on the subject under Governor Deukmejian. Strong opposition from the building industry to mandatory inclusionary programs has tended to weaken the consensus that had developed in Sacramento for affirmative actions in the housing field as well as discourage some local governments from pursuing that option.[26]

These changes, however, do not suggest a drastic reversal of the trends that have been apparent to this point; rather, it is likely that the scale and character of California's inclusionary housing program is entering a period of stabilization. Those communities that already have inclusionary programs on the books are likely to continue to carry them out, but few major new programs will be enacted.[27] In the absence of a new source of federal subsidies, most local efforts will be directed toward the moderate-income population, a target group which builders find easier to accommodate and whose housing needs are more a matter of political consensus than are the needs of the poor. Inclusionary housing programs have become part of the normal planning vocabulary in California; it is likely, for example, that even where there is no formal ordinance or program in place, inclusionary requirements will be imposed on future developments of particularly large scale or local significance.[28]

Programs Around the Country

When California and New Jersey are put to one side, the picture that emerges in the rest of the country is one of scattered inclusionary housing programs arising out of particular local concerns or circumstances and unrelated to any statewide legislative or judicial mandate or any wider consensus on housing priorities and policies. The absence of statewide concern seems most notable in Maryland, where a highly successful inclusionary program has now been in effect for nearly a decade, during which time, however, not one other jurisdiction in the state has chosen to follow Montgomery County's lead.

In view of the number of jurisdictions with land use control powers in the United States, it would be nearly impossible to determine the precise number of inclusionary housing programs in existence, but a reasonable approximation based on references in the literature would suggest that the total outside California and New Jersey is between twenty and thirty, most of which are voluntary density bonus programs rather than mandatory inclusionary programs.[29] These programs are scattered around the nation with no discernible overall geographic pattern; most are, however, located in affluent suburban jurisdictions. Examples are Newton, a suburb of Boston; Montgomery County, Maryland, a suburb of Washington, D.C.; and Lewisboro, New York, an outer suburb of New York City. Others appear to be affluent college communities or scenic resort areas, such as Aspen or Boulder, Colorado; or Eugene, Oregon.

The outstanding program among this group is that of Montgomery County, Maryland, a program which has already been discussed in chapter five of this book. Montgomery County is a large, affluent, and mostly suburban county to the north and northwest of Washington, D.C. It contains such well-known suburban areas as Bethesda, Chevy Chase, and Silver Spring. The county program, known as the Moderately Priced Housing Program (MPHP) was initially enacted in 1973; after a variety of amendments, mostly technical, the form of the program today is as follows:

- All developments of 50 units or more must provide 12.5 percent of their units as Moderately Priced Dwelling Units (MPDUs);
- Developers have the option of donating land to the county, in an amount adequate to provide for the construction of the number of units otherwise required, in lieu of constructing MPDUs;
- The county maintains a waiting list of qualified moderate income buyers or renters, and for a ninety-day period after completion of a new unit, has the ex-

clusive right to refer potential buyers or renters from its lists. If the unit is not sold (under contract) after 90 days, it is offered to the general public at the price established by the county;

- 5 percent of the units in any development (40 percent of the MPDUs) must be offered by the developer at a reduced price to the Montgomery County Housing Opportunities Commission (HOC), the county housing authority;
- Resale controls are in effect for a period of ten years after initial occupancy, during which time resale price is controlled on the basis of the consumer price index, and the county and/or HOC have the exclusive right to refer buyers or to purchase for a sixty-day period. Rent levels and tenant selection are also subject to control for the same ten-year period.[30]

The county establishes maximum prices for both sale and rental units, as well as income ceilings for moderate-income households which it adjusts annually. For 1983, representative maximum prices included $52,948 for a three-bedroom townhouse, or $36,649 for a one-bedroom condominium flat. Maximum rents, where utilities are paid separately by the tenant, are $583 per month for the three-bedroom townhouse and $436 per month for the one-bedroom condominium apartment.[31] Moderate-income limits for the same period ranged from $27,900 for a single person to a maximum of $35,900 for a household of five or more members.[32] Although no effort is made by the county to key its income determinations to those of the Department of Housing & Urban Development, these ceiling incomes are roughly comparable to the current median income in the county.

More notable than the formal structure of the Montgomery County program, which is not unusual, is the level of effort that the county maintains in support of the MPDU program and of affordable housing generally. As was noted in chapter five, the county's record is an outstanding one in terms of the extent of its affirmative action for lower-income housing. One activity is particularly notable: a rental housing subsidy program using revenues raised locally. The county has enacted a 4 percent tax on the sale of converted condominium and cooperative units. A substantial part of the proceeds of this tax is invested and the income is used to create a rental housing subsidy fund. The fund, in turn, is used to make 20 percent of the units in selected rental developments affordable to households earning 80 percent or less of the area median. Affordability of the rental housing developments is further enhanced by tax-exempt bond financing, which is provided through the county or the state of Maryland, and through ownership of the land under the developments by the county which leases it to the developer at a modest rate.[33]

In Montgomery County, as in other jurisdictions with highly successful inclusionary housing programs, that program is only one part of an overall housing strategy and not the entirety of the strategy. In addition to nearly 2,000 occupied moderately priced dwelling units in the county and an additional 4,000 to 5,000 planned or committed,[34] the county contains over 7,000 units of subsidized housing under the Public Housing, Section 236, and Section 8 programs.[35] While that may not be a great amount in a county with over 200,000 total housing units, it is a substantially larger share than is found in other comparable jurisdictions.

The Montgomery County program is in many ways a model program. It has adhered consistently to its general policy goals and principles for a decade while maintaining enough flexibility to adjust specific program features as appropriate. Apparently in response to developer pressure, the program was amended soon after its inception to permit developers to donate land rather than build MPDUs.[36] Resale controls, which were apparently not contemplated in the initial draft ordinance, were first set for a five-year period, and subsequently increased to have a ten-year duration.[37] As noted previously, the program has actively sought out resources with which to support the program and facilitate the provision of MPDUs. Finally, the county has taken the necessary steps to establish administrative machinery capable of carrying out the program.

Although no other program outside California has had the level of sustained success of the Montgomery County program, a number have significant achievements to their credit. One notable program, operating under the legal constraints imposed by the *DeGroff* decision of the Virginia Supreme Court, is that of Arlington County, Virginia. Arlington County has had a voluntary density bonus provision in its zoning ordinance since 1972, which provided for a 10 percent increase in density in return for ensuring that 10 percent "of the total residential units which would otherwise be allowed on the site qualify as moderate income housing units."[38] The ordinance provided further that units could be built either on-site or at acceptable off-site locations, and that "adequate guarantees exist as to the continued availability of such units to families of moderate income."[39] In 1981, the zoning ordinance was amended to increase the density bonus from 10 percent to 15 percent, and the low- and moderate-income requirement from 10 percent to 15 percent.[40]

In view of the experience elsewhere with such density bonus programs, it is not surprising that the ordinance provisions just summarized have generated few moderate-income units. Eleven years after enactment of the ordinance amendments, three projects had qualified for bonus densities under the provisions, which yielded a total of 73 low- and moderate-income units.[41] The significance of the Arlington County program lies in its development of alternative approaches. Recognizing that the density bonus provisions were relatively ineffective and, one can assume, that a mandatory program was impermissible under Virginia case law, the county chose to negotiate for low- and moderate-income units on a more informal basis with any large-scale developer who needed significant zoning changes or other discretionary actions in the course of development approval, whether or not the development came under the bonus provisions of the zoning ordinance. This negotiation process was also extended to a developer who needed variances as a part of a condominium conversion process.[42]

The outcome of the negotiation process was substantially more successful than the results emerging from the density bonus. In negotiations on four separate projects, 757 low- and moderate-income units were provided. These include 300 units of senior citizen housing constructed as part of the massive Pentagon City project, 200 units with ten-year affordable rental commitments, and two low-equity tenant cooperatives — one with 72 units and another containing 60 units.[43]

Although many reasonable people may find such broadly discretionary negotiating processes objectionable, many local officials feel strongly that it is a far more effective means of providing lower-income housing in a manner acceptable both to the community and the developer than the enforcement of an explicit ordinance with quantifiable standards. For this reason, many California communities, including Palo Alto, Orange County, and San Francisco, have deliberately refrained from adopting ordinances to implement their inclusionary housing policies.[44] The negotiating process allows the parties to identify mutually acceptable ground around which a program can be devised. Abuses of the discretionary process, at least in the California examples cited, were limited by virtue of the fact that negotiation could take place only within the framework of a formally adopted policy and body of standards.

The extent to which a municipality can legally and responsibly implement an inclusionary housing program through a negotiated process is likely to vary significantly, depending at least in part on the structure of land use law in each individual state. It would appear that Arlington County's negotiating approach was dictated in part by the prohibition on mandatory ordinances imposed by the Virginia Supreme Court. In New Jersey, by contrast, there is no bar to a mandatory ordinance, but any process grounded in general policies and informal negotiation could easily be found illegal under the general state land use law, which requires that all standards governing land use be set forth explicitly in the muncipal zoning or land use ordinance. California land use law, by comparison, provides a municipality or county with a wider variety of legally acceptable routes to the same end.

Most of the inclusionary housing programs outside California or New Jersey are voluntary programs based on the use of a density bonus. Some such programs have yielded lower-income housing units, either where federal or state subsidies were available or where the design and implementation of the program made use of the bonus attractive to developers. At least some units have been built or committed under programs such as those of Eugene, Oregon (134 units); Newton, Massachusetts (73 units); and Pitkin County (Aspen), Colorado (82 units).[45] Although these are not large jurisdictions, neither are these substantial numbers. It may well be that while a voluntary density bonus program is capable of generating a small number of units, usually only with substantial effort by local officials, it is not likely to be able to create a steady or substantial flow of housing affordable to lower-income households; it is by its nature a "retail" program. Newton has, for example, used a wide variety of techniques to achieve even its modest number of units, including allowing units both on- and off-site, accepting payments in lieu of housing units, and leasing units to the city Housing Services Department to be offered as subsidized housing to the elderly.[46]

Also in Massachusetts, the state has been carrying out one of the largest inclusionary housing programs, using the term broadly, in the United States. Unique among state housing finance agencies, the Massachusetts Housing Finance Agency has adopted a general policy that a minimum of 25 percent of the units in any development financed with tax-exempt bonds issued by the agency must be rented to low-income households. The agency's policies further include the following:

> To promote the development of mixed-income housing by selecting sites and development teams that will produce housing with certain units that are marketable with minimum subsidies; and
>
> To administer available subsidy programs so that they serve to encourage as broad a range of incomes among residents as is possible.[47]

Although some agency projects are entirely low- and/or moderate-income, particularly among those built within inner-city areas, a substantial number of the projects contain a significant income mix. The income mix and the high level of satisfaction on the part of market-rate, moderate-income and low-income residents with both the units and the developments have been documented in a careful study.[48] By 1980, the agency had financed over 37,000 rental housing units, of which 38 percent were rented to low-income persons and 54 percent to moderate-income persons.[49]

A voluntary density bonus program in Lewisboro, New York, has produced a single project of some interest. As was noted in chapter five, the density bonus offered under this program is unusually generous in its ratio of lower-income units to bonus market rate units, although the overall site density remains quite low in view of the arguably semi-rural character of the community. Units must be affordable to households earning between 90 and 200 percent, depending on family size, of the median *municipal salary*, an interesting variation on customary practice and one prompted by the priority given in the program to town employees, followed by local school district employees.[50] This translated in 1982-1983 to a maximum income of $27,000 for a family of four, which is slightly over 80 percent of the area median income.

One project has been developed under the Lewisboro program — a condominium development called Oakridge, which when complete will contain roughly 40 moderate-income units out of a total of 300 units. Within a single multifamily development, located in an area still dominated by single-family homes on large lots, moderate-income units selling at a price range between $29,000 and $56,000 have been effectively integrated with units selling up to $135,000; as one article noted, the project "shows that price-restricted units — some sold for $100,000 less than the market-rate condos — can be integrated into a high-quality suburban project without creating buyer — or builder — resistance."[51] The buyers of the moderate-income units included a mix of retirees, including households who could no longer afford to maintain a single-family home, municipal employees, and a substantial number of single-parent, younger families.[52] This development is well worth study by communities or developers looking for examples of successful inclusion of moderate-income units in a high-quality suburban setting.

A similar bonus density program has recently been enacted by a neighboring community in Westchester County, the town of New Castle, as a part of the outcome of the *Berenson* case, in which the town's zoning ordinance was found to be exclusionary. The ordinance adopted as a result of the decision created a number of multifamily zones in close proximity to the hamlets of Millwood and Chappaqua, in which a substantial density bonus of up to a maximum of a 50 percent increase in overall site density is provided for development of "apartments designed for and limited in occupancy to low/moderate income families."[53] The amendatory ordinance also created a low-density multifamily zone in outlying parts of the town, in which no bonus for lower-income housing was offered.[54] This ordinance was subsequently challenged by a landowner in a low-density zone, and the entire ordinance was affirmed by the New York courts, both with regard to its general constitutionality and its soundness as a response to the *Berenson* decision.[55] No development which incorporates lower-income housing units has taken place to date under the ordinance. While the bonus provisions are on their face substantial, their effect is limited by (1) the relatively high density permitted by right in the districts to which the bonus provisions apply; and (2) the availability of bonus density increases for a wide variety of other features unrelated to lower-income housing, including underground parking, recreation facilities, dedication of public land, construction of off-site improvements, energy efficient features, and "such other special design features or facilities as may be requested or approved by the Planning Board."[56]

By contrast, the municipality of Lakewood, Colorado, a suburb of Denver, administered for a period in the 1970s an inclusionary housing program, albeit on an informal negotiated basis, but has since abolished the program and has no plans to reinstate it. The issue was examined by a housing task force which evaluated the city's housing plans and policies during the second half of 1982. The task force concluded that legal problems, administrative problems, and the opposition of the local builder/developer community meant that "neither the mandatory nor voluntary programs appeared to be worth the administrative, legal, and public relations efforts necessary to sell the program."[57] The analysis of the task force, however, is tendentious in the extreme; it relies heavily on un critical acceptance of doubtful authorities, such as Ellickson or the *DeGroff* deci sion, and contains considerable misinformation about the substance of the California programs.

Notwithstanding such considerations, it can readily be acknowledged that there are many features of inclusionary housing programs which trigger opposi tion. In the absence of an explicit mandate to do so, either legislative or judicial, many communities may hesitate to adopt such programs. As the Lakewood task force noted, "inclusionary programs, however, face two problems: cities are under no judicial or legislative obligation to impose inclusionary programs, and they can often not implement programs without Federal housing subsidies."[58] The second part of that statement is factually inaccurate, but the first part is the more important one. In a social environment where many suburban municipalities have yet wholeheartedly to accept multifamily housing of any kind, an inclusionary housing program is often a drastic step. In the absence of a mandate imposed from above, it is likely only to be prompted by an equally drastic perception of the need or a strong conviction of the justice of the inclu sionary objective.[59] Those criteria are likely to limit the reach of inclusionary housing programs to a minority of potential jurisdictions.

New Jersey Before and After Mount Laurel II

Even before the *Mount Laurel II* decision was handed down early in 1983, more inclusionary housing programs had been adopted in New Jersey than in any other state with the obvious exception of California. The first jurisdictions to in itiate inclusionary housing programs did so in the middle 1970s, often as a re sponse to the generalized low- and moderate-income housing obligation set forth in the initial *Mount Laurel* decision. By 1983, a survey had identified a total of sixteen inclusionary housing programs around the state, of which thirteen were administered by individual municipalities and three by state-level regional plan ning or development agencies under circumstances reminiscent of those govern ing the California Coastal Commission.[60] Notwithstanding these efforts, there is no question that *Mount Laurel II* changed the zoning rules in New Jersey funda mentally and in the process created a significant new role for inclusionary hous ing programs.

Inclusionary Housing Programs Before Mount Laurel II

During the 1970s the forces affecting state government, which in turn dictated the manner in which the state would seek to influence municipal consideration of inclusionary zoning ordinances, were substantially different in New Jersey from those in California. The political and social character of New Jersey has always strongly discouraged a state-level affirmative approach to meeting lower-income housing needs. New Jersey politics, perhaps more than in any other state, are dominated by suburban interests, whose political priorities are shaped to a large degree by their shared flight from the deteriorating central cities. The racial and economic contrasts between New Jersey's core cities and its suburbs are correspondingly extreme. The sharpness of this contrast has undoubtedly played a significant part in fostering the exclusionary land use practices for which the state has become known, although other factors, among them the reliance of suburban municipalities on the local property tax as an almost exclusive revenue source, are not irrelevant. Still, one commentator has written,

> In New Jersey, where local property taxes provide a particularly large share of all local revenues, a state planner believes that most local land use controls are "designed for the purpose of trying to avoid the costs implied in residential growth and its effect on public school growth." Even in New Jersey, however, relatively few suburbs base their housing and land use policies solely on tax calculations. Instead, concern over the implications of housing development for local taxes tends to reinforce, and to be reinforced by, exclusionary behavior rooted in community, property-value, class and racial considerations. Equally important, the workings of the property tax provide suburbanites with a respectable rationale to justify the exclusion of lower-income groups, subsidized housing, and blacks, regardless of the actual mix of motives which underlie a particular local policy.[61]

In this political environment, state legislative and executive efforts to provide affirmatively for lower-income housing, at least outside the central cities which had historically been repositories for subsidized housing projects, were halting and generally unsuccessful. A modest proposal was made in 1969 to add generalized language dealing with lower-income housing needs to the municipal land use law,[62] and a more extensive effort was made in 1972 to mandate a regional fair share allocation procedure.[63] Neither was able to reach the floor of either house of the state legislature. Another fair share allocation bill, seeking to take advantage of the more receptive climate ushered in by the *Mount Laurel* decision, was introduced in 1975; although it appeared briefly to have some possibility of passage, especially after extensive revisions were made in an effort to secure the support of the New Jersey League of Municipalities, it too failed.[64]

During all of this period, executive support both for state legislation and for local affirmative action was limited. All three New Jersey administrations prior to the present one had given nominal support to the principles set forth in the *Mount Laurel* decision. The legislation mentioned above was, in each case, introduced with the support of the existing administration. In no case, however, did any governor make a serious effort to obtain passage of any law that would have had the effect of mandating low- and moderate-income housing development in suburban New Jersey, whether through inclusionary programs, fair share housing allocations, or otherwise. There is no reason to believe, however, that such an effort would have been any more successful.

The most substantial gesture by a New Jersey governor was that of Governor Byrne, who issued Executive Order No. 35 in 1976 in the wake of *Mount Laurel*, ordering the preparation of a fair share allocation plan by the Department of Community Affairs to guide New Jersey municipalities in providing an appropriate variety and choice of housing for all the state's citizens.[65] Although a fair share allocation plan was submitted to the governor late in 1976, the imminent arrival of an election year prompted the issuance of another executive order deferring consideration of the plan until December 1977, conveniently after the gubernatorial election.[66] This procedure, which was widely characterized at the time as a charade, was terminated by Governor Kean in 1982, when he rescinded the initial executive order of 1975.[67]

During the period following the initial *Mount Laurel* decision and Executive Order 35, the Department of Community Affairs made some modest efforts to encourage affirmative action by local government including, but not limited to, inclusionary housing programs. The fair share housing allocation report that was eventually published in 1978 contained some discussion of and recommendations for inclusionary housing programs, voluntary and mandatory.[68] At roughly the same time, the department gave demonstration project grants to two municipalities, South Brunswick and Princeton Township, to design "model" inclusionary programs. In 1981, shortly before the end of the Byrne administration, the department published an *Affordable Housing Handbook*, which contained considerable discussion of inclusionary housing programs.[39]

A substantially more forthright state voice than that of either the governor or the Department of Community Affairs during this period was that of the Department of the Public Advocate. This agency, something like a broadly-empowered state *ombudsman*, under the direction of its outstanding Commissioner, Stanley Van Ness, took a leading role in prompting suburban communities to respond constructively to the precepts of the *Mount Laurel* decision through constant advocacy from its establishment in 1974 into the early 1980s.[70] The agency's role, however, was more significant in the courts than elsewhere; its advocacy of public interest positions in the *Mount Laurel* remand and in other cases is considered a significant element in bringing the New Jersey Supreme Court to the position that it eventually adopted in *Mount Laurel II*. A second important role of the Department of Public Advocate was as a voice for stronger positions and for affirmative action within state government, a role which was particularly significant in its effect on the Department of Environmental Protection's administration of the coastal zone program.

Under an expansive interpretation of the powers granted the state by the Coastal Area Facilities Review Act (CAFRA),[71] the Department of Environmental Protection both imposed inclusionary requirements on a number of developments as a condition of their approval and adopted a general rule holding that ''new residential developments shall provide an appropriate amount of affordable housing for low and moderate income households, where needed and feasible.''[72] Low-income households were defined as those with incomes under 80 percent of the area median, and moderate income as those with incomes between 80 and 95 percent of the area median, the ceiling income for the Federal Section 235 program.[73] The *Egg Harbor Associates* case, which was discussed in some detail in chapter two of this book, affirmed the legality and constitutionality of this rule, although it is grounded in a statute that makes no mention of affordable housing.

After adopting the inclusionary housing policy, the Division of Coastal Resources, the agency responsible for administering CAFRA, directed its efforts to the Atlantic City area and in particular to the large-scale residential developments seeking approval in order to take advantage of the anticipated massive housing demand arising from casino openings. The largest developments subject to inclusionary requirements—being required to provide 10 percent of their units as low-income housing and 10 percent as moderate-income housing—are Bayshore Center, containing roughly 1,500 units, and the Towne of Historic Smithville, a 6,800-unit development. The developer of Bayshore Center was responsible for the unsuccessful *Egg Harbor Associates* litigation.

By late 1983, the inclusionary policy had shown few results. The reasons for this were numerous; indeed, one could argue that the outcome was overdetermined. As was the case with the California Coastal Commission, the New Jersey Department of Environmental Protection has no affirmative powers; it could prevent development through permit denial but could not facilitate development or provide incentives and assistance. Federal subsidy funds, on which the policy had been at least in part predicated, were no longer available. Most importantly, however, the massive market demand which the state planners had anticipated would make the meeting of inclusionary goals economically feasible, had failed to materialize. By the end of 1983 groundbreaking had yet to take place in Bayshore Center, and development at Smithville had slowed to a trickle. Indeed, the only units at Smithville that were selling were those priced at the lowest levels at which the developer could build them and not literally lose money, ranging from one-bedroom condominiums selling for roughly $40,000 to three-bedroom zero-lot-line detached houses selling for slightly more than $60,000. Although some of these units qualified as moderate-income units under the

CAFRA rule when combined with tax-exempt bond financing, it was clear that the development was generating neither the profits nor the volume that would support an inclusionary target of the sort set forth in the CAFRA permit. By 1982, the large Canadian corporation which had developed the Smithville project was actively seeking to sell the entire project.[74]

The other regional agencies adopting inclusionary housing policies are the Pinelands Commission[75] and the Hackensack Meadowlands Development Commission.[76] Inasmuch as no lower-income housing has been built under the policies of either agency, they need not be discussed in detail. They are mentioned, however, to indicate that by the late 1970s, well before the *Mount Laurel II* decision, the inclusionary housing approach had become an accepted part of a regional housing development strategy in New Jersey, although it was still the exception rather than the rule at the local level. Rather than seeing policies such as those adopted by these regional agencies as suggesting directions for them to allow, local government tended to treat them as unwarranted impositions in clear violation of the time-honored New Jersey tradition of "home rule."[77] Atlantic County officials mounted an intense attack on the Pinelands Commission and on the provisions of the act establishing the commission which required municipal and county master plans to be in conformity with the overall Pinelands master plan. By the end of 1983, more than four years after the beginning of the Pinelands planning process, the conflict between the commission and a number of its constituent municipalities and counties was still going on.

During the 1970s and early 1980s a number of suburban municipalities adopted inclusionary housing programs. Some of these programs were enacted as a result of exclusionary zoning litigation directed against the municipality, as was the case in Bridgewater and Bedminster Townships. Other municipalities appeared to be in part motivated by the wave of exclusionary zoning litigation sweeping New Jersey and at least in part by a desire, often not carefully thought out or analyzed, to achieve positive social ends. In other cases, one interest appeared to be the desire to protect the municipality against prospective exclusionary zoning challenges.

Few of these undertakings could be considered programs in a meaningful sense. In most cases the inclusionary provisions were added to the zoning ordinance and subsequently ignored. The realm of supportive actions and incentives pursued by communities such as Orange County, California, or Montgomery County, Maryland, were largely absent. Of the more than a dozen municipalities with inclusionary zoning ordinances, perhaps the only one in which a coherent program to facilitate development under the ordinance was implemented was East Brunswick, which achieved substantially more with its voluntary inclusionary housing program than did any other New Jersey jurisdiction during this period.

East Brunswick Township, which enacted its voluntary density bonus program in 1976, has provided considerable support to developers seeking to use the program as well as to non-profit organizations seeking to provide low- and moderate-income units under federal housing programs. Assistance has included, in addition to the density bonus itself, tax abatement, assistance in obtaining federal subsidies, reduced utility hook-up fees, and accelerated processing.[78] Three developers have taken advantage of the density bonus program, which has resulted in 168 units of federally-assisted housing under the Sections 236 and 235 programs, and 40 units of housing without federal subsidies designed to be affordable to households earning 105 percent or less of the area median income.[79] At least half of the developments taking place in the township, however, have not chosen to participate in the density bonus program, so that the number of units generated during the seven years during which the program has been in effect has not been a substantial part of the total growth of the township.[80]

The only other communities adopting inclusionary zoning ordinances in New Jersey in which lower-income units have been built to date are South Brunswick[81] and Cherry Hill.[82] In the latter case, the absence of a coherent program resulted in a situation in which, when units built under the inclusionary ordinance were put on the market, most households falling within the income limits set by the township could not qualify for a large enough mortgage to purchase the units. According to an executive with one builder, the units ultimately were sold to middle-class people, "widows, widowers, or divorcées, who had some cash but did not make that much income." One of the buyers was a medical resident whose parents helped with the down payment.[83] The township has since amended its ordinance in an effort to target the units more effectively as well as to establish resale controls.[84]

Many of the other ordinances appear to have been drafted in a manner designed to discourage the production of lower-income housing; indeed, a number of these ordinances have been reviewed in that context in chapter five of this book. They have included patently excessive inclusionary requirements, such as in Bridgewater Township; clearly unreasonable overall development standards, such as in East Windsor Township;[85] or administration of an acceptably drafted ordinance in a way inconsistent with its stated objectives, as in Franklin Township. A further example would be the Old Bridge ordinance, which provides a density bonus of 6 percent or less to a developer willing to produce a minimum of 10 percent of the units as lower-income housing, and is replete with other unreasonable provisions.[86]

The experience of inclusionary housing programs in New Jersey between the initial *Mount Laurel* decision and the *Mount Laurel II* decision eight years later cannot but reinforce the conclusion that the court came to in the latter decision that their initial statement of the constitutional obligation had not been enough to motivate New Jersey local government to take the steps needed to provide for their fair share of regional lower-income housing needs. The equivocation and lack of good faith that can be seen in the small group of inclusionary zoning ordinances discussed here is characteristic of the suburban climate during the period; although individual municipalities here and there took affirmative steps to meet their housing obligations, the fundamental change in the practice of land use regulation that the initial *Mount Laurel* decision had sought did not take place. The unusually explicit nature of the conditions and requirements of *Mount Laurel II* as well as the generous provision for builder's remedy were a dramatic reversal of the prior New Jersey judicial posture and a direct outcome of the failure of the New Jersey local government to respond constructively to the earlier decision. As the court put it,

> After all this time, ten years after the trial court's initial order invalidating its zoning ordinance, Mount Laurel remains afflicted with a blatantly exclusionary ordinance. Papered over with studies, rationalized by hired experts, the ordinance at its core is true to nothing but Mount Laurel's determination to exclude the poor. Mount Laurel is not alone; we believe that there is widespread non-compliance with the constitutional mandate of our original opinion in this case.[87]

Here then is a decision, consciously crafted to bring about a basic change in the manner in which New Jersey municipalities provide for growth and development. It remains to be seen whether it will have that outcome; the beginnings of such a change, however, already appear to be taking place.

Mount Laurel II, the Builder's Remedy, and Inclusionary Housing Programs

The central place of inclusionary housing programs in the *Mount Laurel II* decision, which all but mandates the adoption of such programs as the means by which suburban municipalities are to meet their obligation to provide housing for their fair share of regional lower-income housing needs, has been discussed extensively in chapter two of this book. A further facet of the decision, which is likely to have a particularly significant impact in the coming years, is the expansive position taken by *Mount Laurel II* on the subject of builder's remedy: specifically, whether a builder-plaintiff who has successfully challenged an exclusionary zoning ordinance is entitled to a court order directing the municipality to approve his development proposal, or whether the court should limit its remedial action to invalidating the ordinance and setting down guidelines for enactment of a non-exclusionary ordinance by the municipality.

Although the builder's remedy is well enshrined in exclusionary zoning case law in Pennsylvania,[88] it has not been a major part of New Jersey cases. The first substantial grant of a builder's remedy in an exclusionary zoning case in New Jersey took place in the Supreme Court opinion in *Oakwood at Madison v.*

Township of Madison in 1977.[89] In this decision, the court ordered that the township issue permits to the developer-plaintiff, noting that "corporate plaintiffs have borne the stress and expense of this public-interest litigation, albeit for private purposes, for six years, and have prevailed in two trials and on this extended appeal, and yet stand in danger of having won but a pyrrhic victory."[90] In the event that a reader may not have fully appreciated the extent to which the court considered the builder's remedy an outcome of the special circumstances of this particular case, a footnote was added:

> This determination is not to be taken as a precedent for an automatic right to a permit on the part of any builder-plaintiff who is successful in having a zoning ordinance declared unconstitutional. *Such a relief will ordinarily be rare*, and will generally rest in the discretion of the court, to be exercised in the light of all attendant circumstances.[91] [Emphasis added]

The effect of the *Oakwood* decision, as a result, was to discourage trial judges from granting specific relief to developers, notwithstanding the substantial arguments and the substantial support in legal commentary for such relief.[92] The solitary exception of note occurred in the *Allan-Deane Corporation v. Township of Bedminster* litigation, with significant consequences that will be discussed below.

The *Mount Laurel II* decision took a different position, and in so doing, tied the grant of a builder's remedy closely to the inclusionary housing approach, holding that,

> where a developer succeeds in *Mount Laurel* litigation *and proposes a project providing a substantial amount of lower income housing*, a builder's remedy should be granted unless the municipality establishes that because of environmental or other substantial planning concerns, the plaintiff's proposed project is clearly contrary to sound land use planning. We emphasize that the builder's remedy should not be denied solely because the municipality prefers some other location for lower income housing, even if it is in fact a better site. Nor is it essential that considerable funds be invested or that the litigation be intensive.[93] [Emphasis added]

The court then appended a lengthy footnote dealing with the question of what amount of lower-income housing can be considered a "substantial" amount; while giving substantial discretion to the trial courts, the opinion does note that "20 percent appears to us to be a reasonable minimum."[94]

This facet of the *Mount Laurel II* decision offers developers a powerful weapon in their dealings with recalcitrant local governments. A developer thwarted from building in a community that has yet to meet its *Mount Laurel* obligations (which includes nearly every community in the state) and who concludes that the economics of his development will permit him to provide 20 percent of his units as lower-income housing can now petition a court to award him building permits at a density and under standards that will permit him to develop his site efficiently. Under the majority of circumstances, he will obtain what he is seeking from the courts. This potential sequence of events significantly changes the perspective from which a developer is likely to look at the inclusionary housing target. Rather than an externally imposed condition, it becomes an element in his internal calculus of costs and benefits: Are the economic advantages in the increased number of units and reduced standards that he can hope to obtain from the courts equal to or greater than the cost of providing the lower-income units that the court requires as its *quid pro quo*? The court leaves no doubt that the inclusion of the lower-income units is an absolutely necessary condition of the builder's remedy, warning developers that "the courts not be used as the enforcer for the builder's threat to bring *Mount Laurel* litigation if municipal approvals for projects containing no lower-income housing are not forthcoming."[95]

Although the Supreme Court carefully refrained from setting an explicit standard for the percentage of lower-income housing that would justify a builder's remedy, in resolving the status of the developer-plaintiff in the *Mount Laurel* case itself, the court held that building permits for that plaintiff would be subject to the condition that,

> If Davis [the developer-plaintiff] is not able to obtain the Section 8 subsidies being sought, the developer must use whatever other means are available to make certain that *at least* [the court's emphasis] 20 percent of the units built are affordable by lower income households, with *at least* [the court's emphasis] half of these being affordable by low income households.[96]

Translating these minimums into maximum standards, as the author of the opinion may have anticipated, most developers and their attorneys have concluded that the threshold lower-income requirement for a builder's remedy is that 10 percent of the units be affordable to households earning between 50 and 80 percent of the area median income, and 10 percent to households earning under 50 percent of that income. More and more developers are coming to the conclusion that at appropriate densities and development standards those percentages can be accommodated in an economically feasible and profitable development.

The *Mount Laurel II* decision, therefore, in the interest of generating the production of lower-income housing, provides two tracks for the achievement of its objectives. First, municipalities must provide for their fair share of regional lower-income housing needs. Although they may seek to achieve their obligation through means other than the adoption of inclusionary zoning ordinances, that is considered unlikely. Second, to the degree that municipalities do not do so, developers may obtain building permits for their projects by incorporating a reasonable percentage of low- and moderate-income units in those projects.[97] The effect of this second track is that the inclusionary zoning ordinance, at least with regard to the particular project, is imposed on the municipality by the courts.[98]

The Response to Mount Laurel II

By the end of 1983, it had become apparent that a large number of builders and developers had concluded that the inclusionary *quid pro quo* represented sound business practice. Dozens of landowners and developers had served notice to suburban municipalities that unless they were given greater density and more reasonable development standards, they would bring suit under *Mount Laurel II* to be awarded a builder's remedy. In all cases, the inclusion of 20 percent of the units for lower-income households was an explicit element in the development proposal. Numerous suits had already been brought; by the end of 1983, six separate developers or landowners had been joined into the remand proceedings in the *Urban League of Greater New Brunswick v. Borough of Carteret et al.* litigation, a case that had been remanded by the supreme court back to the trial court for further proceedings as a part of the *Mount Laurel II* decision.[99] A major corporate developer, owner of over four square miles of land in a central New Jersey suburb, announced that he had broken off protracted negotiations with the municipal government regarding the conditions under which he was to be allowed to build and was filing a *Mount Laurel II* lawsuit in anticipation of a builder's remedy. A successful outcome of that suit could result in over 2,000 lower-income housing units being built on the site.[100]

In another related turn of events, a group of professionals active in the development industry organized a corporation whose rationale arose directly out of the supreme court position on the builder's remedy. This corporation has begun to seek out exclusionary suburban municipalities in order to obtain control of parcels zoned for low density or nonresidential use but suitable for multifamily development. If approval from the municipality is not forthcoming, they bring *Mount Laurel II* suits in anticipation of obtaining approval from the courts. By the end of 1983, this corporation was involved as principals or partners in seven separate development proposals.[101]

In contrast to developers who were widely responding to the new circumstances created by the *Mount Laurel II* decision, local government tended to adopt a more passive, even inert posture toward the decision and toward their lower-income housing obligations. It is not clear why, a full year after the decision had been handed down, there had been so little municipal response. A number of factors can be suggested, however, which cumulatively may account for the absence of municipal government action. Some municipalities may have placed excessive faith in an abortive effort to adopt an amendment to the New Jersey constitution to nullify the *Mount Laurel II* decision; this undertaking, a project of the Republican minority in the state legislature, was rendered academic when the Democrats retained control of both houses in the 1983 legislature elections.[102] Other municipalities, accustomed to the tradition of considerable judicial deference for their actions, asserted that past efforts or historic circumstances relieved them of any responsibility under the *Mount Laurel II* doctrine, often taking positions patently inconsistent with the clear letter of the decision. Some local officials may have remembered that the supreme court itself had compromised many of the principles of the initial *Mount Laurel* decision in its subsequent *Madison* decision, one of which was the fair share doctrine itself.[103]

Beyond those communities whose inaction was grounded in simple wishful thinking, considerations of prudence, both substantive and political, were a significant factor. Many municipalities were reluctant to take an initiative on matters such as the determination of region or fair share, or the affordability standards to be used to establish what was to be meant by "lower income housing," before the lower courts had clarified and amplified on the supreme court language. In an effort to expedite this process, the New Jersey League of Municipalities and the New Jersey Builders Association jointly funded an analytical study of *Mount Laurel II* technical issues by the Center for Urban Policy Research at Rutgers University. The study was released in late 1983.[104]

Prudence may be called for from the perspective of the local official, even more on political than on substantive grounds. *Mount Laurel II* is not a popular decision with most suburban electorates. In a municipality that is not itself the subject of litigation, there is no political advantage to be obtained and considerable potential disadvantage to be suffered by taking the initiative to adopt a "Mount Laurel" ordinance. Even where an inclusionary development proposal has been made or a lawsuit filed, it may still be politically more palatable to fight the development proposal or the lawsuit vigorously, so that the outcome is delayed and any future lower-income housing built can be seen as having been imposed on the community rather than voluntarily accepted or encouraged. Few local officials are unaware of the fact that the first *Mount Laurel* suit was filed in 1970 and that by 1984 there was still almost no low-income housing yet in place.

By the end of the first year after the decision, the most significant developments were those arising from the courts and in particular those emerging from the developer/builder reaction to the decision. The two most notable examples were in Mahwah Township and Bedminster Township. In Mahwah, the remand from the *Mount Laurel II* decision had progressed to the point where extensive negotiations over the manner in which the township would achieve its fair share goal were taking place, and seven separate developers had come forward to propose inclusionary housing developments. In Bedminster, a development proposal that had been approved as part of litigation preceding *Mount Laurel II*, but which was subsequently recast to conform to the standards and requirements of that decision, was under construction. Groundbreaking for the lower-income housing units, which will make up 20 percent of the total development, was scheduled to take place in spring 1984.

Mahwah Township is an affluent suburban township with a population of roughly 12,000 located in Bergen County along the New Jersey/New York state line. Mahwah was been involved in exclusionary zoning litigation for over a decade. As one of the cases in the *Mount Laurel II* decision, the New Jersey Supreme Court reversed the Mahwah trial judge opinion and remanded the case to the trial judge to establish Mahwah's fair share and secure revision of the township's zoning ordinance to comply with the decision and the fair share goal. The trial judge appointed an expert, Philip Caton, a Trenton architect and planner, who submitted a report on Mahwah's fair share to the court in July 1983. A hearing on fair share was held in September, which was followed by an order adopting the fair share figure proposed by Caton in his report.[105] Caton was subsequently appointed to be the master by the court, and the township was ordered to submit a revised zoning scheme to the court, prepared under his supervision, in ninety days, to which an additional thirty-day period was subsequently added at the township's request.

A developer holding an approximately 27-acre parcel in the township moved to intervene in the case during the summer of 1983, prior to the conclusion of the fair share proceedings. Between the adoption of the fair share allocation and the end of the initial ninety-day period, six additional developers had submitted proposals to the township to build under a 20 percent inclusionary requirement. The seven developments ranged in size from 190 to 1,395 dwelling units, including between 38 and 280 lower-income units, for a total of 4,520 units of which 923 would be lower-income housing.[106] From a community in which there was no lower-income housing at all, Mahwah had become one with a potential embarrassment of riches, inasmuch as the fair share target set by the court was 699 units, at least some part of which the township proposed to meet through means other than inclusionary housing developments.[107]

The developer response is notable, particularly in view of the stringent lower-income housing standards that each developer had to meet and the particularly low median income in effect for Mahwah at this time, as given in Exhibit 4.[108] The author prepared an analysis for one of the prospective developers determining the maximum sales prices that could be charged for housing units affordable to low- and moderate-income households (see Exhibit 5). The prices were based on the availability of tax-exempt mortgage revenue bonds with a projected interest rate of 10½ percent and a buy-down that would enable purchasers to qualify on the basis of an initial interest rate of 9 percent.[109] If mortgage interest rates were higher, the prices would have to be lower. One developer submitted documentation to the effect that units would be priced low enough so that a one-bed-

EXHIBIT 4
Low- and Moderate-Income Ceilings (in Dollars) by Household Size,
Applicable to Mahwah, New Jersey
Effective in 1983

	Low Income	Moderate Income
1 person	10,000	15,200
2 persons	11,400	17,400
3 persons	12,800	19,550
4 persons	14,250	21,750

Source: U.S. Department of Housing & Urban Development, Newark Area Office, March 1983

EXHIBIT 5
Maximum Proposed Sales Prices
for Low- and Moderate-Income Units (in Dollars)
In Mahwah, New Jersey

	Low Income	Moderate Income
1 bedroom	20,000	31,000
2 bedroom	25,000	38,500

Source: Analysis by the author

room low-income unit could be bought with a mortgage no larger than
$12,500.[110] Although it is possible that one of the seven developers was unaware
of the pricing required for the lower-income units, [111] this was not generally the
case. Each of the remaining group had concluded that the pricing did not preclude an economically feasible development.

The developer utilizing the pricing analysis given in the preceding exhibits
subsequently prepared a detailed development proposal and financial feasibility
analysis and balance sheet which were submitted to the master. This development proposed to provide 22 percent of its units as lower-income housing, made
up of one-bedroom units at 568 square feet and two-bedroom units at 774 square
feet. Based on a detailed market analysis by a nationally-known firm which established prices for the market rate units, a comprehensive architectural scheme
by a firm experienced in the design of multifamily housing, and a professional
costing of that design, the developer concluded that he could provide the lower-
income housing as described above (equally divided between low- and moderate-income units) and still achieve a pretax profit on the entire development of
14.5 percent.[112]

The developer indicated that in order to meet the inclusionary standard and maintain economic feasibility, a development density of approximately 15 units per acre was required as well as a number of modifications of development standards in effect in the township, including expedited processing, reduction of standards for internal streets, reduction of sewer/water hook-up fees, and modification of certain setback and building distance requirements. Similar densities and modifications were requested by most of the other developers submitting proposals to the township. As has been discussed previously, these considerations appear reasonable with regard to both density and development standards.

The developers proposing to provide low- and moderate-income housing in Mahwah had no intention of constructing particularly expensive units as their market-rate housing on the balance of their proposed development sites. The development discussed immediately above proposes to sell market-rate units ranging from 800 to 1,107 square feet for prices from $57,600 to $72,000. Another developer has proposed a price range for market-rate units of approximately $48,000 for a one-bedroom unit to $76,000 for a three-bedroom unit, generally comparable to the other proposal. Although Mahwah is an affluent area in which there is a market for more expensive units, the developers appear to have concluded that volume production, which is needed to achieve cost efficiency, dictates a high rate of market absorption, which can take place only with a more "affordable" market-rate product.

The outcome of the Mahwah rezoning and compliance procedure is still unclear. There is substantial civic and political opposition to the entire process and to the entire idea of lower-income housing in the township.[113] A group of residents have organized the Mahwah Concerned Citizens Committee Against Mount Laurel II and begun to issue a professionally printed newsletter and hold meetings with the assistance of township government.[114] It is likely that the township will appeal either the fair share determination or the forthcoming compliance order, or both. Although all of this is significant, it goes beyond the central point of the Mahwah experience so far; namely, that the stringent *Mount Laurel II* inclusionary standards appear to be economically workable, even in an area where the regional median income is substantially lower than in most parts of the state. The Mahwah experience so far represents an unequivocal validation of the economic soundness of the basic *Mount Laurel II* principles.

The Bedminster Project

By the end of 1983, it appeared nearly certain that the first housing development to be constructed under the *Mount Laurel II* rules would be started early in 1984 in Bedminster Township, New Jersey. Although that outcome was coincidental, it nonetheless had considerable symbolic significance since Bedminster had been one of the most exclusive as well as exclusionary communities in the state. It is a large township in the north-central part of the state and contained fewer than 2,500 residents in 1980, many of whom lived in magnificent estates dotting the rolling countryside.[115] It is otherwise distinguished by the fact that it is the location of AT&T Communications (formerly Long Lines), a complex employing some 5,000 workers and is the point at which Interstate Highways 287 and 78 meet, forming a major transportation node in central New Jersey.

As a result of protracted and exceptionally expensive litigation, the court ordered the township in 1980 to provide suitable development densities and standards to a developer plaintiff, a subsidiary of the Johns-Manville Corporation, in order that it could construct a large-scale planned development on a part of its holdings in the township.[116] In keeping with the trial judge's interpretation of the *Madison* decision, which was the governing supreme court decision at that point, the development was made conditional on 20 percent of the units being "least cost" housing as the term was used in the *Madison* decision.[117] Although strongly supporting the builder's remedy, the Department of the Public Advocate, which was a party to the litigation, appealed the failure of the court to impose requirements on the "least cost" units that would have ensured both their initial and continued occupancy by lower-income households. This appeal was pending at the time of the *Mount Laurel II* decision. In the meantime, a new development corporation was formed, known as The Hills Development Company,[118] and construction began on the first market-rate units in the 1,287-unit planned development, known as The Hills, in 1982. Under the terms of the ordinance adopted by Bedminster to comply with the court order, the developer was permitted to construct the first 25 percent of the market-rate units prior to receiving approval for any of the least-cost units required by the ordinance.[119] By the time that the *Mount Laurel II* decision was handed down, The Hills Development Company had reached the point where receiving approval and beginning construction of the least-cost units was a matter of some urgency since the point was not far off when they would have to cease work on the market-rate units if those approvals were not in hand.

With considerable corporate reluctance, the company decided in late spring of 1983 that it would have to construct these units under the *Mount Laurel II* standards rather than the considerably more easily attained least-cost standards. This decision was prompted in large part by an opinion from the firm's legal counsel that the *Mount Laurel II* decision had drastically reduced their likelihood of prevailing in the public advocate's pending appeal. The planning and design process for the low- and moderate-income units began in May 1983, and the first version of the complete project plan was submitted in September. After a number of modifications, the most important of which was deletion of rental housing from the development program, the project was approved for tax-exempt bond mortgage financing by the New Jersey Mortgage Finance Agency in December 1983. A procedure for settlement of the public advocate appeal, which had been

EXHIBIT 6
Low- and Moderate-Income Housing Program
at The Hills, Bedminster, New Jersey

Type	Square Footage	Low Income	Moderate Income	Total Units
1 Bedroom	558	68	—	68
2 Bedroom Loft*	658	44	24	68
2 Bedroom	760	—	80	80
3 Bedroom	990	18	26	44
Total		130	130	260

Note: *Loft units contain one conventional bedroom and a sleeping loft

remanded by the appellate division back to the trial court, was underway during the same period.[120]

The final plan that was submitted provided for 260 condominium apartment units in two-story buildings containing between eight and sixteen units per building, divided as shown in Exhibit 6 by number of bedrooms and target population. This mix, which was considered by both the developer and the public advocate consistent with area housing needs, required a waiver of a high arbitrary bedroom mix provision of the Bedminster ordinance.[121] The units themselves are small, as can be seen from the table, but are attractively designed and laid out; each unit has a deck or patio and has direct access to the outdoors.

Sketch floor plans and elevations of two of the building types are given in the drawings in Exhibit 7. The lower-income units were designed by a well-known

EXHIBIT 8
Profile of Development Types at The Hills,
Bedminster, New Jersey

Number	Name	Bedrooms	Square Footage	Price Range
222	Knollcrest	2-3	1900 - 2200	$190,000 - $225,000
255	Stone Run	1-3	1250 - 1650	138,000 - 167,000
355	Fieldstone	2-3	935 - 1400	95,000 - 132,000
194	Mayfields	1-2	682 - 954	66,000 - 89,000
260	Lower-Income Units	1-3	558 - 990	26,500 - 55,500

Source: The Hills Development Company. Prices as of September 19, 1983 and subject to change.

EXHIBIT 7
**Low- and Moderate-Income Housing, Floor Plans and Elevations, The Hills,
Bedminster, New Jersey**

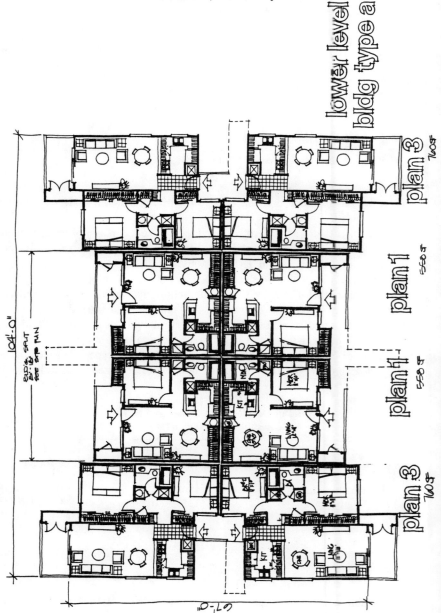

EXHIBIT 7 (cont'd)

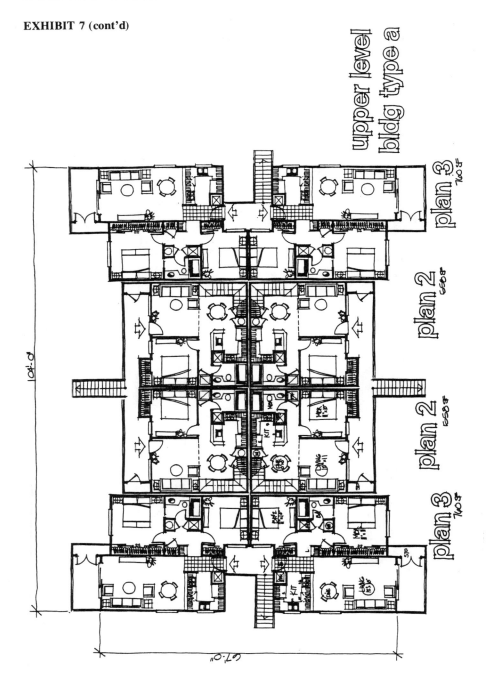

EXHIBIT 7 (cont'd)

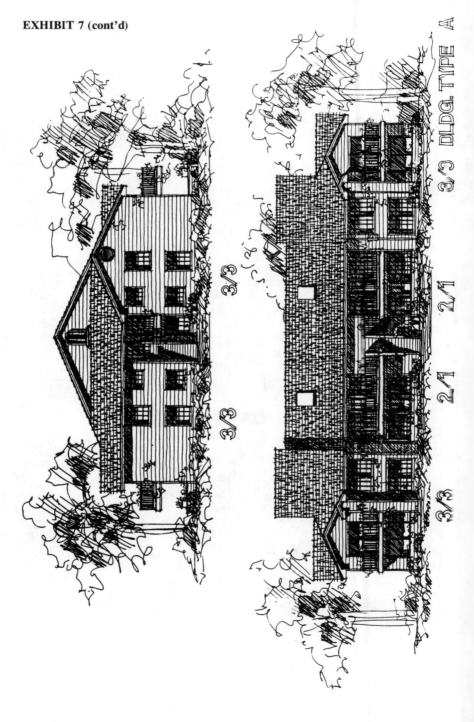

EXHIBIT 7 (cont'd)

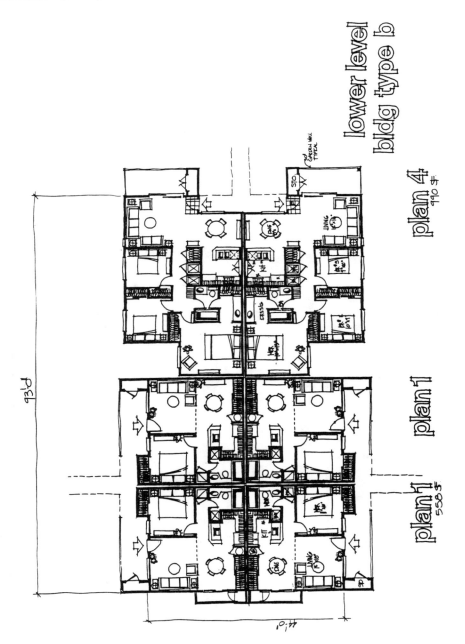

lower level
bldg type b

plan 4

plan 1

plan 1

EXHIBIT 7 (cont'd)

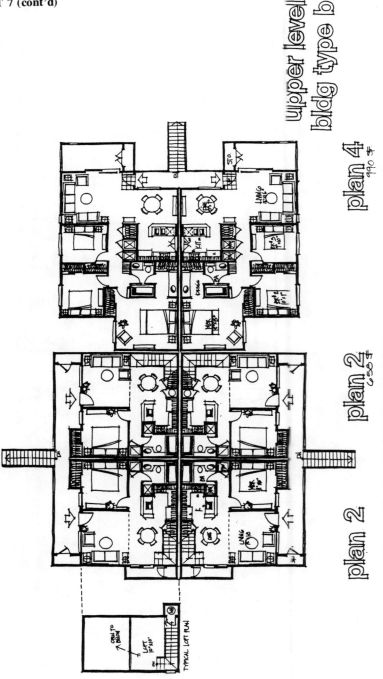

EXHIBIT 7 (cont'd)

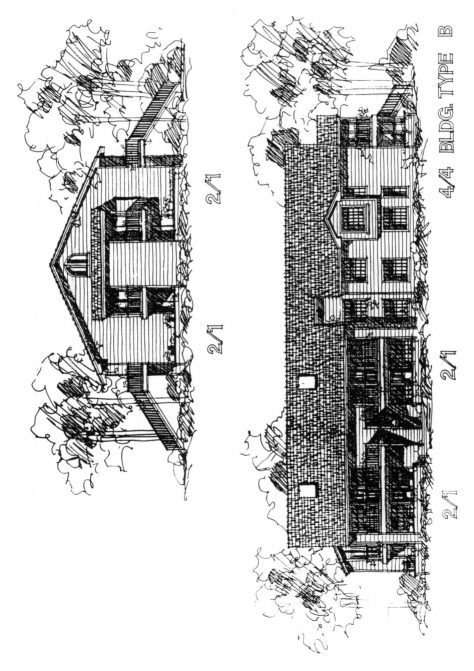

EXHIBIT 7 (cont'd)

California architectural firm, and were designed to conform to the outward appearance of the market-rate units. This was particularly important in this development since The Hills is being built at an overall density of 10 units per acre, a density which provides no opportunities for physical distance or significant visual separation between the lower-income units and the market-rate units.

The sensitivity of the physical and visual integration of the project is made more important by the unusually wide price range proposed to be incorporated in the development which is on a relatively confined site. The project includes units selling at prices up to $225,000, as shown in the breakdown in Exhibit 8.

Units in the more expensive Knollcrest and Stone Run Sections, principally townhouses, sold successfully during 1983. Although disclosure of the 20 percent lower-income housing condition was made in the public offering statement filed by the Hills Development Company, it is not clear to what degree early purchasers were aware of the condition. In any event, the developers anticipate that by the time the lower-income units are marketed, the character of the development will already have been clearly established as one attractive to affluent households and that the lower-income units can be sold without negative effects on the marketability of the balance of the development.

Under the *Mount Laurel II* rules, the low-income units were targeted to households earning below 50 percent of the area median income, adjusted for family size; and the moderate-income units were directed at households earning between 50 to 80 percent of the area median, similarly adjusted. The actual price of the units was derived by working backward from affordability calculations based on a particular interest rate; the interest rate was derived on the basis of the Mortgage Finance Agency (MFA) commitment of tax-exempt bond mortgages coupled with a further buydown, the cost of which was incorporated into the total project cost of the lower-income units. Based on an MFA commitment of mortgage funds at 11 percent, a buydown was provided to set the first year interest rate at 9½ percent on the basis of which prospective buyers would qualify for the units.

The structure of a mortgage buydown has been discussed in chapter three. It was decided, in this project, to limit the buydown to 1½ percent (from 11 to 9½ percent) so that the rate of increase in the amount of the mortgage payment from years 1 through 4 would be modest and not require any significant increase in homeowner income in order to enable the owners to make the rising mortgage payments. A buy-down program in which the rate of increase is too great is likely to impose hardships on a substantial number of households since many will not have income growth in keeping with the assumptions made in the buy-down program.

The factors used to determine affordability were, in addition to the 9½ percent mortgage interest rate, the current local property tax rate, which was unusually low by New Jersey standards,[122] and projected homeowners' association fees.

EXHIBIT 9
Price and Affordability of Lower-Income Units
at The Hills, Bedminster, New Jersey

Category	Price	Annual Carrying Cost*	Minimum Qualifying Income†	Maximum Eligibility Income‡
Low-Income Units				
1 BR	$26,500	$3,168	$11,300	$13,100
2 BR Loft	29,500	3,526	12,600	14,700
3 BR	33,500	4,004	14,300	17,650
Moderate-Income Units				
2 BR Loft	$47,000	$5,617	$20,050	$22,700
2 BR	52,500	6,275	22,400	25,200
3 BR	55,500	6,623	23,650	26,750

Notes: *Mortgage payments @ 9½%, property taxes, homeowners association fees and hazard insurance
　　　†Based on paying 28% of gross income for carrying costs
　　　‡As defined by Department of Housing & Urban Development for Newark, New Jersey SMSA, effective March 1, 1983

Residents of the lower-income housing would be members both of a neighborhood association exclusive to those units and of a master community association made up of the entire planned development. Some modest savings were realized by arranging that a blanket hazard insurance policy would be obtained through the neighborhood association rather than separately for each individual unit. The affordability target was to ensure that each unit would be affordable to a household at the ceiling income for the applicable household size and income category spending 25 percent of gross income for shelter expenses (mortgage payments, taxes, insurance, and homeowners' association fees), and beyond that, that there be an adequate band of affordability to provide a reasonable market for the units.

As Exhibit 9 illustrates, the band of affordability, which is the range between the minimum qualifying income and the maximum eligibility income, tends to fall in the area of $2,000 to $3,000; for example, the band of affordability for the low-income two-bedroom loft unit is from a minimum of $12,600 needed to qualify for the unit to a maximum income ceiling of $14,700. This is the ceiling income for a low-income family of three as defined by the Department of Housing & Urban Development. Although this is not a wide range, the circumstances of this development as the first housing built in this price range within a large geographic area strongly suggest that marketability should not be a problem. The mere notion that units will be available to households with incomes ranging from

EXHIBIT 10
Cost Analysis for Proposed Lower-Income Units
at The Hills, Bedminster, New Jersey

Land		0
Off-site and development-wide improvements		0
Site improvements to lower-income section		
at maximum $5000/dwelling unit (DU)		$1,300,000
Landscaping, hookups, etc. at maximum $3000/DU		780,000
Construction		5,315,632
Architecture & Engineering @ 3.4%	$180,731	
HOW warranty & service*	143,000	
Legal & Consulting Fees	75,000	442,131
Property taxes during construction	13,400	
Permits, fees & misc.	30,000	
		$ 7,837,763
Construction financing @ 13% for 8 months		404,403
Financing fees & financing contingency @ 4%		373,582
Supervision & administration @ 3%		280,187
Marketing & advertising @ 3%		280,187
Closing & title @ 1%		93,396
Nonprofit corporation fee† @ 0.75%		70,047
DEVELOPMENT COST		$ 9,339,565
Mortgage buydown		244,550
Profit, risk & contingency @ 9%		840,561
TOTAL PROJECT COST		$10,424,676

Notes: *HOW represents funds set aside for post-closing repairs under Home Owners Warranty program
    †Fee to be used to support purchaser screening program, administration of future resale controls, and related matters.

$11,000 to $17,000 in one of the most affluent and expensive sections of the state is widely considered to be remarkable.

In the final analysis, however, the pricing of the units was also dependent on the actual development cost of the lower-income project and the level of internal subsidy which the developer felt capable of sustaining from the balance of the development. Two premises were adopted by the developer in establishing the pricing of the units: (1) Certain costs, specifically the land costs and the cost of development-wide infrastructure and off-site improvements, would be borne entirely by the 80 percent of the units that would be market-rate units;[123] and (2) maximum cost levels would be set for all elements in the lower-income housing development process, with a commitment by the developer that any costs in excess of those maximum costs would be absorbed within the profit margin allowed or by the other 80 percent of the units. The developer, therefore, was guaranteeing a price which would be achieved without further subsidy and with a modest profit *if actual costs did not exceed projections*.[124] The approved development pro forma, or cost analysis, is presented in Exhibit 10.

In the final submission, which was approved by the MFA and tentatively approved by the court, all of the lower-income units were to be condominium units Substantial effort had been devoted to planning for one-third of the units to be rental units, both at the behest of the public advocate and in view of provisions of the Bedminster zoning ordinance.[125] In the end, however, plans for rental housing were reluctantly abandoned with the consent of all parties. The reasons for doing so are instructive. First, it became apparent that it was nearly impossible, without some source of further subsidy, to meet the target of 50 percent low-income and 50 percent moderate-income occupancy, even after all of the projected syndication proceeds had been applied to the project as a rental subsidy.[126] Second, no means were available to ensure that operating and maintenance increases in future years would not force the rents beyond low- and moderate-income levels, nor could the developer realistically offer an open-ended commitment to prevent that from taking place. Finally, if the project were to be syndicated, which was necessary if funds were to be obtained for rental subsidies during the initial years of the project, the investors sought a commitment that the project could be converted to condominiums after ten years. Without the syndication proceeds, the objective of 50 percent low-income and 50 percent moderate-income occupancy was not even remotely achievable.

In order to be released of the obligation to provide rental units, which the public advocate had insisted on, the developer offered to provide down payment assistance for the number of low-income units that would be switched from rental units to condominiums, so that low-income households without down payment funds could purchase the units. This proposal, however, was vetoed by the representatives of the private mortgage insurer, who made clear that under their rules they would not accept any mortgagor who did not put up at least 5 percent of the value of the units, *in their money*. Lease-purchase transactions, in which the tenant would accumulate a down payment with which to purchase the unit after a relatively short period, were unworkable because the tax-exempt bond mortgage financing could be used only for owner-occupied units and could not be placed ''on hold'' until the lessors had accumulated the necessary down payment funds.

There is little doubt that the effect of these constraints will be to limit the potential qualifying population for the units and possibly exclude substantial numbers of households who would significantly benefit from the opportunity.

A further element of the Bedminster program is the establishment of a nonprofit corporation to take responsibility for both the screening of potential buyers and the administration of the resale controls to be imposed on the project. The proposal calls for creation of a corporation, tentatively entitled the Bedminister Hills Housing corporation, which will contain three representatives of the Hills Development Company, two representatives of Bedminster Township, and two representatives of the Department of the Public Advocate. The corporation will receive up to approximately $70,000 in seed money from the project development budget.

The resale controls are designed to remain in effect for a 30-year period. They provide for both a formula resale price and a 60-day period at the time of each resale transaction during which the corporation will have the exclusive right to purchase the unit or refer prospective buyers from its waiting list.[127] An unusual feature in the resale control scheme designed for the project is that should the 60-day period expire and the unit be sold on the open market, it must be sold (1) at the formula price; and (2) subject once again to the resale controls for the *next* transaction. The corporation will, therefore, have a second opportunity to restore the unit to the ranks of the housing stock affordable to lower-income households. In order to reduce the risk that changes in the relationship between house price and affordability could make it difficult for a lower-income buyer to qualify for the unit in the future, the corporation will share in the appreciation of the unit. Funds thus obtained by the corporation will be used to ensure continued affordability of the units on resale.[128]

The Bedminster project shows at a stage considerably further advanced than any of the Mahwah proposals that the inclusionary goals set forth in *Mount Laurel II* can be made to work. At the same time, the project as the first of its kind has brought to light a series of questions that must be addressed as the *Mount Laurel II* doctrine gradually becomes a statewide policy. Many of the issues seem to arise from the lack of alternatives to Bedminster-type inclusionary programs; i.e., from an environment in which inclusionary housing programs are perceived as *the* low- and moderate-income housing program, rather than simply *a* low- and moderate-income housing program among others. The most significant one is that of the "reach" of the program. The Bedminster units, although all targeted to the low- and moderate-income population, are accessible in reality only to a very small fraction of that population. Specifically, they are accessible only to potential homebuyers, and among homebuyers, only to those at or near the ceilings of their respective income ranges. Instead of providing housing for households earning from 0 to 50 percent of median, and from 50 to 80 percent of median, adjusted by family size, the project is actually affordable to households earning from 42 to 50 percent of median, and from 71 to 80 percent of the area median, adjusted for family size.[129] Thus, no more than 10 to 15 percent of the universe of low- and moderate-income households are potential candidates for the Bedminster units. This is not likely to pose a concrete problem for the Bedminster project since it is the first project of its sort and is located in an exceptional area, but it does raise a serious issue. The long-term benefits of inclusionary housing programs could be significantly compromised if all future New Jersey projects are targeted to the same narrow segments of the broader lower-income universe.

Some technical improvements are clearly possible within the same basic model. Instead of dividing the universe into two categories, 0 to 50 and 50 to 80 percent, which tends to encourage the "skimming" process, affordability standards could be broken down into finer categories, such as 35 to 50 percent, 50 to 65 percent, and 65 to 80 percent. This would broaden the eligible population as well as recognize that for an inclusionary program to reach substantially below households earning 35 percent of the area median income is patently unrealistic in the absence of outside subsidy funds. Still, this is clearly only a limited improvement. The fact remains that inclusionary housing programs, in the absence of federal or state subsidies, are only one part of a housing strategy that will be realistically capable of meeting the housing needs of all lower-income households. Except in unusual cases, it is unreasonable to expect that more than a token amount of rental housing will be built through inclusionary programs until, or unless federal subsidies are available. If the course of recent federal housing policy is a guide, if and when subsidy funds again reappear, it is more than likely that a condition of their use will be that they be used in an inclusionary setting.

Other issues are of a more technical nature and are many in number: Is a buydown an appropriate means of making units more affordable to low-income households, or do the risks that household incomes will not keep pace with payment increases outweigh the benefits of enabling more families to qualify? Is the proposed division in allowable appreciation between the owner and the corporation really adequate for fairness to the owner? Is a local nonprofit organization of the sort contemplated an appropriate and effective vehicle for administering a program of this nature? Other issues will undoubtedly emerge once the units are built and occupancy begins.

In the final analysis, not only is it in all probability not possible for these questions to be answered definitively, but it is most probably not desirable as well. The nature of these questions is that reasonable men and women may legitimately differ on their answers; there is no particularly compelling reason why a program which is by its nature decentralized should be forced to conform to highly specific standards and conditions for each of its facets. Within certain general standards of what is reasonable, which in most cases can be determined through a common sense application of the basic principles and premises set forth in *Mount Laurel II*, each community should be free to develop specific procedures and requirements that best reflect the needs and concerns of the community.

The Future of Inclusionary Housing Programs in Housing and Land Use Policy

Prudence dictates that one take great care before predicting the future. Predictions that a particular modest phenomenon is about to become a wave that will sweep the country are particularly risky. In the area of land use, such predictions have a particularly bad record. During the past few decades, commentators have identified a number of such waves: state control of land use, development or growth timing, or transfer of development rights. None have swept the country; in some cases, such as with development timing, even some of the original advocates have since had second thoughts.

Short of sweeping the country, the most important threshold that a particular land use approach or technique can pass through is that of normality, where the approach comes to be perceived as part of the "normal" body of tools and methods available to the sophisticated practitioner or the adventuresome municipality. The evidence from our survey of inclusionary housing programs is that it is rapidly approaching that threshold. This is not to suggest that it is only a matter of moments before the thousands of municipalities and counties with land use regulatory powers adopt inclusionary zoning ordinances and establish inclusionary housing programs, as in California or New Jersey. On the contrary, that is very unlikely. What *is* happening, instead, is that inclusionary housing programs are being seen more and more as a reasonable and effective means by which a community can address a need for more affordable housing. This applies clearly to suburban communities and to many urban centers as well. *If a community reaches the conclusion that it should actively intervene to promote the production of affordable housing in the 1980s, it will give serious consideration to adopting an inclusionary zoning ordinance.* It may or may not enact such an ordinance. Indeed, it is quite possible that it will choose not to initiate an inclusionary housing program more often than it will do so. The central point, however, is that inclusionary housing programs are entering the normal vocabulary of the worlds of housing policy and land use regulation. As they do so more and more, the programs themselves are likely to become more widespread.

An unlikely actor encouraging this trend is the federal government. In recent years, at least since the Housing and Community Development Act of 1974, the vocabulary and philosophy of inclusionary housing policy has become a major theme of federal housing legislation. The 1974 act specified that an objective of federal subsidy funds for low-income housing would be:

> promoting greater choice of housing opportunities and avoiding undue
> concentrations of assisted persons in areas containing a high proportion of
> low income persons.[130]

The act also provided with regard to the newly enacted Section 8 rental subsidy
program that the Department of Housing & Urban Development could give preference to projects in which no more than 20 percent of the units were assisted
with Section 8 rental subsidies.[131] In practice, the project mentality of both HUD
area office personnel and the personnel of state housing finance agencies, with a
few notable exceptions such as Massachusetts, led to little use being made of this
provision.

Although the 1974 act may have approached inclusionary policy somewhat
diffidently, subsequent enactments were more forthright. In 1980, Congress
enacted the Mortgage Bond Subsidy Tax Act, a law dealing with the circumstances under which tax-exempt bonds could be issued by state and local governments to finance housing development.[132] Although this act dealt primarily
with the sale of tax-exempt bonds to finance homeownership, it included a significant provision governing the use of tax-exempt bonds to finance rental housing: *Any rental development financed with tax-exempt bonds must provide that 20
percent of the units be affordable to and occupied by low-income households.* In
certain inner city and economically distressed areas, known as "targeted areas,"
the requirement was reduced to 15 percent of the units. Although experience with
rental projects affected by the act has not been extensive or widely documented, a
substantial number of developments have been financed in which the 20 percent
requirement was met through use of Section 8 subsidies, and a smaller number in
which either internal subsidies or funds derived from local resources were
used.[133]

Most recently, the same policy has been incorporated into the newly enacted
Section 17 Rental Rehabilitation and Development Grant program, sometimes
referred to as the Dodd-Schumer Bill.[134] This legislation, which provides capital
grants for the construction and substantial rehabilitation of housing for rental occupancy, provides that:

> The owner of each assisted structure agrees that, during the 20-year
> period beginning on the date on which 50 per centum of the units in the
> structure are occupied or completed, at least 20 per centum of the units the
> construction or substantial rehabilitation of which is provided for under the
> application shall be occupied, or available for occupancy. by persons and

families whose incomes do not exceed 80 per centum of the area median income.[135]

The act further provides that, in order to ensure that "skimming" the households at or near the ceiling of the low-income population does not take place, "the grantee shall provide that the rents of such [units available for lower-income occupancy] units are not more than 30 per centum of the adjusted income of a family whose income equals 50 per centum of the median income for the area, as determined by the Secretary with adjustments for smaller and larger families."[136]

This program has just been enacted, and there is no way to tell whether it will be any more successful, either in creating rental housing or in fostering economic integration, than its predecessors, particularly the Section 236 program, whose failures in that regard provided at least part of the impetus for developing inclusionary housing programs. It contains a "prevailing wage" requirement for developments containing more than twelve units that may discourage builders from using the program in conjunction with conventional construction projects. It represents, however, a major milestone on a route being followed by federal housing policy, a route which is leading directly toward the targeting of federal housing funds into inclusionary housing developments.

The effect of federal initiatives such as Section 17 is likely to be limited; whatever the shifts may be in national politics during the coming decade, it is hard to imagine any administration, Democratic or Republican, implementing a new housing production program on a scale comparable to those of either the Section 235/236 programs, or the Section 8 program, in their peak years. A production approach which is targeted toward limited and more carefully defined housing objectives and geographic areas is a more likely prospect. Section 17 may be a step toward such a program.

Federal policy, therefore, will tend to strengthen the trend that has already been noted: the gradual filtering of the inclusionary housing vocabulary into the language of planning and land use regulation, and an ongoing modest increase in the number of jurisdictions in which inclusionary programs are put into effect. A major parallel trend, also fostered by the emerging federal policy, will be that inclusionary objectives will be more and more widely applied in settings where no formal inclusionary housing programs are in place. Many rental housing projects have historically accommodated households of widely varying economic level; the step from that point to a public policy that explicitly targets a percentage of rental units in new developments for lower-income households is narrower today than it may have seemed only a short while ago. Similarly, the notion that large-scale developments, whether residential or mixed use, should include some lower-income housing has become more generally accepted and less of a visionary idea as it appeared when it was first suggested some fifteen or more years ago, and first incorporated in the planning of communities such as Columbia, Maryland, or Roosevelt Island, New York.[137] Many of the communities planned in the 1960s and 1970s have grown and matured and demonstrated that the idealistic goals of economic and racial integration initially expressed by their planners and developers are workable and fully consistent with the creation of attractive, livable communities.[138]

Although it may seem almost intolerably naive, one wonders whether in the America of the 1980s, in which the fantasy of permanent economic growth and upward mobility has finally been laid to rest, economic differences will come to be seen less as a stigma and more as an inevitable part of economic and social reality. As more and more Americans realize that the "nouveau poor"[139] are us — or if not ourselves, then our children — they may become more accepting of the presence of the less affluent around them. If that is the case, then there is a possibility of achieving a national housing policy in which inclusionary housing techniques and strategies are coupled with public and private resources to provide greater housing opportunities and economic opportunities for all Americans.

NOTES

1. In view of the extent to which programs are enacted and abolished, generally on short notice, in local jurisdictions, any complete survey would be an artifact of a particular moment and of little genuine significance. The time and energy that would be needed to assemble such a survey would be vastly out of proportion to its value.

2. The tabulation of programs identified in the literature, bearing in mind that it is neither complete nor definitive, may be of some moderate interest: California (38), New Jersey (16), Colorado (5), Massachusetts, Illinois, and New York (2 each), Connecticut, Delaware, Florida, Maryland, Oregon, Virginia, and Washington (1 each). This tabulation includes state programs such as the New Jersey coastal program.

3. State of California, Department of Housing & Community Development, *101 Steps to Better Housing: The California Housing Plan, 1982* (Sacramento, 1982).

4. It is likely that in no other state was the affordability crisis felt so strongly on a statewide, or nearly statewide, basis. In most other states, the most severe problems tended to be limited to relatively small parts of the state, e.g., in Maryland, where the greatest pressures were largely limited to the suburbs of Washington, D.C., thereby providing little impetus for the growth of a strong statewide consensus on the issue.

5. This priority has since shifted and more recent legislative sessions have been more concerned with deregulation; interview with Ruth Schwartz, California Department of Housing & Community Development.

6. California Government Code, *Planning and Zoning Law*, Sec. 65583(c).

7. Ibid., Sec. 65584.

8. Ibid., Sec. 65913.1.

9. Ibid., Sec. 65913.3.

10. Ibid., Sec. 65915.

11. James Longtin, *California Land Use Regulations: 1980/1981 Supplement* (Westlake Village, CA, 1980); Sec. 1.22(3), p. 4; also see the polemic against the Department of Housing & Community Development generally, and its guidelines in particular, in Ward Connerly & Associates, *The Implications of Inclusionary Housing Programs*, a study conducted for the California Building Industry Association (Sacramento 1979), pp. 1-26.

12. Memorandum from Carolyn Burton, Esq., to I. Donald Terner, Director, "Legality of In-clusionary Zoning Ordinances," dated September 11, 1978; memorandum to "All Interested Par-ties" from Legal Division, Department of Housing & Community Development, "Legality of Deed Restrictions," dated December 19, 1978.

13. Carolyn Burton, Esq., "California Legislature Prohibits Exclusionary Zoning, Mandates Fair Share: Inclusionary Housing Programs a Likely Response," *San Fernando Valley Law Review*, Vol. 9 (1981). This article also provides a good overview of the scope of the major California housing legislation enacted during this period.

14. Public Resources Code, Sec. 30000 *et seq.* A summary is provided in Longtin, *California Regulations*, pp. 52-55

15. Ibid., Sec. 30213.

16. California Coastal Commission, *Draft Interpretative Guidelines on New Construction of Housing* (San Francisco, January 24, 1980), pp. 8-12. These guidelines superseded those issued Oc-tober 4, 1977.

17. Interview with Ruth Schwartz, DH&CD. A major analytical study of the housing policies and actions of the California Coastal Commission, conducted by Seymour Schwartz and his colleagues at the University of California at Davis, is expected to be published in 1984.

18. SB 626 (Mello, Chapter 1007 of 1981). This amendment became effective in January 1982.

19. Seymour Schwartz, Robert Johnston, Geoffrey Wandesforde-Smith, and Kirk Savage, *The Implementation of SB 626 in Southern California: A Summary of Findings* (Davis, CA, 1983).

20. The actual procedure was indirect; the Air Resources Board imposed growth controls in parts of Orange County as a result of air quality problems. These growth controls were implemented through a moratorium on hookups carried out by the Water Resources Control Board at the instigation of the ARB. Thus, the provision of affordable housing was required in order to obtain approval of sewer hookups. Interview with Victor Rea, California Department of Housing & Community Devel-opment.

21. Interview with Victor Rea. See, also, California Coastal Commission, *New Construction*, p. 6.

22. Orange, County of, California, Southeast Orange County Housing Task Force, *Report of the Southeast Orange County Housing Task Force* (Santa Ana, 1977), p. 1-2.

23. Ibid., p. VI-2.

24. Kenneth Leventhal & Co., *Bench Mark Villas: A Demonstration of Affordable Housing*, report prepared for the Orange County Chapter of the Building Industry Association of Southern California (Santa Ana, 1983). Twenty percent of the 124 units in this project were sold to households earning 80 percent of the area median or less, with *all* of the remaining units sold to households earning between 80 and 120 percent of the area median income. The project and the report represent an outstanding effort to achieve savings through efficiency and economy rather than subsidies and to document the savings obtained for the use of other developers, local officials, and housing advocates.

25. For example, it is difficult to determine precisely how many units represented by the "several hundred" that Santa Cruz County reported to the state are under commitment. Similarly, among the roughly 2,600 units that have been or are being produced under the San Francisco program, it is not certain how many should be considered "built" or considered "committed."

26. Interview with Ruth Schwartz, Department of Housing & Community Development.

27. One major factor which could change this is the course of litigation now in the courts regard-ing inclusionary housing programs. A suit has been brought challenging Orange County's disman-tling of its inclusionary housing program; other suits have been brought to compel affirmative actions under the state laws in municipalities that have failed to meet their fair share of regional housing needs. Given the scope of the state laws described earlier, there is a substantial legal argument that can be made to the effect that a municipality which does not have an inclusionary program in place has a heavy burden to prove that it can meet lower-income housing needs otherwise; alternatively, that a municipality, having adopted such a program, cannot repeal it unless it has put in its place something comparably effective as a means of delivering lower-income housing. Interview with Crystal Sims, Esq., Legal Aid Society of Orange County.

28. California law makes this easier than in many states; many large-scale developments are ap-

proved through a procedure of general plan amendment, during the course of which the municipality has broad discretion to impose specific development conditions or requirements, whatever may cr may not have previously existed in their plans or ordinances. Many of the inclusionary housing programs described in this chapter are administered without a formal ordinance, as such under the gereral powers associated with the general plan, or the housing element.

29. A survey of the literature identified 21 programs, of which 14 were clearly voluntary density bonus programs. It is likely, however, that there are a number of unreported ordinances and programs.

30. Montgomery County Code, Chapter 25A, Moderately Priced Dwelling Unit Law, as amended.

31. Office of the County Executive, Montgomery County, Maryland, Executive Regulation No 29-82, *Maximum Sales Price Limits for Moderately Priced Dwelling Units;* No. 31-82, *Maximum Rental Limits for Moderately Priced Dwelling Units,* February 1, 1983.

32. Office of the County Executive, Montgomery County, Maryland, Executive Regulation No 30-82, *Maximum Income Limits for Applicants for Moderately Priced Dwelling Units,* Feb. 1, 1983.

33. Described in Leadership Council for Metropolitan Open Communities, *Recent Developments in Housing,* Vol. 18, October 1982, p. 6.

34. Department of Housing and Community Development, Montgomery County, MD., *Moderately Priced Housing in Montgomery County* (undated).

35. Department of Housing and Community Development, Montgomery County, Md., *Assisted Units in Montgomery County,* March 1983.

36. Kleven, "Inclusionary Ordinances," footnote 32, p. 1443. This characterization is Kleven's, and not the author's.

37. Ibid., p. 1445, for reference to initial draft ordinance. The ten-year period for resale controls became effective on October 1, 1981. Office of the County Executive, Montgomery County, Md., Executive Regulation No. 44-81, *Administrative Procedures and Requirements for the MPDU Program,* Oct. 15, 1981.

38. Arlington County, Virginia, Zoning Ordinance, Section 36, Subsection H5c.

39. Ibid.

40. Amendatory ordinance, adopted March 21, 1982.

41. Letter from Larry J. Brown, County Manager, Arlington County, Virginia, September 30, 1983.

42. Ibid.

43. Arlington County, Virginia, Office of the County Manager, untitled chart of developments providing moderate-income units, 1983.

44. This point was made separately in interviews with officials in all three jurisdictions.

45. Brooks et al., *Housing Choice,* pp. 126-128.

46. Joel T. Werth, "Inclusionary Zoning Regulations: An Update," *PAS Memo* 80-3 (Chicago: American Planning Association, March 1980).

47. Quoted in Brooks et al., *Housing Choice,* p. 93.

48. William Ryan et al., *All In Together: An Evaluation of Mixed-Income Multifamily Housing* (Boston: Massachusetts Housing Finance Agency, 1974).

49. Brooks et al., *Housing Choice,* p. 94.

50. Town of Lewisboro, N.Y., Community Development Committee, *Table of Costs for Middle Income Units,* March 30, 1982 (effective date).

51. Barbara Behrens Gers, "The City Hall Solution," *Housing,* July 1981, p 70.

52. Ibid., p. 71.

53. Town of New Castle, New York, Zoning Ordinance (as amended by Local Law 16, Oct. 29, 1979), Sec. 60-417.2121(1). Low/moderate-income families are defined in the ordinance as having an income at the following multiple of $17,000 (in 1979), as that figure is adjusted annually based on the consumer price index:

1 person	0.7
2 person	0.9
3 person	1.0
4 person	1.1
5 person or more	1.2

This represents a very low gradient of income increase with increased family size; coupled with a zoning ordinance in which the permitted density of development drops drastically as the number of bedrooms increases (an exclusionary feature which has been singled out as illegal by the New Jersey courts), the ordinance strongly discourages the construction of large units, or the housing of large families.

54. Ibid., Sec. 60-437.9.

55. *Joseph Blitz et al. v. Town of New Castle*, 463 NYS2d 832, decided by the New York Supreme Court, Appellate Division, June 6, 1983.

56. Town of New Castle, New York, Zoning Ordinance Sec. 60-417-2121 (5), (6), (8), (9), (10) and (11).

57. City of Lakewood, Colorado, *Findings and Recommendations of the Affordable Housing Task Force* (Lakewood, Col: February 1982), pp. 26-27.

58. Ibid., p. 22.

59. There are other inclusionary housing programs, or zoning ordinances, worthy of brief mention. *Windsor, Connecticut* has a provision in its New Neighborhood Design Development district (similar to a planned development district) under which at least 10 percent of the units must be provided to lower-income households (Section 8-eligible) or an equivalent amount of land deeded to the Windsor Housing Authority; Zoning Ordinance, sec. 11.2.3.B(3). *Highland Park, Illinois* has a density bonus provision, discussed briefly in chapter five, under which a number of Section 8 units have been provided in the community. *King County, Washington* has recently adopted development criteria for a large underdeveloped section of the county requiring that 10 percent of newly developed units be low-income (under 80 percent of median), 10 percent moderate income (80 to 100 percent of median), and 10 percent "median income," or 100 to 120 percent of area median. If no public subsidy funds are available, the low-income units may be waived, but the developer is required to set aside land for future construction of those units if and when subsidies become available for up to five years. King County Code, 20.12 addendum, *The Newcastle Community Plan* (adopted May 31, 1983 by Ordinance no. 6422). *Boulder, Colorado* has a program whereby any developer seeking annexation in order to obtain city water and sewer for developments of more than 50 units must ensure that fifteen percent of the units, either on- or off-site, are set aside for lower-income households. Described in Allen Porter, Esq., & Gerald Muller, Esq., *A Legal Analysis Updating and Supplementing the Princeton Housing Proposal*, prepared for the Princeton Regional Planning Board (Princeton, NJ, December 1979).

60. The municipalities identified as having inclusionary housing programs in New Jersey, as of mid-1983, were the following (V = voluntary density bonus program; M = mandatory inclusionary program): Bedminster (M), Bridgewater (M), Cherry Hill (M), Cranbury (V), East Brunswick (V), East Windsor (M), Franklin (in Somerset County) (M), Mt. Laurel (M), Old Bridge (V), Piscataway (V), Raritan (in Hunterdon County) (V), South Brunswick (M), and West Windsor (V). A survey of features of most of these programs is found in Robert W. Burchell et al., *Mount Laurel II: Challenge & Delivery of Low-Cost Housing* (New Brunswick, N.J.: Center for Urban Policy Research, 1983), pp. 384-388.

61. Michael Danielson, *The Politics of Exclusion* (New York: Columbia University Press, 1976), p. 45.

62. S.803 (introduced May 12, 1969).

63. The Voluntary Balanced Housing Plan Act, A.1421 (introduced Nov. 13, 1972). The history of this effort is discussed in Alan Mallach, "Do Lawsuits Build Housing: The Implications of Exclusionary Zoning Litigation," *Rutgers-Camden Law Journal*, Vol. 6, No. 4, Spring 1975.

64. S-3100. After the modifications had been made to this bill, which resulted in the substance of the legislation being largely removed, the sponsor, Sen. Martin Greenberg, received assurances from New Jersey League of Municipalities representatives that they would support it and as a result, it passed in the state senate. Subsequently, the League reversed its position, and the bill was killed in the assembly.

65. Executive Order No. 35, issued April 2, 1976.

66. Executive Order No. 46, issued December 8, 1976. See also article in *New York Times*, "Byrne, with his eyes on a second term, drops support of open housing in suburban areas," Dec. 10, 1976.

67. Executive Order No. 6, issued May 4, 1982.

68. New Jersey Department of Community Affairs, *A Revised Statewide Housing Allocation Report for New Jersey* (Trenton, N.J., 1978), pp. 27-28.

69. New Jersey Department of Community Affairs & Tri-State Regional Planning Commission *Affordable Housing Handbook* (Trenton, N.J., 1981), pp. 28-29.

70. The author was closely involved with this work as the principal advisor to the Department of the Public Advocate on housing and land use during this period. See, also, Martin Bierbaum, "On the Frontiers of Public Interest Law: The New Jersey State Department of Public Advocate–The Public Interest Advocacy Division," *Seton Hall Law Review*, Vol. 13, No. 3 (1983).

71. N.J.S.A. 13:19-1 *et seq.*

72. N.J.A.C. (New Jersey Administrative Code) 7:7E-7.2(e)2.i, adopted January 6, 1981.

73. Ibid., Sec.(e)1.iii and iv.

74. The information and conclusions in this paragraph are based on the personal experience of the author who was closely involved with the parties mentioned during the period under discussion.

75. Pinelands Protection Act, N.J.S.A. 13:18-1 *et seq.* This agency was established in 1979 principally to protect the environmental balance in the Pinelands Region of New Jersey, an area covering a large part of the southern half of the state. The agency has broad master planning powers over this region as well as the power to supersede local land use controls in the event that a municipal plan and zoning ordinance fail to conform to the standards of the Pinelands master plan. See *Pinelands Comprehensive Management Plan*, Sec. 6-1201 to Sec. 6-1203.

76. This agency was established in 1970 to direct both planning and development in a large under-utilized area of northern New Jersey in close proximity to New York City whose development had lagged because of difficult environmental conditions and fragmentation of the area which was divided among eighteen separate municipalities. The agency has full planning and zoning controls within the district and has established an inclusionary policy for certain areas designated as Specially Planned Areas in its master plan. There has been only one large-scale residential development application made under these regulations; at the time, however, and in view of the pioneering nature of this proposal and its economic uncertainties, the commission chose to waive the inclusionary conditions of its ordinance. This was strongly opposed by a number of housing and community organizations in the area. Personal experience, discussions with James Sacher, Esq., formerly attorney for the Bergen County Fair Housing Council.

77. Although there is no "home rule" in the legal sense in New Jersey; i.e., state enabling statutes delegating broad fiscal managerial powers to local government, there is a time-honored tradition, known as "home rule," which provides that state government will refrain from interjecting itself in matters of concern only to local government, of which one of the most jealously protected has been land use control.

78. Memorandum from Carl E. Hintz, Director of Planning & Community Development, to Bertram Busch, Esq., Township Attorney, East Brunswick Township, December 11, 1980; also, "East Brunswick Planner Prepares Mount Laurel Defense," New Brunswick *Home News*, February 20, 1983.

79. These projects included 15 units of Sec. 235 townhouses, built by a nonprofit organization to whom a developer had deeded land; a 153-unit senior citizen housing project built under the Sec. 236 program; and forty townhouse units, which will be priced at $58,000.

80. According to the Hintz memorandum, note 78, two of four developers by 1980 had chosen the density bonus option. A more recent overview, *New York Times*, May 22, 1983, indicates that another large-scale development is underway which will not include lower-income housing under the density bonus provision. Furthermore, where the density bonus has been utilized, the developers have not utilized it up to the maximum allowed by the ordinance.

81. According to Burchell et al., *Mount Laurel II*, p. 386, two developments with a total of 172 lower than market cost units have been built under the South Brunswick inclusionary ordinance.

82. Approximately 40 lower-income units have been produced under the Cherry Hill ordinance; see "Cherry Hill Needs to Tackle Legal Challenge in Housing," *Philadelphia Inquirer*, Feb. 20, 1983.

83. Ibid., statement by Gary Schaal, Marketing Director, Scarborough Corporation.

84. Ibid.

85. In addition to the negative program features described in chapter five governing the so-called

inclusionary program, East Windsor Township offered substantially more attractive zoning opportunities, in terms both of higher density and fewer unreasonable standards and conditions, in other zoning districts of the township which did not have inclusionary housing requirements.

86. Old Bridge Township, Land Development Ordinance, Sec. 9-5:2.1.3. Specifically, in return for development of 10 percent of the units as "affordable housing," a density increase from 3.4 units per acre to 3.6 units per acre is permitted. This ordinance also, in a manner similar to that of the New Castle, New York ordinance (see note 53) allows density bonuses for a wide variety of amenity features or facilities unrelated to affordable housing.

87. 92 NJ at 198-199.

88. See, e.g., *Casey v. Zoning Hearing Board of Warwick Township*, 328 A2d 464, (1974), or *Township of Williston v. Chesterdale Farms, Inc.* Pa. Cmwlth 300 A2d 107 (1973), Pa.Sup.Ct. 341 A2d 466 (1975).

89. 72 NJ 481 (1977).

90. Ibid., at 549-550.

91. Ibid., at 551-552.

92. This footnote was cited by the trial judge as the basis for denying specific relief to the plaintiff city of Newark, acting as a landowner, in *Newark v. Township of West Milford* (unpublished opinion issued Feb. 19, 1981, Docket No. L-25413-77 PW), notwithstanding findings that the ordinance was exclusionary and that substantial parts of Newark's acreage were suitable for development. For legal commentaries, see Jan Krasnowiecki, "Zoning Litigation and the New Pennsylvania Procedures, *U.Pa.L.Rev.*, Vol. 120 (1972); Arnold Mytelka & Rosalind Mytelka, "Exclusionary Zoning: A Consideration of Remedies," *Seton Hall Law Review*, Vol. 7 (1975).

93. 92 NJ at 279-280.

94. Ibid., fn 37 at 279.

95. Ibid., at 280.

96. Ibid., at 308-309.

97. It can reasonably be assumed that in the event federal or state subsidy programs for lower-income housing are re-established, any housing development proposed under such a subsidy program would have the same status under *Mount Laurel II*.

98. It should be emphasized that the award of a builder's remedy to a developer-plaintiff does not modify the continuing municipal obligation to provide for its fair share allocation — in this case the total fair share less the amount which the developer-plaintiff proposes to build. It is likely that in cases brought by a developer and where the municipality is found not to have met its obligation, the court will simultaneously order that building permits be granted to the plaintiff *and* that a rezoning take place to provide for the balance of the fair share obligation, most probably under the supervision of a court-appointed master.

99. The *Urban League* case had initially been brought in 1974 with the assistance of the National Committee against Discrimination in Housing against 23 of the 25 municipalities in Middlesex County, a major central New Jersey suburban county, and was tried early in 1976. At that time one municipality was dismissed, 11 were conditionally dismissed on the basis of settlement with plaintiffs, and 11 were ordered to rezone to meet their *Mount Laurel* obligations. Seven of the 11 municipalities appealed, and in 1979 the appellate division reversed the trial court on the basis of technical issues dealing with the determination of region and fair share. This decision in turn was reversed by the supreme court as a part of the *Mount Laurel II* package; the case was remanded back to the trial court, although not the original trial judge, to establish each municipality's obligation under the new standards and order them to rezone accordingly. The hearings on liability and remedy as they affected the seven municipalities were scheduled for spring 1984.

100. Discussion with Mr. Lloyd Brown, Executive Vice President, O & Y Old Bridge Development Corporation.

101. Discussion with Carl Bisgaier, Esq.

102. Discussion with Kenneth Meiser, Esq., New Jersey Department of the Public Advocate.

103. The 1977 *Madison* decision effectively undermined a great deal of the substance of the *Mount Laurel* decision that the court had handed down two years earlier. In particular, we note the need to establish a fair share allocation to serve as a basis for a municipality's subsequent rezoning (see 72 NJ at 498-499), and the need to provide housing explicitly for lower-income households, for which the *Madison* court substituted the notion of "least cost" housing (ibid. at 510-514). Although

there is no evidence that the court was consciously or deliberately "backing off" the *Mount Laurel* decision, there is no question that the *Madison* decision had that effect, especially on conservative trial judges reluctant to reverse municipal actions. See Williams, *op. cit.*, 1983 Supplement to Volume 3 Sec. 66-12e, pp. 12-18. This was notable in the trial opinions in the *Mount Laurel* remand, and in the *Mahwah* case. A careful reading of *Mount Laurel II* shows in many places a painstaking effort by the court to extricate itself from the difficulties created by *Madison* in order to return to the clarity of the initial *Mount Laurel* principles.

104. This study has been published as Burchell et al., *Mount Laurel II: Challenge & Delivery of Low-Cost Housing.* It is unclear what effect it will have on the process of implementing the *Mount Laurel II* decision.

105. Philip Caton, Clarke & Caton, *Mahwah Township Fair Share Allocation Report*, July 1983. Letter opinion and order of Judge Harvey Smith, J.S.C., dated September 16, 1983.

106. Michael F. Kauker Associates, *Mount Laurel II: Private Development*, preliminary report to township of Mahwah, December 9, 1983, p. 1. Mr. Kauker was the township's planning consultant at this time.

107. Ibid., attachment entitled "Tabulation — Mount Laurel II." The township proposes to meet between 40 to 50 percent of its fair share obligation through other means, including scatter-site public housing, creation of accessory apartments in single family dwellings, and use of Section 8 certificates. The plaintiffs have indicated that they consider the township's estimates of the number of units to be provided through these other resources patently unrealistic.

108. Until mid-1983 Bergen County, in which Mahwah is located, was considered part of the New York City SMSA (which also included Rockland County, New York). The overwhelming weight of New York City in this SMSA tended to result in an areawide median income substantially lower than that of Bergen County by itself. Bergen County is now part of a smaller PMSA made up of Bergen and Passaic Counties, which can be anticipated to have a higher median income than the New York City SMSA. No revised income figures, however, have yet been published.

109. Other assumptions included (1) a 5 percent down payment; (2) property taxes at 1.965 percent of true market value, the current township rate; (3) insurance at $40 per $10,000 house value; and (4) condominium association fees at $180 per $10,000 house value per year. The units are proposed to be condominium apartments.

110. Memorandum from Scott Radway, AICP, planning consultant to James MacIsaac, Esq., attorney for Franklin Commons development, entitled "Mount Laurel Feasibility Analysis," dated February 29, 1983.

111. Discussion with Philip Caton, Mahwah rezoning master.

112. Confidential submission to Mahwah rezoning master.

113. See "Mahwah mayor says poor will bring crime," *Bergen Record*, October 3, 1983, in which the following appeared: "Referring to crime-ridden public housing projects in New York and Philadelphia, Kent [the mayor of Mahwah] said, 'I assure you these are the type of people [Mount Laurel-type] housing will attract. To me, the quickest way to develop a slum is to let this kind of housing in here.' Kent added that his position was that of the township committee. 'Therefore, it represents the view of the entire community,' he said. None of the four other township committee members challenged the mayor's assertion."

114. *The Insider*, Vol. 1, No. 1, December 1983. This newsletter notes that "Mayor Frederick Kent has put the resources of his office at the disposal of the committee, but will not be eligible to become a committee member until the conclusion of his term as mayor."

115. Bedminster is the center of fox hunting in the northeastern United States. The annual meet of the Essex Hunt, in fact, held each fall, is a major social event for the entire area

116. The case was formed from the consolidation of two cases, one brought by a group of low- and moderate-income citizens, under the auspices of the Suburban Action Institute and the New Jersey chapter of the American Civil Liberties Union (*Cieswick et al. v. Township of Bedminster*, Docket No. L-28061-71 P.W.), and the second brought by the landowners and prospective developers, who were a subsidiary of the Johns-Manville Corporation (*Allan-Deane v. Township of Bedminster*, Docket No. L-36896-70 P.W.). The initial trial was held in 1974 and the decision rendered against the township in 1975. After an unsuccessful appeal by the township to the supreme court, the township was ordered to amend its zoning ordinance in 1977. The revised ordinance was inadequate in the eyes of both parties of plaintiffs, and a second trial was held in 1979, at which time the trial

court found the amended ordinance invalid, ordered that the developer-plaintiff be given suitable zoning for development, and appointed a master to superintend the rezoning process. The order approving the revised zoning was entered in 1980, at which time the office of the public advocate (which had taken responsibility for the public interest part of the case from the ACLU) appealed on the lower-income housing issue.

117. See *Madison*, 72 NJ 481 at 510-514.

118. This was a partnership in which the Manville Corporation (formerly Johns-Manville Corporation) held a 50 percent interest.

119. The Bedminster Township Land Development Ordinance, Sec. 13- 805.3h, specifies that "final approval shall not be granted for any section of the development until the following ratio of required subsidized and/or least cost to market dwelling units is conceptually approved by the subsidizing agency in the case of subsidized dwelling units and/or constructed or under construction in the case of least cost dwelling units:

	% Subsidized Units and/or Least Cost Units	% Market Units
	0%	up to 25%
At least	25%	up to 50%
At least	50%	up to 75%
At least	100%	more than 75%"

120. Much of the information in this paragraph, as well as elsewhere in this section, is based on the personal experience of the author, who has acted as consultant to The Hills Development Company, responsible for development of the low- and moderate-income housing program, since May 1983.

121. Ibid., Sec. 13-606.4.j, required that all such developments contain a minimum percentage of four-bedroom units, at least 5 percent in rental developments, and 10 to 20 percent in sales units.

122. The combination of exceptionally high house values with the effect of the AT&T facility, a $50+ million rateable in a very small community, has maintained the property tax rate in Bedminster at consistently low levels. For 1983, property taxes were 1.22 percent of equalized or market value.

123. The land and site improvement costs associated with the project were considerable. The land was acquired at considerable cost by Johns-Manville in 1969. Infrastructure improvements included construction of an advanced wastewater treatment plant costing in excess of $4 million as well as a loop road for the development at arterial road standards.

124. Under the proposed settlement, the developer will be able to seek price increases, with court approval, if and when the Department of Housing & Urban Development increases the low- and moderate-income ceilings for the area in which Bedminster is located.

125. Bedminister Township Land Development Ordinance, Sec. 13-606.4.j.2, required that 35 percent of the least cost units either be subsidized rental units, or, if subsidies were unavailable, rental units "rented at a cost not exceeding the Fair Market Rents established for Bedminster Township by the Department of Housing & Urban Development." This is a very liberal and not particularly relevant standard, since the fair market rents are a reflection of market conditions and are not necessarily affordable in themselves by low- and moderate-income households.

126. One particular problem associated with this outcome was the fact that the New Jersey Finance Agency, which provides tax-exempt bond financing for rental projects, has a statutory requirement that projects be built under "prevailing wage" standards. Applying this standard to the Bedminister project would have raised development costs considerably, well in excess of the savings resulting from the tax-exempt bond financing. The project would, therefore, have had to rely on conventional mortgage financing, in the area of 13 to 14 percent.

127. It was the intention of the planners of the project to impose resale controls for a longer period than 30 years; since the mortgage commitment from the MFA included a condition that project approval be obtained either from FMA or FHLMC, both of which have regulations setting a 30-year limit on resale controls, the project plans have been accordingly modified, unless a change can be negotiated with the applicable secondary mortgage market agency.

128. There are a number of ways in which these funds can be used, including further mortgage buydowns, cost writedowns, or down payment assistance. The corporation will also be allowed to retain some part of the funds collected to cover its operating expenses.

129. The actual ranges vary with regard to each different low-income unit, from 42 to 50 percent for the one-bedroom unit, 44 to 50 for the two-bedroom loft unit, and 45 to 50 for the three-bedroom unit. All of the moderate-income units provide for the same 71 to 80 percent range.

130. 42 U.S.C. Sec. 5304(a)(4).

131. Cited in Herbert Franklin, David Falk, and Arthur J. Levin, "Inclusionary Programs and the Larger Public Interest" in Rose & Rothman, eds., *After Mount Laurel*.

132. Public Law 96-449, enacted December 5, 1980.

133. The latter have taken place in Montgomery County, Maryland, and in Atlantic City, New Jersey, among other locations. In the latter case, proceeds from a hotel room occupancy tax were used to provide the necessary subsidies. For reasons unrelated to this provision, however, the volume of tax-exempt bond issuing for rental housing dropped significantly during the 1980s.

134. Housing Act of 1937, As Amended, Sec. 17. Enacted as Sec. 301 of the Housing and Urban-Rural Recovery Act of 1983, enacted November 17, 1983.

135. Sec. 17(d)(4)(E).

136. Sec. 17(d)(8)(A).

137. The economic mix on Roosevelt Island has been characterized as "rich and poor and those in between living within a few hundred yards of each other." Over half of the units built so far in this project are low- and moderate-, principally moderate-, income housing. See Mildred F. Schmertz, ed. *Apartments, Townhouses and Condominiums*, Third Edition (New York: McGraw-Hill, 1981), p. 2.

138. Many aspects of the "new towns" boomlet of the late 1960s and early 1970s now appear, in retrospect, misguided; indeed, most of the communities supported by the federal government under their 1970 new communities program turned out to be highly unsuccessful. The problems with that program and the "new towns" idea generally, however, had nothing to do with the economic integration objectives of the program, but a variety of other reasons.

139. A credit to Ruth Price, Housing Authority of the city of New Haven, Connecticut, for this apt usage.

Bibliography

Abrams, Charles. *The City is the Frontier*. New York: Harper & Row, 1965.

American Society of Planning Officials. "Planning Agency Ideas for Encouraging Low- and Moderate-Income Housing." *PAS Memo*, No. 77-12. Chicago: American Society of Planning Officials, 1977.

Association of Bay Area Governments. *Working Paper #1 - Review of Inclusionary Land Use Measures*. San Francisco, 1979.

―――. *Working Paper #2 - Issues Surrounding Adoption of Inclusionary Land Use Measures and Preliminary Strategies*. San Francisco, 1979.

Baade, John A. "Required Low-Income Housing in Residential Developments: Constitutional Challenges to a Community Imposed Quota." *Arizona Law Review*, Vol. 16, No. 3, 1974.

Bozung, Linda J. "Inclusionary Housing: Experience Under a Model Program." *Zoning and Planning Law Report*, Vol. 6, No. 1, Jan. 1983.

Brooks, Mary et al. *Housing Choice: A Handbook for Suburban Officials, Non-Profit Organizations, Community Groups, and Consumers*. New York: Suburban Action Institute, 1980.

―――. "Lessons to Learn from Inclusionary Zoning." Paper presented at *Inclusionary Zoning Moves Downtown: A Legal Symposium*, New York, November 18, 1983.

―――. "The San Francisco Office/Housing Production Program." Unpublished ms., August 1983.

Buchsbaum, Peter. "The Irrelevance of the 'Developing Municipality' Concept." In *After Mount Laurel: The New Suburban Zoning*. Rose, Jerome G. and Rothman, Robert E., eds. New Brunswick, N.J.: Center for Urban Policy Research, 1977.

Burchell, Robert W. et al. *Mount Laurel II: Challenge and Delivery of Low-Cost Housing*. New Brunswick, N.J.: Rutgers University, Center for Urban Policy Research, 1983.

265

Burton, Carolyn. "California Legislature Prohibits Exclusionary Zoning, Mandates Fair
    Share: Inclusionary Housing Programs a Likely Response." *San Fernando
    Valley Law Review*, Vol. 9, 1981, pp. 19-46.
California, Coastal Commission. *Draft Interpretative Guidelines on New Construction of
    Housing*. San Francisco, January 1980.
————. Department of Housing & Community Development. "Legality of Deed Re-
    strictions." Unpublished memorandum, December, 1978.
————. Department of Housing & Community Development. "Legality of Inclusionary
    Ordinances." Unpublished memorandum. September 1978.
————. Department of Housing & Community Development. *Model Inclusionary Ordi-
    nance*. Sacramento, 1978.
————. Department of Housing & Community Development. *101 Steps to Better Hous-
    ing: The California Housing Plan 1982*. 2 vols. Sacramento, 1982.
————. Department of Housing & Community Development. *Advisory Memorandum on
    Coastal Zone Housing Requirements in Government Code Section 65590*. Sac-
    ramento, 1982.
————. Office of Appropriate Technology. *The Affordable Housing Book*. Sacramento,
    1982.
————. Office of Planning & Research. *Planning Zoning and Development Laws, 1982
    Edition*. Sacramento, 1982.
Caton, Philip. *Mahwah Township Fair Share Allocation Report*. Trenton, N.J.: Clarke &
    Caton, 1983.
Central Naugatuck Valley Regional Planning Agency. *Least Cost Housing: Minimizing
    the Fiscal Impact of Zoning and Subdivision Regulations*. Waterbury, CT,
    1978.
Connerly, Ward & Associates. *The Implications of Inclusionary Housing Programs*.
    Sacramento: California Building Industry Association, 1979.
————. *The Feasibility of the Density Bonus in Relation to Inclusionary Housing Pro-
    grams*. Sacramento: California Building Industry Association, 1980.
————. *Inclusionary Housing in Orange County: A Look at Preliminary Results*. Sac-
    ramento: California Building Industry Association, 1981.
Danielson, Michael N. *The Politics of Exclusion*. New York: Columbia University Press,
    1976.
Davidoff, Paul & Davidoff, Linda. "Opening the Suburbs: Toward Inclusionary Land
    Use Controls." *Syracuse Law Review*, Vol. 22, 1971, pp. 509-536.
"Developments in the Law — Zoning." *Harvard Law Review*, Vol. 91, No. 7, 1978, pp.
    1427-1708.
Downs, Anthony. *Opening Up the Suburbs: An Urban Strategy for America*. New Haven,
    CT: Yale University Press, 1973.
Ellickson, Robert. "The Irony of 'Inclusionary' Zoning." In *Resolving the Housing
    Crisis*, M. Bruce Johnson, ed. San Francisco: Pacific Institute for Public Policy
    Research, 1982.
————. "Inclusionary Housing Programs: Yet Another Misguided Urban Policy?" Paper
    presented at *Inclusionary Zoning Moves Downtown: A Legal Symposium*, New
    York, November 18, 1983.
Fishman, Richard P., ed. *Housing for All Under Law*. Cambridge, MA: Ballinger, 1978.
Franklin, Herbert M.; Falk, David; and Levin, Arthur J. *In-Zoning: A Guide for Policy-
    Makers on Inclusionary Land Use Programs*. Washington D.C.: The Potomac
    Institute, 1974.

————. "Inclusionary Programs and the Larger Public Interest." In *After Mount Laurel: The New Suburban Zoning*. Rose, Jerome G. & Rothman, Robert E. eds. New Brunswick, N.J.: Center for Urban Policy Research, 1977.

Frieden, Bernard J. *The Environmental Protection Hustle*. Cambridge, MA: MIT Press, 1979.

————. "The Exclusionary Effects of Growth Controls." In *Resolving the Housing Crisis*. M. Bruce Johnson, ed.

Fox, Gregory Mellon, and Davis, Barbara Rosenfeld. "Density Bonus Zoning to Provide Low and Moderate Income Housing." *Hastings Constitutional Law Quarterly*, Vol. 3, 1976, pp. 1015-1071.

Gailey, J. Benjamin. "Municipal Regulation of Housing Costs and Supply." *Zoning and Planning Law Report*, Vol. 4, No. 3, Feb. 1981.

Gans, Herbert J. "The Balanced Community: Homogeneity or Heterogeneity in Residential Areas?" In *Housing Urban America*, Jon Pynoos, Robert Schafer, and Chester W. Hartman, eds. Chicago,: Aldine, 1973.

————. *The Levittowners*. New York, N.Y.: Pantheon Books, 1967.

Gers, Barbara Behrens. "The City Hall Solution." *Housing*, July 1981.

Glazer, Nathan. "The Bias of American Housing Policy." In *Housing Urban America*. Jon Pynoos, Robert Schafer, & Chester W. Hartman, eds. Chicago: Aldine, 1973.

Hagman, Donald G. "Taking Care of One's Own: Bootstrapping Low and Moderate Income Housing by Local Government." *Urban Law & Policy*, Vol. 5, 1982.

———— and Dean J. Misczynski, eds., *Windfalls for Wipeouts: Land Value Capture and Compensation*. Chicago: American Society of Planning Officials, 1978.

Irvine, City of, California. "Low and Moderate Income Housing in Irvine, California: A Status Report." Irvine, 1979.

Kilduff, Marshall. "San Francisco's Novel Scheme to Provide Affordable Housing." *California Journal*, May 1982.

King, David S. "Inclusionary Zoning: Unfair Response to the Need for Low Cost Housing." *Western New England Law Review*, Vol. 4, 1982, pp. 597-621.

Kleven, Thomas. "Inclusionary Ordinances — Policy and Legal Issues in Requiring Private Developers to Build Low Cost Housing." *UCLA Law Review*, Vol. 21, 1974, pp. 1432-1528.

————. "Inclusionary Ordinances and the Nexus Issue." Paper presented at *Inclusionary Zoning Moves Downtown: A Legal Symposium*. New York, November 18, 1983.

Lakewood, Colorado, Affordable Housing Task Force. *Findings and Recommendations of the Affordable Housing Task Force*. Lakewood, CO: 1983.

Lesk, Ann Berger. "Theater Fund and Housing Trust Fund Issues." Paper presented at *Inclusionary Zoning Moves Downtown: A Legal Symposium*, New York, November 18, 1983.

Leventhal, Kenneth & Co. *Bench Mark Villas: A Demonstration of Affordable Housing*. Santa Ana, CA: Orange County Chapter, Building Industry Association of Southern California, 1983.

Longtin, James. *California Land Use Regulations: 1980/81 Supplement*. Westlake Village, CA: Local Government Publications, 1980.

Mallach, Alan. "Do Lawsuits Build Housing: The Implications of Exclusionary Zoning Litigation." *Rutgers-Camden Law Journal* Vol. 6, 1975, pp. 653-688.

————. "Exclusionary Zoning Litigation: Setting the Record Straight." *Real Estate Law*

Journal, Vol. 9, 1981, pp. 275-310.

Marcus, Norman. "Zoning Exactions Employed to Solve Housing Problems." *New York Law Journal*, October 5, 1983.

Mayer, Martin. *The Builders*. New York: W.W. Norton & Company, 1978.

Muth, Richard. "Condominium Conversions and the 'Housing Crisis'." In *Resolving the Housing Crisis*, edited by M. Bruce Johnson. San Francisco: Pacific Institute, 1982.

New Jersey, Department of Community Affairs. *A Revised Statewide Housing Allocation Report for New Jersey: For Public Review and Comment*. Trenton, N.J., 1978.

———. Department of Community Affairs and Regional Planning Board of Princeton. *The Princeton Housing Proposal: A Strategy to Achieve Balanced Housing Without Government Subsidy*. Trenton, N.J., 1977.

———. Department of Community Affairs and Tri-State Regional Planning Commission. *The Affordable Housing Handbook*. Trenton, N.J., 1981.

Orange, County of, California, Southeast Orange County Housing Task Force. *Report of the Southwest County Housing Task Force*. Santa Ana, CA, 1977.

———. Environmental Management Agency. *Principles and Guidelines for an Inclusionary Housing Program*. Santa Ana, CA, 1978.

———. Environmental Management Agency. *History, Rationale, Implementation and Alternatives Regarding the Anti-Speculation and Continued Affordability Policies for Affordable Housing*. Santa Ana, CA, 1981.

———. Environmental Management Agency. *Orange County's Inclusionary Housing Program*. Santa Ana, CA, 1982.

———. Environmental Management Agency. *Orange County's Inclusionary Housing Program Assessment*. Santa Ana, CA, 1982.

Palo Alto Housing Corporation, *Semi-Annual Report January-June 1983*. Palo Alto, CA, 1983.

Pazar, Charles E. "Constitutional Barriers to the Enactment of Moderately Priced Dwelling Unit Ordinances in New Jersey." *Rutgers-Camden Law Journal*, Vol. 10, 1979, pp. 253-276.

Pilon, Roger. "Property Rights and a Free Society." In *Resolving The Housing Crisis*, M. Bruce Johnson, ed. San Francisco: Pacific Institute for Public Policy Research, 1982.

Polikoff, Alexander. *Housing The Poor: The Case for Heroism*. Cambridge, MA: Ballinger, 1978.

Porter, Allen, Esq., and Gerald Muller, Esq. *A Legal Analysis Updating and Supplementing the Princeton Housing Proposal*. Unpublished legal memorandum prepared for the Regional Planning Board of Princeton. Princeton, N.J., 1979.

Princeton University, Research Center for Urban & Environmental Planning. *Planning and Design Workbook for Community Participation*. Princeton, N.J., 1969.

Professional Builder. "Affordable Housing Ideas." Denver, 1982.

Real Estate Research Corporation. *The Costs of Sprawl*. Chicago, 1974.

Rodger, Ruth. *Creating a Livable Inner City Community: The Vancouver Experience*. Vancouver, British Columbia: False Creek Development Group, 1976.

Ryan, William, et al. *All In Together: An Evaluation of Mixed-Income Multi-Family Housing*. Boston: Massachusetts Housing Finance Agency, 1974.

Sager, Lawrence. "Tight Little Islands: Exclusionary Zoning, Equal Protection, and the Indigent." *Stanford Law Review*, Vol. 21, 1969.

San Diego, County of, California, Board of Supervisors. Policy I-75, *Inclusionary Housing Policy*. San Diego, 1979.

San Francisco, City of, California. *Citywide Affordable Housing Program*, San Francisco, 1982.

———. Office/Housing Production Program. *Interim Guidelines for Administering the Housing Requirements Placed on New Office Developments*. San Francisco, 1981.

Santa Cruz, City of, California. Ordinance No. 80-06, "Income, Asset and Housing Cost Guidelines." Santa Cruz, 1980.

Schmertz, Mildred F. *Apartments, Townhouses & Condominiums*, Third Edition. New York: McGraw-Hill, 1981.

Schwartz, Seymour I. and Johnston, Robert A. with Burtraw, Dallas. *Local Government Initiatives for Affordable Housing: An Evaluation of Inclusionary Housing Programs in California*. Davis, CA: Institute of Governmental Affairs and Institute of Ecology, University of California, Davis, 1981.

——— and Johnston, Robert A. "Inclusionary Housing Programs." *APA Journal*, Winter 1983, pp. 3-21.

——— and Johnston, Robert A.; Wandesforde-Smith, Geoffrey; and Savage, Kirk. *The Implementation of SB 626 in Southern California: A Summary of Findings*. Davis, CA: Institute of Governmental Affairs, University of California, Davis, 1983.

Sedway, Paul H. "The San Francisco Office Housing Production Program." Paper presented at *Inclusionary Zoning Moves Downtown: A Legal Symposium*, New York, November 18, 1983.

Southern California Association of Governments. *Methods to Increase Housing Supply: A "How To" Manual for Local Government*. Los Angeles, 1981.

———. *Costs, Causes and Consequences of the Housing Shortage*. Los Angeles, 1981.

Sternlieb, George & Hughes, James W., eds. *America's Housing: Prospects and Problems*. New Brunswick, N.J.: Rutgers University, Center for Urban Policy Research, 1980.

———. *The Future of Rental Housing*. New Brunswick, N.J.: Rutgers University, Center for Urban Policy Research, 1981.

Taylor, Barbara. "Inclusionary Zoning: A Workable Option for Affordable Housing?" *Urban Land*, March 1981.

Tegeler, Phil and Davidoff, Paul. "Zoning Reforms Pushed." *The Neighborhood Works*, Vol. 6, 1983.

Torrance, City of, California, Planning Department. *Discussion Paper on the Principles of Inclusionary Housing Ordinances*. Torrance, 1979.

Trout, Lake S. "Low Cost Housing — Resale Controls." Unpublished legal memorandum, dated March 15, 1979, included in Southern California Association of Governments, papers distributed for Inclusionary Zoning Conference held September 1980.

United States Government, Department of Housing & Urban Development. *Final Report of the Task Force on Housing Costs*. Washington, D.C.: Government Printing Office, 1978.

———. Dept. of Housing & Urban Development. *The Affordable Community: Growth, Change and Choice in the 80s*. Washington D.C.: Government Printing Office, 1982.

———. Dept. of Housing & Urban Development. *Affordable Housing: How Local Regulatory Improvements Can Help*. Washington, D.C.: Government Printing Office, 1981.

————. Congressional Budget Office. *Homeownership: The Changing Relationship of Costs and Incomes, and Possible Federal Roles*. Washington, D.C.: Government Printing Office, 1977.

————. The President's Commission on Housing. *The Report of the President's Commission on Housing*. Washington, D.C.: Government Printing Office, 1982.

Urban Land Institute. *Residential Development Handbook*. Washington, D.C.: Urban Land Institute, 1978.

Werth, Joel T. "Inclusionary Zoning Regulations: An Update." *PAS Memo* No. 80-3. Chicago: American Planning Association, 1980.

Westchester County, New York. *Affordable Housing: The Westchester Approach*. White Plains, N.Y.: County of Westchester, 1980.

Williams, Norman Jr. *American Land Planning Law: Land Use and the Police Power*. 5 vols. Chicago: Callaghan & Co., 1974.

INDEX